Table of Contents

THE KINGDOM JOURNEY · BOOK ONE

THE HEART OF VICTORY

A Daily Journey Through
the Book of Revelation

CARL COPSEY

PILGRIM'S PATH
PRESS

Published by Pilgrim's Path Press
For permissions or inquiries, contact: pilgrimspathpress@outlook.com

Library of Congress Cataloging-in-Publication Data
Copsey, Carl.
The Heart of Victory: A Daily Journey Through the Book of Revelation / Carl Copsey.
Includes bibliographical references. (if applicable)

1. Bible. Revelation—Devotional literature. 2. Bible. Revelation. 3. Christian life—Biblical teaching. I. Title.
   Dewey Decimal Classification: 228 (Primary), 242.64 (Devotional)

Library of Congress Control Number: 2026909101
ISBN (print): 979-8-9953900-0-8

First edition, February 2026
Printed in DeRidder, LA, United States of America

Cover design, interior layout, and typesetting by Carl Copsey
Editing by Carl Copsey

Dedication

To my beautiful wife, Rebecca, **whose unwavering faith and endless encouragement have been my anchor through every season. Your love reflects Christ's heart in ways that words cannot capture.**

To my son, MoeCharles and his wife Camille, who inspire me with their passion for truth and their commitment to building a godly legacy that will impact generations to come.

To my son, Quinten and his wife Bella, whose love for God's kingdom and Christ-centered integrity demonstrate the victory this book proclaims.

You have each shown me that Revelation's greatest truths are not found in distant visions but in daily faithfulness, sacrificial love, and lives surrendered to the King who makes all things new. This book exists because you believed its message long before it was written and lived its truths when they were costly, reminding me that victory belongs to those who hold fast to the end.

With all my love and deepest gratitude.

Author's Note

Let's address this up front: this is a large book. I know that.

You're holding 84 daily readings through the entire book of Revelation, plus introductions, a conclusion, and resources designed to deepen your understanding. The scope is intentional—Revelation deserves this kind of sustained attention.

But here's what I want you to know: you don't have to read it all at once.

This book is structured to be read one day at a time. Each daily reading stands on its own—complete, digestible, and designed to fit into your morning coffee or evening wind-down. The part introductions and conclusion? Read them when you get there. The appendices? Use them as you need them.

Think of this not as a massive volume to conquer, but as 84 conversations about the most hopeful book in Scripture. One day, one reading, one step forward in understanding Christ's victory.

By the time you finish, you won't just have read about Revelation — you'll have lived with it for twelve weeks. You'll know this book. And there's deep satisfaction in that kind of sustained engagement with God's Word.

So don't let the size intimidate you. Let the structure serve you. One day at a time, you'll get there. And when you do, you'll have accomplished something significant.

Now let's begin.

"The Book of Revelation cannot mean for us what it did not mean for them."

— Matt Chandler

The 'them' in this statement is the original first-century churches who first received Revelation. Before we ask what the book means for our moment, we must first ask what it meant for theirs. Only then can we apply it faithfully to our own lives and contexts. For a pastoral walk through Revelation with this same emphasis, Matt Chandler's Revelation sermon series at The Village Church is a helpful example.

Preface: The Heart of Victory

Before you begin this 84-day journey through Revelation, I need to explain what I mean by "the heart of victory." Understanding this phrase will shape how you read every page that follows.

What Victory Actually Is

When most people hear "victory," they think of winning — defeating an enemy, overcoming an obstacle, achieving a goal. And while Revelation certainly has enemies defeated and obstacles overcome, the victory it proclaims is something deeper and more radical than most of us realize.

The heart of victory isn't something we're waiting for. It's something we're living in.

This might sound strange at first. After all, the world around us doesn't look particularly victorious. Christians still suffer and evil still rages. Death hasn't stopped claiming its victims.

How can we talk about victory as a present reality when so much remains broken?

But here's what Revelation wants you to see: The Lamb isn't going to win someday. He has already won. The decisive battle wasn't fought at the end of history — it was fought at the cross. Christ's death and resurrection didn't just make victory possible; they accomplished victory completely in principle. What remains is not whether Christ will triumph, but how that already-secured triumph will unfold and be revealed in history.

This is the first layer of what "heart of victory" means: the core of what victory actually is. Not future escape or distant hope, but present reality in Christ's current reign.

The Source of Victory

Think of the heart in your chest right now. It's pumping blood through your body, sustaining life with every beat. You don't consciously control it. It just works—faithfully and consistently giving life to every part of you.

That's the second layer: the source from which victory flows. The throne room of heaven — which you'll encounter in Part Two of this journey — is the heart of all reality. And at the center of that throne stands the Lamb who was slain. His sacrifice isn't just a past event. It's the ongoing source from which all victory pulses through history.

Every judgment and every promise in Revelation flows from the throne. Every act of redemption, every vindication of the martyrs, every defeat of evil — all of it flows from the heart of heaven where the Lamb reigns.

You don't create this victory or earn it. You don't even contribute to accomplishing it. You receive it, participate in it, and live from it. It flows to you from the throne.

Where Victory Lives

The third layer might be the hardest for us to grasp: Victory isn't located in our circumstances.

The churches in Revelation 2-3 are under pressure. Some are persecuted. Some are seduced by false teaching. Some are lukewarm and barely alive. Their circumstances don't look victorious at all.

And yet Christ walks among them. He holds the churches in His hand. He calls them to faithfulness and promises them triumph. The victory isn't found in their circumstances improving — it's found in Christ's character and faithfulness remaining constant regardless of their circumstances.

This means the martyrs under the altar in Revelation 6 aren't defeated — they're victorious. The two witnesses in Revelation 11 who are killed and lie in the street aren't victims — they're conquerors. The saints in Revelation 13 who refuse the mark of the beast and face economic ruin or death aren't losing — they're winning.

Victory in Revelation looks nothing like the world's version of victory. It's located in faithful witness, costly obedience, patient endurance, and unwavering worship. It's found in dying well more than living comfortably. It's measured by conformity to the Lamb, not by earthly success.

What Gives Us Heart

The fourth layer is intensely practical: "The heart of victory" is what gives believers heart — courage — to face what's in front of them.

This isn't "hang on until the rapture comes and rescues you from all this." It's "Christ reigns now, right now, over everything including your Monday morning, so live accordingly."

When your alarm goes off tomorrow and you step into another day of trials, you're not stepping into chaos. You're stepping into the kingdom of the reigning King. The difficult conversation you're dreading? He's sovereign over it. The diagnosis that terrifies you? He's still on the throne. The relationship that's falling apart, the finances that won't stretch, the children who've walked away, the suffering that makes no sense — Christ reigns. Now. Over all of it.

And that changes everything about how you face tomorrow. Literally, everything.

Monday Morning Reality

This brings us to the point of this whole journey: Revelation isn't theoretical theology for academic discussion. It's battle-tested truth designed for your actual life.

The difficult coworker who makes every day harder isn't just an annoyance to endure. They're someone who is made in the image of God, and your patient love might be the only gospel they ever see clearly. Your response to them is participation in Christ's victory — choosing to reflect the Lamb rather than the beast.

The financial stress that keeps you awake at 3 AM isn't merely overwhelming. Instead, it offers a chance to show that your security is rooted in an everlasting kingdom, not in an ever-changing bank balance. Faith in God during difficult times enables you to operate from a place of victory rather than being driven by defeat.

The news headlines that spark anxiety aren't proof that the world is collapsing. They serve as reminders that earthly kingdoms rise and fall, yet Christ's kingdom lasts forever. Every empire that once seemed unbeatable has turned to dust, and every tyrant who appeared invincible is now swept into history. Every system that demanded worship has disappeared. Yet the Lamb continues to reign.

This is what "the heart of victory" produces in real life:

Worship that transforms ordinary moments into acts of eternal significance. When you choose integrity at work, you're casting your crown before the throne. When you extend forgiveness to someone who wounded you, you're echoing the Lamb who prayed for His executioners.

Endurance that outlasts trials because it's rooted in Christ's finished work, not your fluctuating strength. You're not trying to survive until He returns — you're conquering through His power, adding your testimony to the great cloud of witnesses.

Witness that boldly proclaims truth even when the cost is high. You can risk loving difficult people because you know love wins. You can pursue justice when it costs you because you know God's justice prevails.

Hope that anchors your soul when everything around you is shaking. Every tear you cry now will be wiped away personally by God Himself. Every injustice you witness will be corrected by perfect justice. The victory is certain.

Living from the End

You're about to spend 84 days learning how the story ends. And here's what you'll discover: Christ wins. His kingdom comes and death is defeated. Evil is judged, and love triumphs.

Knowing the end changes how you live today.

You can risk everything for the kingdom because you know it's the only kingdom that lasts. You can endure temporary hardship because you've seen the eternal glory. You can face suffering with courage because you know it doesn't have the last word, and you can say no to sin's empty promises because you've tasted Christ's fullness.

This knowledge — this certainty — this vision of the victorious Lamb enthroned — this is what I mean by the heart of victory.

It's not a concept to understand. It's a reality to live.

Not someday, but today. Not just Sunday — Monday morning.

The Journey Ahead

The Introduction that follows will show you how this book is organized and what to expect structurally. But I wanted you to understand the beating heart beneath all of it before you begin.

For the next 84 days, every passage you read, every truth you encounter, every challenge, comfort and promise — all of it will pulse with this same reality: Christ reigns. His victory is certain. And you, because you belong to Him, share in that triumph.

That's the lens through which you'll read Revelation, and the truth that will transform your Monday mornings, and every day, for the rest of your life.

That's the heart of victory.

Carl Copsey
February 2026

Introduction: Come and See

There's something about the book of Revelation that makes most of us nervous.

Maybe it's the strange imagery — beasts with multiple heads, stars falling from the sky, a woman clothed with the sun. Or maybe it's the history of wild speculation, failed predictions, and confident declarations about the "end times" that never quite panned out. Whatever the reason, Revelation feels different from the rest of the New Testament. The Gospels tell us about Jesus' life and teaching. The Epistles explain Christian doctrine and practice. But Revelation? It's… apocalyptic. And that word alone can feel intimidating.

So we avoid it. We skip over it in our Bible reading plans. We let others tell us what it means while we focus on more "practical" books. And we quietly wonder if we're missing out on something important by steering clear of the one book in Scripture that explicitly promises a blessing to those who read, hear, and keep it (Revelation 1:3).

If that describes you, this book is your invitation to stop avoiding Revelation and start discovering what John actually wrote. Not through the lens of sensationalist prophecy charts or fear-mongering speculation, but through careful, pastoral engagement with the text itself.

What You'll Find in Revelation

Revelation isn't what most people think it is.

It's not primarily a roadmap for the future, predicting specific events in chronological order. It's not a coded message about current events or political figures. And it's definitely not meant to generate fear, confusion, or endless debates about timelines and tribulation periods.

Revelation is, first and foremost, a revelation of Jesus Christ. That's how it opens: "The revelation of Jesus Christ..." (1:1). Everything that follows — every vision, every symbol, every dramatic scene — serves that purpose. John wants you to see Jesus clearly: His authority, His love for His Church, His judgment against evil, and His certain victory over every power that opposes Him.

When you see Jesus rightly, everything else comes into focus. The trials you face make sense in light of His sovereignty. The temptations to compromise lose their appeal when you've seen His glory. The chaos of the world stops feeling so overwhelming when you've glimpsed the throne room of heaven where He reigns, right now, over all things.

This is what Revelation offers: not speculation about the future, but clarity about the present. Not escape from the world's troubles, but strength to endure them faithfully. Not a puzzle to solve, but a Person to worship.

How This Book Works

Over the next 84 days, we're going to walk through all of Revelation together. Not in a rush, but at a pace that lets the text breathe and the message sink in.

The journey is organized into eight parts, each focusing on a major section of Revelation:

Part One: The Glorious Christ Among His Churches (Days 1-12) Christ walking among the seven churches, addressing their strengths and weaknesses, calling them back to faithfulness.

Part Two: The Throne and the Scroll (Days 13-22)
The throne room of heaven, where worship reframes everything, and the Lamb who is worthy to open the scroll of history.

Part Three: The Seals and the Sealed (Days 23-32)
The opening of the seven seals, revealing both the brokenness of history and the security of God's sealed people.

Part Four: Trumpets, Prayers, and Witness (Days 33-43)
Seven trumpets sound as warnings, emphasizing the power of prayer and the call to faithful witness.

Part Five: The Dragon, the Beasts, and the Lamb (Days 44-53)
The cosmic conflict unveiled—Satan's rage, the beast's blasphemy, and the Lamb's victory.

Part Six: Bowls, Babylon, and the Coming King (Days 54-66)
The seven bowls of final judgment, the fall of Babylon, and the return of Christ as conquering King.

Part Seven: The Thousand Years, Judgment, and New Creation (Days 67-78)
Final judgment, the defeat of death itself, and the arrival of the new heaven and new earth.

Part Eight: Echoes of the Old Testament (Days 79-84)
Stepping back to see how Revelation gathers and fulfills the hopes, visions, and promises of the Old Testament prophets.

Each day follows the same basic structure:

- A **Scripture passage** to read
- A "**Heart of Victory**" statement that captures the day's essence
- **Exposition** that explains what the text means
- **Application** that connects it to your daily life
- A **prayer** to help you respond

The goal isn't to make you an expert in Revelation's details. The goal is to help you see Jesus more clearly and live more faithfully in light of His victory.

How to Read Revelation

Before we begin, we need to address something important: **how you approach Revelation matters as much as how much you read of it.**

This book treats Revelation's imagery as **symbolic truth that reveals spiritual realities** rather than literal predictions of future events. The beasts aren't specific political figures we can identify on the nightly news. The numbers aren't mathematical codes we can calculate to determine when Jesus will return. The visions aren't giving us a chronological timeline of events that haven't happened yet.

Instead, Revelation uses vivid, symbolic language—drawn heavily from the Old Testament—to reveal timeless truths about Christ's authority, the Church's calling, and the certain triumph of God's kingdom. The symbols are meant to be understood in light of their Old Testament background and their theological significance, not decoded like a puzzle or mapped onto current events.

Revelation doesn't move in a straight line from chapter 1 to chapter 22. Instead, it **recapitulates**—it covers the same ground multiple times from different angles. The seven seals, the seven trumpets, and the seven bowls aren't three consecutive series of judgments, one after another. They're three different ways of depicting the same realities of this present age, viewed from different angles and with increasing intensity.

This means Revelation is less like a documentary unfolding chronologically and more like a symphony, where themes are introduced, developed, and returned to with new depth and intensity. John is showing you the same truths from multiple angles, each time adding new layers of meaning and application.

A Word About Interpretation

If this interpretive framework is new to you, that's understandable. Much of contemporary evangelicalism has been shaped by a different approach to Revelation—one that emphasizes future predictions, detailed timelines, and attempts to match prophetic symbols to current events. If you've grown up hearing about the rapture, the seven-year tribulation, or identifying a future Antichrist, the approach in this book may feel unfamiliar, perhaps even surprising.

I'd encourage you to read **Appendix A** either before or after you complete the 84 days. It traces the history of how Christians have read Revelation across two millennia and explains why the approach in this book, while it may feel new to you, actually represents the historic mainstream of Christian interpretation across many centuries. You might be surprised to discover how "old" this "new" way of reading actually is—and how the approach that feels familiar to you is, historically speaking, quite recent.

For now, I'm simply asking you to read with an open mind and heart. Let the text speak. See what John is actually showing you. And trust that the Holy Spirit who inspired this book can guide you into its truth, even if it challenges what you've previously been taught.

While this book approaches Revelation from a particular interpretive framework, you don't have to share all of those convictions to benefit from it. Faithful Christians have differed on the details of timelines and millennia, but Revelation offers far more than an interpretive system to defend. Its substance—the glory of Christ, the call to faithful witness, the warning against compromise, and the comfort of His certain victory—is for every believer. My aim here is not to win you to a position, but to help you see Jesus more clearly and live more courageously in light of His reign.

Who This Book Is For

This book is written for anyone who wants to understand Revelation but has felt intimidated by it.

You don't need seminary training or expertise in biblical languages. You don't need background in apocalyptic literature or first-century Roman history, though we'll provide that context when it's helpful.

You just need to show up, one day at a time, ready to see Jesus and let His word shape your life.

Whether you're a new believer wanting to understand all of Scripture, a mature Christian who's avoided Revelation and is ready to engage it thoughtfully, someone confused by other approaches and looking for clarity, or a church leader looking for a resource to guide your people through Revelation faithfully — this book is for you.

How to Use This Book

The best way to use this book is simple: one day at a time, in order, at a steady pace.

Don't try to read it all at once or skip around. And don't rush through it just to say you've finished. Revelation is meant to be received slowly, pondered deeply, and allowed to do its work in your soul.

Each day's reading is designed to take about 10-15 minutes. Read the Scripture passage first. Then work through the exposition and application. Spend time with the "Heart of Victory" statement — memorize it if you can. And don't rush past the prayer. Let it shape your own conversation with God.

If you can, read aloud. Revelation was meant to be heard, not just silently scanned. There's power in hearing these words spoken — it engages your mind and heart in a different way than silent reading alone.

Take notes if that helps you process. Underline. Highlight. Write in the margins. This isn't a coffee table book meant to stay pristine — it's a tool meant to be used.

Consider reading this book with others. Revelation was written to churches, not just individuals. If you can gather a small group to walk through these 84 days together, discussing what you're learning and encouraging each other to hold fast, you'll experience Revelation the way it was meant to be experienced — in community.

And when you finish, read it again. You'll see things you missed the first time. Connections will become clearer. Themes you didn't notice will jump out at you. Revelation rewards re-reading.

A Word About "Boxes"

As you read through the 84 days, you'll occasionally encounter notes in **"boxes."** These highlight moments when Revelation is recapitulating — going back over the same ground from a different angle.

For instance, when you get to the seven trumpets and they sound remarkably similar to the seven seals, a "box" note will point that out and help you see that John isn't describing new events but is showing you the same realities from a fresh perspective.

These notes aren't distractions — they're guideposts, helping you recognize Revelation's structure and avoid getting confused when themes repeat. Pay attention to them. They'll help you see the forest while you're examining the trees.

Translations Used

This book primarily uses the **Christian Standard Bible (CSB)** for its clarity and accuracy. Occasionally, the **English Standard Version (ESV)** is used when it captures a particular nuance especially well. Unless otherwise noted, the CSB is being used.

Ready to Begin

Revelation opens with a promise: *"Blessed is the one who reads aloud the words of this prophecy, and blessed are those who hear, and who keep what is written in it, for the time is near"* (Revelation 1:3 ESV).

You're about to receive that blessing.

Not because you'll decode hidden mysteries or figure out when Jesus is returning. But because you'll see Him clearly. You'll hear His voice speaking to His Church. You'll learn to worship Him in the throne room of heaven, to hold fast through trials, to resist the seductions of Babylon, and to wait with confident hope for the day when He makes all things new.

The heart of Revelation is victory. Christ's victory. Certain, unstoppable, eternal victory. And because you belong to Him, that victory is yours.

Let's begin the journey.

PART ONE: The Glorious Christ Among His Churches

Revelation 1–3

Heart of Victory: Christ walks among His churches—knowing, correcting, and calling them to overcome—because He holds the keys to death and Hades, and no darkness can extinguish His lampstands.

Before the cosmic battle unfolds and judgment falls, before empires crumble, John sees something foundational: Jesus walking among His churches.

This is where Revelation begins — not with terror but with presence. Christ is here, right in the midst of His people, knowing them completely, seeing them clearly, and speaking to them with both comfort and correction. He knows their struggles, compromises, faithfulness, and failures. He walks among the lampstands (His churches), tending the light, calling them back to their first love, and promising victory if they will hold fast (Revelation 1:13; 2:1).

The seven letters to the seven churches aren't just ancient history. They're also a mirror held up to every church in every age, including ours. We see ourselves in Ephesus's lost love, Smyrna's suffering, Pergamum's compromise, Thyatira's tolerance of false teaching, Sardis's spiritual deadness, Philadelphia's faithful weakness, and Laodicea's lukewarm self-satisfaction. And in seeing ourselves, we hear Christ's voice — calling us back to faithfulness, urging us to hold fast and overcome.

This is the foundation for the rest of what follows. Before we can understand the cosmic conflict or the ultimate victory, we need to know this: Jesus is with His church. He hasn't abandoned or forgotten us. He walks among us, even now, and His eyes of fire see everything — both our failures and our faithfulness. To those who overcome, He makes promises that will echo through the rest of this book— the tree of life, the crown of life, hidden manna, a white stone, authority over the nations, white garments, pillars in God's temple, and the right to sit with Him on His throne (Revelation 2–3).

The heart of victory begins here, in the presence of the risen Christ who knows His churches and loves them enough to speak truth, offer grace, and promise glory to those who conquer.

Welcome to Part One.

Day 1 – The Heart of Revelation

Scripture Reading: Revelation 1:1–3

Heart of Victory: The blessing of Revelation isn't found in decoding its mysteries but in seeing Jesus as He truly is — the risen, reigning King whose victory reshapes how we live.

There are books you read once and set aside. And then there are books that read you — books that search you out, confront you, and won't let you go. The book of Revelation is one of those. For many of us, though, it sits on the shelf of our Bibles like a locked room we're afraid to enter. We've heard it's confusing, full of beasts and bowls and numbers that don't add up. We've been told it's about the end of the world, and honestly, that sounds terrifying. So we stay away.

But what if Revelation isn't meant to confuse or frighten you? What if it's meant to bless you?

Look at how the book begins: "Blessed is the one who reads aloud the words of this prophecy, and blessed are those who hear the words of this prophecy and keep what is written in it, because the time is near" (1:3). This isn't just a warning. It's a warm invitation to see things from a different perspective. Revelation opens with a promise of blessing — not for the super-spiritual or the end-times experts, but for anyone who will read it, keep it, hear it, and live by it. The very act of engaging with this book, of letting it shape your heart and your life, carries a blessing.

That's worth pausing over. John doesn't say, "Blessed are those who decode every symbol" or "Blessed are those who can draw a timeline of the tribulation." He says blessed are those who hear and keep. The blessing is in the encounter, in letting this revelation of Jesus Christ do its work in you.

And notice what this book actually is. "The revelation of Jesus Christ" (1:1). Not the revelation of the future, though the future is part of it. Not the revelation of tribulation or judgment, though those realities are here too. This is the revelation — the unveiling, the disclosure — of Jesus Christ. Everything in this book exists to show you who He is: His beauty, His authority, His love for His church, His unstoppable victory over every power that sets itself against Him and His people. When you read Revelation rightly, you don't walk away with a chart. You walk away with a clearer vision of Jesus.

God gave this revelation to Jesus, who sent it through an angel to John, who wrote it down for the churches. It's a chain of grace — Father to Son to angel to apostle to you. The content of this revelation is described as "what must soon take place" (1:1). That phrase has confused some readers. Two thousand years later, how can we say these things happen "soon"? The point isn't that everything in Revelation was fulfilled in the first century. The point is that we live in the time of fulfillment. The decisive victory has been won — Christ has died and risen, the kingdom has broken into the world, and Satan has been defeated. Revelation shows us the ongoing outworking of that victory in the age we now inhabit — and the certainty that Christ will return to consummate what He began.

This is why "the time is near" (1:3). Not because the calendar is running out, but because we live in the overlap of the ages, the time between the cross and the crown, when the victory is sure but not yet fully seen. Revelation pulls back the curtain on this in-between time and shows you what's really happening: Christ reigning from the throne, the church enduring in faithfulness, evil raging in its death throes, and the new creation already breaking in (Revelation 21:1–5).

So the blessing John promises is not reserved for scholars or mystics. It's for you — for the person who feels small and afraid in a world that seems out of control, for the believer who wonders if faithfulness matters when everything feels like it's falling apart, for the church that worships in the shadow of hostile powers and asks, "How long, O

Lord?" Revelation says: Read this and keep it. Hear these words. You will be blessed.

"Keeping" these words doesn't mean mastering every detail. It means letting them shape you. It means living in light of the reality they reveal — that Jesus is Lord, that He walks among His churches and holds history in His hands, that every enemy will fall and He is coming back. To keep these words is to let them anchor your hope and fuel your endurance, to let them direct your worship and shape your life.

You might still feel uncertain about what lies ahead in this book. That's okay. You don't have to understand everything to receive the blessing. You just have to show up. Read aloud, if you can. Hear these words as though they were spoken directly to you — because they were. And then keep them. Let them keep you. Let this unveiling of Jesus steady your heart and sharpen your vision, setting your hope on the One who was, and is, and is to come.

Prayer:

Father, thank You for giving us this revelation of Your Son. We confess that we've been intimidated by this book, afraid of what we might not understand. But You promise blessing to those who read and keep these words, who hear and obey. Open our eyes to see Jesus on every page. Give us ears to hear what the Spirit is saying. And help us to keep — to hold fast — the truth You reveal. We're ready to see Him. Amen.

Day 2 – Grace from the Eternal One

Scripture Reading: Revelation 1:4–6

Heart of Victory: We are loved by the eternal God and freed by the blood of Jesus—made a kingdom of priests by grace that will never run dry.

We live in a world that feels increasingly fragile. Markets shift overnight and governments change without warning. Leaders who seemed untouchable are suddenly gone. Even the ground beneath our feet can shift and crack. In a world like this, we're hungry for something that won't change, something we can count on when everything else slips through our fingers.

John knew that hunger. He was writing to churches under pressure, believers watching their world grow hostile and unstable. So he begins his greeting with these words: "Grace and peace to you from him who is and who was and who is to come" (1:4). Not from Rome. Not from any earthly power. Grace and peace come from the One who stands outside of time yet holds all of it in His hands — utterly, eternally present.

"Him who is and who was and who is to come" is God's unique name, echoing Exodus 3 where He revealed Himself to Moses as "I AM." God does not just exist in a single moment or era; He is eternal and always present, the unchanging One who holds every moment in His hands. He's the God who never wavers or diminishes. When John's readers faced their world falling apart, he reminded them of the unshakable God.

But notice: John doesn't stop with God the Father. Grace and peace also come "from the seven spirits before his throne" (1:4). This is John's way of speaking about the Holy Spirit in His fullness — seven symbolizing completeness and perfection. The same Spirit who hovered over the waters at creation, who filled the prophets and descended on Jesus at His baptism, now dwells in and empowers the church. And grace and peace flow from Him too.

And then there's Jesus. John piles up titles like treasures: "the faithful witness, the firstborn from the dead, and the ruler of the kings of the earth" (1:5). Each title matters. Jesus is the faithful witness — He tells the truth about God and reveals the Father perfectly, testifying even unto death. He is the firstborn from the dead — not the first person ever to be raised (others were raised before Him), but the first to be raised to new, resurrection life that death can never touch again. He's the pioneer, the trailblazer who breaks death's power and opens the way for all who are His. And He is the ruler of the kings of the earth — not Rome, not Caesar, not any president or prime minister or dictator, but Jesus. He reigns now, whether the kings of the earth recognize it or not.

But this becomes personal when John moves from mentioning titles to talking about relationship: "To him who loves us and has freed us from our sins by his blood" (1:5). The present tense emphasizes that He loves us now. It's not a past love to be remembered; it is an active, ongoing, unconditional love. This reflects the constant, unchanging love of the One who is, who was, and who is to come.

And that love has accomplished something. He has freed us. The ESV says "freed," while older translations say "washed." Both are true. By His blood — His death on the cross — Jesus has broken the chains of our sin and cleansed the stain of our guilt. We were captives; He liberated us. We were defiled; He made us clean. This is finished work, completed on the cross and applied to us when we trust in Him.

And more: "He made us a kingdom, priests to his God and Father" (1:6). This is staggering. We're not just forgiven sinners grateful to escape judgment. We are a kingdom — a people who belong to the King, who live under His rule, who share in His reign. We are priests — set apart to approach God, to serve in His presence, to offer worship and intercession. What was once reserved for a few in Israel is now the inheritance of every believer in Jesus. You, if you are in Christ, are part of this kingdom. You are a priest before the living God.

No wonder John bursts into doxology: "To him be glory and dominion forever and ever. Amen" (1:6). When you see who Jesus is and what He's done, worship is the only reasonable response. Glory — honor, radiance, the full display of His worth. Dominion — power, authority, sovereign rule over all things. Forever and ever, with no expiration date and no end to His reign. Amen — so be it, let it be so, we agree, we affirm, we join our voices to the praise.

This is where Revelation begins — not with terrifying visions of judgment (though those will come), but with grace and peace from the eternal God and the faithful witness who loves us and has freed us, with the sure knowledge that we belong to Him as His kingdom and His priests. This is the foundation. Everything else in this book builds on it.

When the world feels unstable, you find grace and peace from the unchanging God. When your sins weigh on you, recall the One who redeemed you with His blood. If you question your significance, remember that you are part of His kingdom, serving as a priest in His presence. And when the forces of this age seem too powerful, hold onto the truth: Jesus is the reigning king of the earth, and all glory and dominion belong to Him forever.

Prayer:

Eternal God — Father, Son, and Holy Spirit — thank You for the grace and peace that flow from Your throne. Thank You, Jesus, for loving us without pause and freeing us from our sins by Your blood, for making us Your kingdom and Your priests. This is pure gift — we could never deserve it or earn it. You've given it freely, and we receive it with grateful hearts. To You be all glory and dominion, now and forever. Amen.

Day 3 – Every Eye Will See Him

Scripture Reading: Revelation 1:7–8

Heart of Victory: The return of Jesus is not a possibility to consider but a certainty to live by — and for those who know Him, it is our hope, not our terror.

Some truths are quietly spoken. Others are loudly declared. Some truths are so profound and certain that they don't require volume — they rest on the foundation of absolute certainty. Revelation 1:7 exemplifies this: "Look, he is coming with the clouds, and every eye will see him, even those who pierced him. And all the tribes of the earth will mourn over him. So it is to be. Amen."

This is not speculation or wishful thinking; it's a declaration. Jesus will return — not secretly or in a way we must decode. He will come visibly, publicly, and undeniably. Every eye will see Him — not only believers or those prepared but everyone. The entire world will witness the coming of the King.

John borrows this imagery from the prophet Daniel, who saw "one like a son of man coming with the clouds of heaven" (Daniel 7:13-14). In Daniel's vision, this figure approaches the Ancient of Days and receives dominion and glory — an everlasting kingdom. Jesus claimed this title for Himself — "the Son of Man" — again and again in the Gospels, and now John declares that what Daniel saw in a vision, the whole world will see in reality. The crucified Jesus, the one who was despised and rejected, will return in glory and power that no one can ignore.

"Even those who pierced him." This is personal. The very people who rejected Him and called for His crucifixion, who drove the nails into His hands and feet — they will see Him. Not because they sought Him out, but because His coming will be unmistakable. There's both warning and tragedy in this phrase. It means no one gets to avoid the question of Jesus forever. History is moving toward a moment when every person who has ever lived will have to reckon with Him.

And what will the response be? "All the tribes of the earth will mourn over him." Some have wondered whether this mourning is repentance or regret. Is it the grief of those who finally recognize their Savior, or the despair of those who realize it's too late? Perhaps both. For those who belong to Him, there will be mourning that we didn't love Him better or serve Him more fully. But there will also be joy — overwhelming, irrepressible joy. For those who rejected Him, the mourning will be different: the realization that they bet their eternity on the wrong thing and lost.

No one will be indifferent. Christ's return will not be met with shrugs or yawns. It will provoke the deepest emotions — relief, awe, joy, terror — one way or another. The question for us today is not whether He's coming — He is. The question is whether we're ready, whether we're living as people who actually believe what we say we believe.

John adds two affirmations: "So it is to be. Amen." In the Greek, it is "Yes, amen" — a double affirmation, like driving the nail all the way in. This is settled. This is sure. God has spoken it, and God does not lie. Amen means "let it be so," and here it carries the weight of divine certainty. It will be so, whether we believe it or not.

And then God Himself speaks: "I am the Alpha and the Omega...the one who is, who was, and who is to come, the Almighty" (1:8). Alpha and Omega are the first and last letters of the Greek alphabet. God is saying, "I am the beginning and the end of all things. I was there when it started and I'll be there when it concludes. I'm sovereign over everything in between — including the seasons that feel most out of control to you." He is the Almighty — not almost mighty, not mostly powerful, but all-powerful. Nothing can stop what He has decreed.

This matters more than we sometimes realize. We live in an age that wants to tame Jesus, to make Him manageable and fit Him into our categories and schedules. We like the Jesus who comforts and heals, but we're less comfortable with the Jesus who comes in clouds and demands an accounting. Yet the Jesus of the Bible is both. He is the Lamb who was slain, tender and full of compassion. And He is the Lion of Judah, the coming King before whom every knee will bow.

The certainty of His return should shape the way we live right now. If you know that one day every hidden thing will be revealed and every person will stand before Jesus to give an account, how does that change your choices today? If you believe that He is the Alpha and the Omega, the Almighty, does that affect your worry and anxiety about the future?

And if you belong to Him — if you are among those who have been freed by His blood and made part of His kingdom — then His return is not a threat. It's a hope. It's the day when faith becomes sight and every tear is wiped away, when the struggle ends and the victory is complete. Yes, we'll mourn that we didn't love Him as we should have. But that mourning will be swallowed up in joy because we'll finally see Him face to face.

So John says, "Look." Pay attention. Don't let this slip past you. He is coming with the clouds. Every eye will see Him. It is certain. And the God who speaks it is the Alpha and the Omega, the Almighty, the One who is, who was, and who is to come (1:8).

Prayer:

Lord Jesus, we believe You are returning, despite the world's mockery and our distractions. Thank You for the certainty of Your return, when every eye will see You, for You are the Alpha and the Omega, holding all things together. Help us to live today mindful of that Day. Prepare us and strengthen our faith. When You come, may we greet You with joy rather than shame. Come soon, Lord Jesus. Amen.

Day 4 – The Son of Man in Our Midst

Scripture Reading: Revelation 1:9–13

Heart of Victory: No exile, no isolation, no suffering can separate us from the presence of the risen Christ who walks among His churches.

John is on Patmos, a rocky island in the Aegean Sea. It's not a vacation. He's there "because of the word of God and the testimony of Jesus" (1:9) — a biblical way of describing persecution. The Roman authorities disliked what John preached, so they exiled him to this barren island, far from the churches he loved and the believers he cared for. If you've ever felt isolated because of your faith, pushed to the margins, or felt that your commitment to Christ has cost you something, John understands exactly what you're going through.

But watch how he describes himself: "I, John, your brother and partner in the affliction, kingdom, and endurance that are in Jesus" (1:9). Your brother — not your superior, not your hero, just your fellow believer. He names what they share: affliction and endurance — the pressures and patient faithfulness of living for Christ in a hostile world — and kingdom, because they belong to the King and share in His realm, no matter what Rome thinks. All of this is "in Jesus" — bound up with Him and sustained by Him, centered on Him alone.

It's the Lord's Day, and John is "in the Spirit" (1:10). We're not entirely sure what this means — maybe deep prayer, maybe an ecstatic state, maybe something like what the Old Testament prophets experienced when God's Spirit came upon them (for example, Ezekiel 2:1–2). What matters is that John is worshiping, attentive to God, in the posture of listening. And that's when he hears it: a voice like a trumpet, loud and impossible to ignore.

The voice tells him to write down what he sees and send it to seven churches in Asia Minor. This isn't a private mystical experience meant just for John. It's a message for the church — for real congregations with real struggles in real cities. And what John sees when he turns around takes his breath away.

He sees "someone like the Son of Man, dressed in a robe and a golden sash around his chest" (1:13). The imagery is vivid; "Son of Man" recalls Daniel's vision of the exalted, glorious figure who is granted authority by God (Daniel 7:13–14). The robe and golden sash symbolize priestly dignity and royal power. This depiction differs from Jesus as the gentle shepherd or suffering servant, though He embodies those roles as well. Here, Jesus appears in His exalted, reigning glory.

And He's standing among seven golden lampstands. Later, we'll learn that the lampstands are the seven churches (1:20). For now, let the image sink in: Jesus is not distant. He's not removed, watching from a safe distance. He's in the midst of His churches. Right there, walking among the lampstands, present with His people even when they feel alone.

Think about what this meant for John. Here he is, exiled and isolated, far from the churches he loves. He might have wondered if Jesus had forgotten him, if the distance between Patmos and those congregations meant he was cut off from Christ's care. And then he turns and sees that Jesus is with the churches. Right there in the middle of them. The exile and isolation — none of it puts Jesus out of reach.

And think about what it meant for those churches. Some were suffering. Some were compromising. Some were lukewarm. Some were faithful under pressure. But wherever they were, whatever they were facing, Jesus was there. Walking among them, seeing and knowing them. Always present.

This is the heart of the vision John is about to receive. Before he sees the cosmic conflict, before the judgments and the beasts and the new creation, he sees Jesus among His churches. That's the foundation. That's what makes everything else bearable. Christ is not absent. He hasn't abandoned His people to figure it out on their own. He's right there, walking among the lampstands, tending and sustaining the light.

You might feel alone in your faith today. Maybe you're the only believer in your workplace or your family. Maybe you've taken a stand that cost you relationships or opportunities, and now you're wondering if it was worth it. Maybe, like John, you feel exiled — cut off from the fellowship and encouragement you long for.

And, like John, you can be sure Jesus is with you. He's not far away, waiting for you to get your act together before He shows up. He's right there in the middle of your struggle, your suffering, your faithfulness, and even your failure. The risen, glorified, reigning Lord who holds all authority in heaven and on earth is walking among His people. And that includes you.

Prayer:

Lord Jesus, we confess that we often feel alone. The world feels hostile, and we wonder whether You see us and whether You're really here. Thank You for this vision — a reminder that You are not distant but present, walking among Your people and sustaining us even when we can't see You. Help us live with confidence in Your presence, endure with patience, and rest in the truth that we are never abandoned. You are our brother and our King, our constant companion. Amen.

Day 5 – Eyes Like Fire, Voice Like Waters

Scripture Reading: Revelation 1:14–20

Heart of Victory: The risen Christ is majestic beyond words and tender beyond measure—He sees us completely, and His first word to the fearful is not condemnation but comfort.

When was the last time you were truly awestruck? Not just impressed. Not merely interested. Awestruck — that overwhelming sense of being in the presence of something so far beyond you that words fail and your knees go weak. That's what happens to John when he gets a full look at the risen Christ.

The description comes at us in waves. His head and hair are white as wool, white as snow — echoing Daniel's vision of the Ancient of Days, the eternal God Himself (Daniel 7:9). Jesus shares the very nature and authority of God. His eyes are like a fiery flame — not warm and comforting, but searching and intense, the kind of gaze that sees straight through every pretense and every hidden thing. You can't hide from eyes like that.

His feet are like fine bronze refined in a furnace, suggesting strength and the capacity to trample every enemy. His voice is like the sound of cascading waters — overwhelming, powerful, the kind of sound you feel in your chest. This isn't the voice of the gentle shepherd calling His sheep by name, though it's the same person. This is the voice of absolute authority, the Word by which all things were made.

And there's more. In His right hand He holds seven stars, which we later learn are the angels — or messengers — of the seven churches. Out of His mouth comes a sharp two-edged sword, an image drawn from Isaiah and Hebrews, representing the word of God that judges and discerns the thoughts and intentions of the heart (Isaiah 49:2; Hebrews 4:12). And His face — His face is like the sun shining at full strength, blazing and radiant, impossible to look at directly.

This is almost too much to take in. We're used to Jesus in the Gospels — walking dusty roads, touching lepers, weeping at a graveside, letting children climb into His lap. We know Jesus, and we love Him. But this Jesus — this exalted, glorious, blazing-in-majesty Jesus — can feel almost like a different person. How do we reconcile the two?

Here's the thing: they're the same. The Jesus who washed the disciples' feet is the Jesus whose face shines like the sun. The Jesus who wept over Jerusalem is the Jesus whose voice sounds like cascading waters. The humble servant and the reigning King are not two different people. They're one Christ in two modes — incarnate humility and eternal glory.

And John's response? "When I saw him, I fell at his feet like a dead man" (1:17). This is the disciple who leaned on Jesus' chest at the Last Supper. The one who stood at the foot of the cross when others fled. The beloved disciple. Even he can't stand before the glorified Christ. He collapses, undone by the sheer weight of holiness and majesty.

But then Jesus reaches down. "He placed his right hand on me and said, 'Don't be afraid. I am the First and the Last, and the Living One. I was dead, but look — I am alive forever and ever, and I hold the keys of death and Hades'" (1:17-18). The same hand that holds the seven stars reaches down to touch the fallen disciple. The voice that sounds like "rushing waters" (NIV) speaks comfort: "Don't be afraid."

Do you see the mercy in this? Jesus doesn't leave John prostrate on the ground. He doesn't stand over him in aloof majesty. He touches him. He reassures him. And He identifies Himself with titles that remind John who this is: the First and the Last (echoing God's own name from Isaiah 44:6; 48:12) and the Living One (the one who has life in Himself and gives life to others) — the one who died but is now alive forevermore.

That last part matters enormously. Jesus doesn't just say, "I'm alive." He says, "I was dead." He doesn't skip over the cross or erase the suffering. The glorified Christ still bears the marks of what it cost to save us. And because He died and rose, He holds the keys of death and Hades. Death isn't a locked door keeping us out of life. It's a locked door that Jesus has the key to. He's been through it and come out the other side, and He holds the power to bring us through too.

Yes, the vision is breathtaking. The majesty is genuine and should inspire awe. Yet it is not cold or remote. It belongs to the One who loves us enough to die for us and who rose to guarantee our future. This presence now moves among His churches, with eyes that see all and a voice that offers comfort to the fearful.

When you feel insignificant and vulnerable, recall that the one holding the seven stars also reaches out to comfort you with a gentle "Don't be afraid." If you feel exposed in your failures, remember that those fiery eyes belong to the one who possesses the keys to death and can open any prison, even the ones you've created for yourself.

Prayer:

Lord Jesus, You are majestic and awe-inspiring, surpassing words in beauty. Though we cannot fully comprehend Your greatness, we see enough to bow before You in reverence. Thank You for reaching down to touch us and offering comfort when overwhelmed by Your holiness. You are the First and the Last, the Living One who was dead but is now alive forevermore. Keep us safe in Your hand and calm our fears with Your peace. We belong to You. Amen.

Day 6 – Remembering Our First Love

Scripture Reading: Revelation 2:1–7

Heart of Victory: The Christ who commends our endurance is the same Christ who won't let us settle for loveless orthodoxy — He calls us back to first love because His victory was an act of love.

You can be right about many things and still be wrong about the thing that matters most.

The church in Ephesus had much going for it. Jesus commends their works, their labor, and their endurance. They haven't grown weary. They've tested those who claimed to be apostles but weren't and found them to be liars. They hate the practices of the Nicolaitans, which Jesus also hates. By almost any measure, this is a faithful church — doctrinally sound, morally vigilant, unwilling to compromise with false teaching or corrupt behavior.

And yet Jesus says, "I have this against you: You have abandoned the love you had at first" (2:4). Not "you've lost your love." Abandoned. The word carries the weight of a choice, a deliberate turning away. Somewhere along the line, in all their labor and resistance to falsehood, they stopped loving the way they used to.

It's not entirely clear what "first love" means here. Is it their love for Jesus? Their love for one another? Their love for the lost? Maybe it's all of those things, tangled together the way they often are. What's clear is that something central has gone cold. The engine's still running — they're still doing the work, still holding the line — but the heart's not in it anymore.

You can become so focused on being right that you forget to love. You can spend so much energy opposing error that you lose the warmth and grace that drew people to Jesus in the first place. In the end, you become so vigilant about what you're against that you lose sight of who you're for.

Jesus doesn't minimize what they've done well. He acknowledges their endurance and hard work, their discernment. But He's clear: this is a fatal problem. "Remember, then, how far you have fallen; repent, and do the works you did at first. Otherwise, I will come to you and remove your lampstand from its place, unless you repent" (2:5). This isn't a minor issue. If they don't turn back and recover their first love, they'll cease to function as a church. The light will go out.

"Remember and repent... do the works you did at first." That's the pathway back. Remember — think back to what it was like when you first came to faith, when everything was new, and Jesus was the center, and love poured out of you like water from a spring. What happened? Where did the shift occur? When did orthodoxy replace love, or duty replace delight?

Repent — which means more than feeling bad about it. It means turning around, changing direction, choosing a different path. Repentance is active. It's saying, "This is wrong, and I'm going to do something about it."

"And do the works you did at first" — not just any works, but the works that flowed from love. Acts of service that aren't obligation but overflow. Truth spoken with grace. Resistance to evil that's rooted in compassion for people caught in it. The kind of Christianity that makes others want what you have because they see Jesus in you, not just your ability to be right.

There's a promise here too, tucked into the end: "To the one who conquers, I will give the right to eat from the tree of life, which is in the paradise of God" (2:7). The tree of life — the symbol of eternal communion with God and the promise of restoration and unending life in His presence (see Genesis 2:9; 3:22–24; Revelation 22:1–2). That's what awaits those who overcome, endure, and return to their first love, holding on to Jesus.

The question for us is uncomfortably personal. We might not be the church in Ephesus, but we can so easily become like them. We can get really good at the mechanics of faith — attending church, reading our Bibles, defending truth, avoiding sin — and somewhere along the way, the love drains out. We're still faithful, technically. But something's missing.

Ask yourself: Do I love Jesus more today than I did when I first believed, or has my faith become more about maintaining standards and less about relationship? Have I become cynical toward other believers or written off the lost as enemies of the truth?

If the answer stings, don't despair. Jesus doesn't say, "Too late, you're done." He says, "Repent." There's a way back. It starts with remembering what it was like when love came first, when Jesus was enough, and everything else was just the overflow of knowing Him.

Prayer:

Lord Jesus, forgive us for the times we've abandoned our first love. We've been so focused on being right and defending truth, on avoiding compromise, that we've lost the warmth and joy that first drew us to You. Bring us back. Remind us of what it was like when knowing You was enough. Renew our love — for You and for Your people, for a world in need of saving. We don't want to lose the lampstand. We want to burn bright with love. Amen.

Day 7 – Faithful unto Death

Scripture Reading: Revelation 2:8–11

Heart of Victory: Faithfulness unto death is met with the crown of life—and the one who calls us to endure has already conquered death and leads the way.

There's no rebuke in this letter. No call to repent, no warning about losing the lampstand. The church in Smyrna is suffering, and Jesus knows it. More than that — He sees what they can't see, and He speaks into their pain with words that refuse to let them drift.

"I know your affliction and poverty, but you are rich" (2:9). They're poor by the world's standards, probably because their faith has cost them economically. Maybe they've lost jobs, been excluded from trade guilds, or had property confiscated. When you refuse to participate in the emperor cult or compromise with idolatry, there are consequences. The world sees poverty. Jesus sees riches — the kind that can't be taken away, the treasure laid up in heaven that thieves can't steal and moths can't destroy.

Then comes the warning: "Don't be afraid of what you are about to suffer. Look, the devil is about to throw some of you into prison to test you, and you will experience affliction for ten days" (2:10). This is remarkable. Jesus doesn't promise to prevent their suffering. He tells them it's coming. The devil is behind it, using human agents to carry out his schemes, and some of them will be imprisoned.

"Ten days" probably doesn't mean a literal ten-day period. In biblical symbolism, ten often represents a complete but limited time — a full measure, but not forever (compare Daniel 1:12–15). The suffering is real, but it's bounded. It has limits. God has set a fence around it, and the devil can't go beyond what God permits. That doesn't make the suffering less painful, but it does mean it's not meaningless and it's not endless.

Then the call: "Be faithful to the point of death, and I will give you the crown of life" (2:10; see also James 1:12). To the point of death. Not just "be faithful while things are hard" or "be faithful until it gets easier." Be faithful even if it kills you. This is martyrdom language, and it's not hypothetical for the church in Smyrna. Some of them will die for their faith.

Why would anyone do that? Why not recant, say the words, burn the incense, save your life, and trust that God understands? Because there are things worse than death, and denying Christ is one of them. Because the "crown of life" Jesus promises is worth more than a few extra years in a broken world. Because faithfulness unto death isn't about grim duty — it's about loving Jesus more than your own life.

Jesus introduces Himself to this church as "the First and the Last, the one who was dead and is alive" (2:8). This isn't random. He's saying, "I know what you're facing, because I faced it too. I died. I tasted death fully. And I came through it to life that never ends. Trust Me. Follow Me. I've already walked the road you're on, and I'm alive on the other side."

The letter ends with another promise: "The one who conquers will never be harmed by the second death" (2:11). The second death — Revelation's term for final, eternal separation from God, the lake of fire, and the ultimate judgment (see 20:14; 21:8). Believers in Smyrna might face the first death, the physical death that comes to all of us eventually (and for some of them, sooner than they'd like). But the second death has no power over them. They're safe. Forever.

This is hard to hear in a culture that treats comfort and safety as the highest goods. We don't like the idea that following Jesus might cost us something serious — reputation, our livelihood, maybe even our lives. We prefer a gospel that promises health and wealth and smooth sailing. But that's not the gospel Jesus preached, and it's not the word He gives to Smyrna.

What He offers instead is honest acknowledgment of suffering and a clear-eyed warning about what's coming, along with a promise that makes it all worthwhile. You're richer than you know. Your suffering has limits. Faithfulness even unto death leads to the crown of life. And the second death — the one that really matters — will never touch you.

Most of us won't be asked to die for our faith. But we're all asked to be faithful in whatever circumstances we find ourselves. And Jesus sees. He knows. He walked this road before us, through death to resurrection life. He promises that no one who trusts Him, no one who holds on to the end, will be lost.

Prayer:

Lord Jesus, You know our afflictions. You see what we face and the cost of following You. Give us the courage to be faithful, even when it's hard, and the shadows deepen. Remind us that You walked through death before us and came out alive on the other side. We don't ask for ease; we ask for endurance. We don't ask to escape suffering; we ask for faithfulness. We trust Your promise: the crown of life awaits. Amen.

Day 8 – Holding Fast Where Satan Dwells

Scripture Reading: Revelation 2:12–17

Heart of Victory: Even where Satan's throne is established, Christ's people can hold fast to His name—and He will sustain them with hidden manna and a new name.

Pergamum was a hard place to be a Christian. It was a center of emperor worship, home to massive temples dedicated to the Roman gods, and a city where political and religious power were so intertwined that they couldn't be separated. Jesus doesn't sugarcoat it: "I know where you live — where Satan's throne is" (2:13). Not just "Satan's influence" or "Satan's presence," but his throne. This is the enemy headquarters.

And yet they're still there, still holding on to Jesus' name, still refusing to deny the faith. Jesus commends them for this: "You didn't deny your faith in me even in the days of Antipas, my faithful witness, who was put to death among you, where Satan lives" (2:13). Antipas — we don't know much about him beyond this verse, but we know enough. He was faithful. He was a witness. And they killed him for it. Right there in Pergamum, where the believers had to watch it happen, where the threat was real, visible, and breathing down their necks.

So they are not playing games. They're living their faith in a place where it's genuinely dangerous, where compromise would be the easy option, where everyone around them is bowing to Caesar, burning incense, and getting on with their lives. And most of them are holding firm.

But not all. "I have a few things against you," Jesus says. "You have some there who hold to the teaching of Balaam... Likewise, you also have those who hold to the teaching of the Nicolaitans" (2:14-15). The specifics of these false teachings are debated, but the pattern is clear: these are people within the church who are advocating compromise, finding ways to participate in the surrounding culture's idolatry and immorality without technically renouncing Christ — very much in the spirit of Balaam's counsel in Numbers 25 and 31. They're saying you can have Jesus and the world at the same time, faithfulness alongside accommodation.

Jesus isn't having it. The sharp two-edged sword that comes from His mouth isn't decorative — it's for cutting and dividing truth from error, for exposing what's really going on beneath the surface. "Repent," He says. "Otherwise, I will come to you quickly and fight against them with the sword of my mouth" (2:16). This is Jesus speaking — the same Jesus who wept over Jerusalem and welcomed sinners, who showed mercy to the broken. But He will not tolerate false teaching that leads His people astray.

The promise to those who overcome is both unusual and beautiful: "I will give him some of the hidden manna and a white stone, and written on the stone is a new name that no one knows except the one who receives it" (2:17). Hidden manna — bread from heaven, nourishment for the journey, and a reminder that God supplies what His people need to persevere. A white stone — perhaps a token of acquittal or a sign of acceptance, a mark of belonging. And a new name, known only to the one who receives it — intimacy and personal relationship, the promise that God knows you fully and calls you His own.

Living for Christ in a hostile environment can be draining, and the urge to compromise persists. Though you're not confronting literal lions, every day involves small choices. How do you respond when others celebrate what you believe is wrong? How can you stay grounded without seeming overbearing? When is silence wise, and when is it cowardice? These questions lack simple answers, and some within the church may accuse you of being too rigid, narrow-minded, or judgmental.

But here's what Jesus says to Pergamum: Don't let go. Hold fast to My name. Don't deny the faith, even when it costs you. And don't tolerate teaching that makes compromise seem acceptable. The road is hard, yes. But the manna is real, the stone is sure, and the new name is coming. What you lose for My sake, you'll gain back a hundredfold. What you cling to instead of Me will turn to dust in your hands.

Prayer:

Lord Jesus, some of us live in places where the pressure to compromise feels relentless. We're tired of standing out and being misunderstood, tired of the cost. Give us the strength to hold fast to Your name and refuse the easy path of accommodation. Help us see false teaching for what it is, even when it comes dressed in Christian language. Sustain us with Your hidden manna. We trust Your promise: You know our names, and You're preparing a new name that only we will hear. Amen.

Day 9 – Tolerating What Christ Condemns

Scripture Reading: Revelation 2:18–29

Heart of Victory: The One whose eyes are like fire and whose feet are like burnished bronze will not tolerate what destroys His people — and His authority to judge is His authority to protect.

Jesus begins with praise. The church in Thyatira has love, faith, service, and endurance — and not merely on the surface. "Your last works are greater than the first" (2:19). They're growing. They're not coasting on past faithfulness but actively increasing in good works. If the letter ended here, we'd think this was one of the healthiest churches in Asia Minor.

But it doesn't end here. "I have this against you: You tolerate the woman Jezebel, who calls herself a prophetess and teaches and deceives my servants to commit sexual immorality and to eat meat sacrificed to idols" (2:20).

Jezebel. The name carries weight. In the Old Testament, she was the villainous queen who guided Israel into Baal worship, persecuted prophets, and symbolized seductive idolatry (see 1 Kings 16:31–33; 18:4; 21:25). It's unclear whether "Jezebel" is the woman's real name or a title Jesus uses based on her symbolism. In any case, the comparison is obvious: she is a false teacher — someone within the church who claims to speak for God but secretly undermines the church's foundation and guides it toward sin.

Sexual immorality and eating food sacrificed to idols likely refer to participation in pagan religious practices that were woven into the social and economic fabric of the city. Thyatira was known for its trade guilds, which regularly held feasts that included the worship of pagan gods and behaviors incompatible with Christian holiness. Jezebel's teaching likely offered a way to participate in these events without feeling like you were abandoning Christ. "It's just business. It doesn't really mean anything. God knows your heart."

But Jesus doesn't buy it. He gave her time to repent, and she refused. Now judgment is coming — on her and on those who've followed her into adultery. The language is stark: "I will throw her into a sickbed, and those who commit adultery with her into great affliction, unless they repent of her works" (2:22). There's still a window for repentance, even now. But the window won't stay open forever.

What's striking isn't just that Jezebel is teaching this, but that the church is tolerating it. They're not endorsing it, necessarily. But they're allowing it to continue, giving her a platform and avoiding confrontation. Maybe they're afraid of causing division or don't want to seem judgmental. Or perhaps they're just tired — hoping the problem will eventually resolve itself if they ignore it long enough.

Jesus is clear: tolerating false teaching that leads people into sin is not neutrality. It's complicity. The church doesn't get credit for their love, faith, and service if they're simultaneously allowing a teacher to lead people astray. Holiness matters. Truth matters. And love that refuses to confront sin isn't really love — it's cowardice dressed up as grace.

But there's hope for those who haven't gone along with Jezebel's teaching: "I will not throw any other burden on you. Only hold on to what you have until I come" (2:24-25). Jesus isn't demanding perfection; He seeks faithfulness. Hold firmly to what you know is true. Don't be influenced by teachings that normalize sin. Keep enduring.

The one who overcomes and remains faithful to Jesus' works until the end will receive a remarkable promise: authority over the nations and the morning star. These images symbolize reigning with Christ, sharing in His victory, and belonging to Him in a way the world cannot influence. The faithful remnant in Thyatira will not only survive but also reign.

The challenge for us is recognizing when we're tolerating what we should confront. We live in an age that prizes tolerance above almost every other virtue and treats any boundary-setting or truth-claiming as inherently oppressive. And the church, wanting to be winsome and gracious, sometimes swings too far toward accommodating ideas and behaviors Scripture clearly condemns.

Loving people caught in sin does not mean endorsing the sin itself. There is a distinction between being patient with those who struggle and supporting those who claim the struggle isn't important. Jesus calls us to embody both grace and truth — and at times, truth means stating, "This teaching is false, this behavior is harmful, and we must acknowledge it."

Hold on to what you have. Don't let the seduction of compromise — dressed up in spiritual language, promising freedom but delivering bondage — pull you away from the path of holiness. The morning star is coming, and He will shine brighter than every false light that tries to lead you astray.

Prayer:

Lord Jesus, give us discernment to recognize false teachings, even when they are cloaked in appealing words. Help us find the courage to confront them, despite potential costs. Enable us to love those deceived without endorsing their false beliefs. We refuse to accept what You condemn; instead, we seek to cling to the truth and walk in holiness. You are the morning star — shine brightly until all false lights are extinguished. Amen.

Day 10 – Wake Up, Strengthen, Hold Fast

Scripture Reading: Revelation 3:1–6

Heart of Victory: Even when spiritual life has faded to embers, Jesus calls us to wake up, remember, and strengthen what remains—there is still hope for revival.

Everyone thought the church in Sardis was doing great. They had a reputation for being alive — probably active, visible, maybe even growing by outward measures. But Jesus sees what others miss, and His assessment is devastating: "You have a reputation for being alive, but you are dead" (3:1).

Dead. Not struggling. Not lukewarm. Spiritually dead. This is a church going through the motions, maintaining the appearance of spiritual vitality while life has drained out. It's possible to have all the machinery of Christianity — worship services, programs, ministries — and still be spiritually lifeless. Sardis had the form without substance, the reputation without the reality.

Jesus identifies Himself as "the one who has the seven spirits of God and the seven stars" (3:1) — He holds the fullness of the Spirit and the messengers of the churches. He's the source of life, the one who can see through every facade. And He's not impressed by reputations.

"Wake up," He says, "and strengthen what remains, which is about to die" (3:2). There's urgency here. Not everything is gone yet. There are still embers, still something that can be revived. But if they don't act quickly, even that will be lost. The call is to wake up — to recognize the danger, to see their condition honestly — and then to strengthen what remains. Don't just lament what's been lost. Work with what's still there. Tend the dying flame before it goes out completely.

The problem isn't just that they've stopped doing certain things. It's deeper: "I have not found your works complete before my God" (3:2). Their works are incomplete, lacking full commitment. Perhaps they begin with enthusiasm but lack perseverance. They may appear impressive on the outside, but lack true depth. In any case, Jesus observes efforts that do not meet God's standards and fall short of His expectations.

And then the remedy: "Remember, then, what you have received and heard; keep it, and repent" (3:3). Remember — go back to the beginning, to the gospel they first believed, to the teaching they first received. What was it like when the faith was fresh, when the truth was new and compelling? What have they drifted away from?

Keep it — don't just remember as a historical exercise. Hold on to it. Live by it. Let it shape you again. And repent — turn around, change course, acknowledge that this slow death isn't acceptable, and choose life instead.

The warning is sobering: "If you are not alert, I will come like a thief, and you have no idea at what hour I will come upon you" (3:3). The image of a thief suggests sudden, unexpected judgment (an image also used of the Lord's coming in passages like Matthew 24:43 and 1 Thessalonians 5:2). For those who are awake and faithful, Christ's coming is a hope. For those who are asleep, it's a terror. Sardis is in danger of being caught unprepared, still playing church while the Lord returns and finds them spiritually dead.

But there's a remnant. "You still have a few people in Sardis who have not defiled their clothes, and they will walk with me in white, because they are worthy" (3:4). Not everyone in Sardis has gone along with the spiritual deadness. A few have stayed faithful, kept themselves from defilement, and held on to genuine faith. And Jesus sees them. He knows their names. He promises them white clothes — purity, honor, the righteousness of Christ — and the privilege of walking with Him.

The promises to the one who conquers are rich: white clothes, a name never erased from the book of life, and a public acknowledgment before the Father and the angels. This is security, vindication, and the assurance that belonging to Christ means a victory that cannot be revoked.

How do you wake up a dead church? How do you revive what's dying? You remember the truth you once believed with passion. You hold on to it fiercely. You repent of the drift and the settling for appearances over reality. And you strengthen what remains — the few who are still faithful, the embers that haven't quite gone out — by fanning them into flame again.

Maybe you're not part of a dead church, but you recognize something of Sardis in your own heart. The routines are still there — Bible reading, prayer, church attendance, missions, worship — but the life has faded. You're going through the motions. The reputation is intact, but the reality is hollow.

Jesus doesn't say, "Too late, you're finished." He says, "Wake up." It's not too late. There's something left that can be revived. But you have to be honest about where you are, willing to remember where you've been, and determined to repent and return. The alternative — staying asleep, coasting on reputation, letting the last embers die — is unthinkable.

Prayer:

Lord Jesus, wake us up. We confess that we can too easily settle for appearances, for the reputation of being alive while the reality is something else. Forgive us for half-hearted works and for drifting from the truth we once held tightly. Strengthen what remains in us. Revive the dying embers of our faith. Clothe us in white and write our names in the book of life. Above all, Lord, keep us alert for Your coming. We don't want to be found asleep. Amen.

Day 11 – The Open Door No One Can Shut

Scripture Reading: Revelation 3:7–13

Heart of Victory: Our weakness does not limit Christ's power to open doors and keep His promises—faithfulness, not strength, is what He requires and rewards.

I know that you have little power" (3:8). That's not usually how Jesus begins a commendation, but for Philadelphia, it's the starting point. By every human measure, they are vulnerable. They have little influence or resources, and by the world's standards — wealth, status, numbers — this church wouldn't register.

But Jesus sees something else. "You have kept my word and have not denied my name" (3:8). That's what matters. In the face of opposition and their own weakness, they've remained faithful. They've held on to Jesus and refused to let go, even when it would have been easier to compromise or fade into the background.

And Jesus makes them a promise: "Look, I have placed before you an open door that no one can close" (3:7). An open door — opportunity and mission. We're not entirely sure what the door represents. Maybe it's the gospel going out into the world despite opposition. Maybe it's entrance into God's presence, the assurance that nothing can keep them from Him. Maybe it's both. What's clear is that the door is open because Jesus opened it, and it will stay open because He's the one holding it.

He identifies Himself as "the Holy One, the true one, the one who has the key of David, who opens and no one will close, and who closes and no one opens" (3:7). The key of David points back to Isaiah 22, where God gives authority to His chosen servant (Isaiah 22:20–22). Jesus holds ultimate authority. What He opens remains open and what He closes remains closed. Human opposition, cultural shifts — even demonic schemes — can't overturn His decision.

This is a word of immense comfort to a weak church. They can't force doors open by their own strength or rely on political power or social influence. But they don't have to. Jesus has already opened the door, and their weakness doesn't change that. What He's set in motion, no one can stop.

Then Jesus addresses the opposition. There are people claiming to be Jews who are really "a synagogue of Satan" (3:9). They're pretending to speak for God but are actually working against His purposes. Jesus promises that they will eventually have to acknowledge the truth: that God loves this weak, faithful church. The persecutors will see that they were wrong and that the people they despised and opposed were actually the ones God favored.

Because they've "kept my command to endure," Jesus promises to "keep you from the hour of testing that is going to come on the whole world to test those who live on the earth" (3:10). This is debated — does it mean protection through the testing or removal before it? Either way, the promise is clear: their faithfulness in small trials prepares them for greater ones, and Jesus will keep them in and through whatever comes. They won't be abandoned.

"I am coming soon," He says. "Hold on to what you have, so that no one takes your crown" (3:11). The crown is the reward for endurance, the prize for faithfulness. It's within reach, but not guaranteed. There's still a fight, still a need to hold on. And — most soberingly — there's still the possibility of losing what they've been given if they drift now.

And the promise to the one who conquers? "I will make him a pillar in the temple of my God, and he will never go out again. I will write on him the name of my God and the name of the city of my God — the new Jerusalem, which comes down out of heaven from my God — and my new name" (3:12). Permanence and belonging. Pillars don't move — they're stable, foundational, essential to the structure. To be a pillar in

God's temple is to be secure forever. The names written on the overcomer speak of ownership and relationship — tangible proof that they belong to God, to His city, and to Christ Himself. They belong completely.

You might be weak. You might not have the resources or influence you wish you had. You might look around at other Christians or other churches and feel small and invisible. Maybe you feel easily overlooked. But if you've kept Christ's word and refused to deny His name, if you've remained faithful in your weakness, then hear this: Jesus has opened a door for you that no one can close. Not your enemies. Not your circumstances. Not even your own doubts about yourself.

He doesn't need you to be strong. He needs you to be faithful. The door He's opened — to mission, to His presence, to eternal security — isn't dependent on your power but on His. Hold on. The crown is within reach, and the pillar is being prepared. The name is ready to be written. You are seen and loved by the one who holds the keys. You are not forgotten.

Prayer:

Lord Jesus, we are weak. We don't have the power or resources we sometimes wish we had. But You've opened a door for us that no one can shut, and that's enough. Thank You for seeing our faithfulness, for keeping Your promises, and for holding us secure even when we feel fragile. Help us hold on to what we have and trust that You will make us pillars in Your temple. We belong to You, and that's all we need. Amen.

Day 12 – Lukewarm Hearts and the Knocking Lord

Scripture Reading: Revelation 3:14–22

Heart of Victory: Lukewarm self-sufficiency repels Christ, but zealous repentance opens the door to intimate fellowship and the promise of reigning with Him forever.

Lukewarm. The word has become shorthand for halfhearted Christianity — and for good reason. Laodicea's water supply came from hot springs several miles away, and by the time it reached the city through the aqueducts, it was lukewarm — not refreshing like cold water, not therapeutic like hot water, just tepid and unpleasant. Jesus uses the image to describe their spiritual state. They're not on fire for Him, but they're not completely cold either. They're just... there, going through the motions. Comfortable in their compromise.

What makes this especially tragic is their self-assessment. "For you say, 'I'm rich; I have become wealthy and need nothing,' and you don't realize that you are wretched, pitiful, poor, blind, and naked" (3:17). They think they're doing great. Laodicea was a wealthy city, a banking center, famous for its textiles and medical school. And the church has absorbed the culture's values. They measure success by the world's standards — comfort and self-sufficiency.

But Jesus sees the truth. Wretched, pitiful, poor, blind, naked. Everything they think they have, they don't actually possess. Their riches are an illusion, their fine clothes nothing but rags, and their clear sight is really blindness. They're spiritually bankrupt and don't even know it.

So Jesus offers them what they really need. "I advise you to buy from me gold refined in the fire so that you may be rich, white clothes so that you may be dressed and your shameful nakedness not be exposed, and ointment to spread on your eyes so that you may see" (3:18). Gold refined in the fire — real wealth, the kind that endures. White clothes — the righteousness and covering they desperately need. And ointment for their eyes, giving them spiritual sight and the ability to see reality as it actually is.

The irony is sharp. Laodicea produces wool garments and eye salve. They're famous for these things. But the church needs to come to Jesus for what they think they already have. All their earthly resources can't give them what matters most.

Then comes the loving rebuke: "As many as I love, I rebuke and discipline. So be zealous and repent" (3:19). This is not condemnation but correction. Jesus rebukes because He loves them, refuses to let them stay in self-deception, and recognizes that lukewarmness is deadly. His goal is to awaken them.

Be zealous — not halfhearted or lukewarm, but passionate and fully committed. And repent — turn around, acknowledge the truth about your condition, and receive what Jesus offers instead of clinging to the illusion of self-sufficiency.

Then comes one of the most beautiful images in all of Scripture: "See! I stand at the door and knock. If anyone hears my voice and opens the door, I will come in to him and eat with him, and he to me" (3:20). This is often used in evangelism, as though Jesus is knocking on the door of an unbeliever's heart. But the context is a church. He's knocking on the door of His own people, the ones who are so self-satisfied they've locked Him out.

He's not barging in. He's knocking, waiting for a response. The invitation is stunning: if you open the door, I'll come in and eat with you. In that culture, sharing a meal was an intimate form of fellowship, the deepest kind of relationship. Jesus isn't offering judgment from a distance. He's offering His presence and companionship. He wants to sit at your table and share life with you.

But you have to open the door. You have to hear His voice through the noise of your self-sufficiency and respond. Ultimately, it means admitting you need Him more than any earthly security or status. True victory begins at the end of ourselves.

The promise to the overcomer is staggering: "To the one who conquers I will give the right to sit with me on my throne, just as I also conquered and sat down with my Father on his throne" (3:21). Sharing His throne. Participating in His victory by reigning with Christ. This is the destiny of those who repent and open the door, who trade their lukewarm self-satisfaction for zealous devotion.

Laodicea's danger is ours. We live in a prosperous age, and the church has often measured success by worldly standards — larger budgets and greater influence. Along the way, we can become comfortable, convinced we have everything we need. Meanwhile, Jesus stands at the door and knocks, and we're too busy congratulating ourselves to hear.

The call is to be honest. To see ourselves as Jesus sees us. To recognize that what we think makes us rich might actually be making us poor. And then to open the door — not conditionally, but fully — and let Him in. He's not coming to condemn but to fellowship, not to tear down but to refine. But He won't force His way in. He knocks and waits for us to respond.

Prayer:

Lord Jesus, forgive us for the times we've been self-satisfied, convinced we have everything we need. We don't. We're poor and blind without You, desperately needing what only You can give. Come in. We open the door. Refine us and clothe us. Give us eyes to see and make us zealous again. We don't want You standing outside knocking — we want You at our table, sharing life with us. Thank You for loving us enough to rebuke us and for knocking even when we've shut You out. We're listening now. Come in. Amen.

PART TWO: The Throne and the Scroll

Revelation 4–5

Heart of Victory: The throne rules all things, the Lamb alone is worthy to open history's scroll, and every creature in heaven and earth bows before Him who was slain and now reigns forever.

Before John can understand the seals and trumpets, the beasts and bowls, and the intensifying conflict, before judgment falls, he needs to see something foundational: the throne room of heaven, where the victory is already decided.

This is where perspective shifts. John transitions from observing the churches on earth — with their struggles, compromises, suffering, and faithfulness — to the throne room in heaven, where all reality is most clearly revealed. What he sees there secures every future victory: a throne occupied by the one whose glory shines like precious stones, encircled by the rainbow of covenant mercy — a sign that his sovereign rule is framed by His promises. Lightning flashes and thunder rumbles as the Spirit burns before the throne with fullness and power. Living creatures, covered with eyes, sing endlessly: "Holy, holy, holy." Twenty-four elders cast their crowns before the Creator of all things.

Then the crisis. A sealed scroll in God's hand, and no one worthy to open it. John weeps, because if the scroll remains sealed, history is stuck — God's purposes for judgment and salvation cannot unfold. But an elder speaks comfort: "Do not weep. The Lion from the tribe of Judah has conquered." John turns, expecting to see a conquering king — and instead sees a slaughtered Lamb, standing in the midst of the throne. The Lion has conquered by becoming the Lamb. Victory comes through sacrifice. Power is revealed in weakness.

The Lamb takes the scroll, and worship erupts. The living creatures and elders fall to their knees. Angels beyond count join the song. Every creature in heaven and on earth declares: "Worthy is the Lamb who was slaughtered!" The prayers of the saints rise as incense. The redeemed sing a new song: "You purchased people for God by your blood from every tribe and language and people and nation."

This is the vision that makes sense of everything that follows. When suffering comes, when evil seems to prosper, when the powers of this world appear unstoppable, we return to this: the throne is occupied. The Lamb has conquered. Worship never stops. And — at the center of it all — the scroll is in His hand.

The heart of victory is seen most clearly here — not in earthly triumph but in heavenly worship, not in avoiding suffering but in trusting the one who conquered through sacrifice, not in human strength but in the power of the Lamb who was slain and now reigns forever.

This is the lens. Everything else in Revelation must be understood from the vantage point of the throne room. God is sovereign. The Lamb is worthy. History unfolds according to His plan. And when you see this — really see it — fear loses its grip, because you know who's in control.

Welcome to Part Two.

Day 13 – A Door Opened in Heaven

Scripture Reading: Revelation 4:1–2

Heart of Victory: When earthly circumstances overwhelm us, heaven's open door invites us to see reality from the throne—and the throne is occupied by the sovereign King.

There's a sudden, dramatic shift here. John has been writing letters to seven churches — letters full of comfort and challenge, encouragement and rebuke. He's been on the ground, addressing real congregations facing struggles. Then he looks up, and the veil between the seen and unseen is torn away.

"After this I looked, and there in heaven was an open door" (4:1).

An open door. Not a window to peek through or a crack to strain toward, but a door standing wide, an invitation to enter. And the voice — the same trumpet-voice of Jesus that launched this whole vision — calls him forward: "Come up here, and I will show you what must take place after this" (4:1).

Come up here. Not "stay where you are and I'll explain things." Not "figure it out from your vantage point on earth." Come up. See from a different perspective. Let Me show you what's really happening, what lies behind the chaos — the blueprint of the victory that is already underway.

This is one of the most important transitions in Revelation. John moves from the church on earth to the throne room in heaven. From human struggle to divine sovereignty. From the immediate pressures of persecution and compromise to the eternal reality that makes sense of it all. What he's about to see will unmask the true nature of power and the ultimate path to victory — shattering the illusion that earthly powers have the final word.

"Immediately I was in the Spirit" (4:2). There's no description of climbing stairs or passing through gates. One moment John is on Patmos, and the next he's standing before the throne of God. This isn't physical travel; it's a vision, a spiritual reality made visible. The same Spirit who hovered over the waters at creation (Genesis 1:2), who filled the prophets (Ezekiel 2:1–2), and who empowered Jesus (Luke 3:21–22) now lifts John out of his earthly context and seats him in the presence of God. And what does he see? "There was a throne in heaven, and someone was seated on the throne" (4:2).

A throne. Not a suggestion box. Not a negotiating table. A throne — the seat of absolute authority and uncontested rule. It's already there, already established, already occupied — not awaiting an election or a challenger but eternally secure. This isn't a throne waiting for someone to claim it. It's the throne, the center of all reality, the place where every earthly power is measured and found wanting.

And someone is seated on it. John doesn't name Him yet — the description will come in the next verses — but the posture says it all. Seated. Not pacing anxiously. Not scrambling to respond to crises. Seated in calm, sovereign authority, ruling over all that is.

This is the vision John needs, the vision the churches need, and the vision we need — not as an escape from reality but as the truest view of it. When the world is falling apart, when the powers of darkness seem to be winning, when suffering feels random and justice seems absent, you need to see the throne. You need to remember that there's a seat of ultimate authority, and it's occupied, and the one seated there is not worried.

The open door isn't just for John. It's for every believer who feels overwhelmed by earthly circumstances — an invitation to see reality from God's perspective and lift your eyes from the immediate crisis to the eternal truth. What looks like chaos from down here looks like a plan from up there. What feels like defeat in the moment is part of a victory already secured. Notice what the voice promises to show John: "what must take place after this" (4:1). This isn't speculation. It's certainty. These things must take place — not might, not could, but must. History isn't careening out of control. It's unfolding according to a plan, and the plan originates from the throne — the same language of divine necessity announced at the very opening of the book (1:1).

Before John sees the seals and trumpets, the beasts and bowls, the judgments and the new creation, he sees the throne. The order matters. You can't make sense of what's coming in Revelation if you don't first grasp who's in control. You can't endure the trials and troubles if you don't know that the throne is occupied, that sovereignty is secure, and that the King is reigning.

John looks up, and there's an open door. He hears the invitation: "Come up here" (4:1). Immediately, he stands in the throne room, face to face with the reality that makes sense of everything else.

The door is still open. The invitation still stands. When the weight of this world presses down on you, when you can't see how things will ever work out, and when your very hope begins to feel like a naive fairy tale — look up. There's a door standing open in heaven. The voice is still calling: "Come up here. Let Me show you what's real. Let Me give you the perspective that will steady your heart and anchor your hope."

You don't have to figure it out from down here or make sense of it all from your limited vantage point. Come up. See the throne. Remember who is seated there. And let that vision reshape everything about how you live.

Prayer:

Father, thank You for the open door and the invitation to see things from Your perspective. We get so caught up in what's happening down here that we forget what's true up there. Lift our eyes to the throne. Remind us that You are seated in authority, that nothing has spun out of Your control, and that history is unfolding exactly as You decreed. When we're overwhelmed, help us come up here and see what You see. Amen.

Day 14 – The Radiant Throne and the Rainbow

Scripture Reading: Revelation 4:3–4

Heart of Victory: The throne radiates both glory and mercy—the rainbow around it reminds us that the sovereign God is also the promise-keeping God.

How do you describe the indescribable? How do you put into words the beauty of the one who created beauty itself? John does his best, reaching for the most radiant, precious things he knows — jasper, carnelian, emerald — but even these fall short. He's trying to capture the uncreated glory of God with created images, and the gap between the two is infinite.

"The one seated there had the appearance of jasper and carnelian stone" (4:3). In John's day, jasper was likely a clear or translucent stone, radiating a light that felt less like a color and more like a presence. Carnelian was a deep red, fiery and warm. The one seated on the throne radiates light and fire, purity and passion. He is both transcendent — so holy and bright you can barely look — and immanent, burning with a warmth that draws you in even as it overwhelms you.

But here's what John sees that calms the storm: "A rainbow that had the appearance of an emerald surrounded the throne" (4:3).

A rainbow. The first time we see a rainbow in Scripture is after the flood (Genesis 9:12–17). God places it in the sky as a sign of His covenant with Noah, a promise that He will never again destroy the earth with water.

The rainbow is a reminder of mercy, of God's commitment to preserve and sustain His creation despite its rebellion. And here, in the throne room of heaven, surrounding the seat of absolute authority, is that same sign.

This rainbow around the throne tells us something crucial. The God who judges is also the God who keeps His promises. The one who holds all power is also the one who made a covenant with His people. Sovereignty and mercy are not in tension; they're woven together in the very fabric of who God is.

And this rainbow looks like an emerald — green, the color of life and growth. Not the full spectrum we see after a storm, but a concentrated brilliance, the promise of life radiating from the throne. Where God reigns, there is hope. Where His authority is established, mercy flourishes.

Then John's eyes move outward. "Around the throne were twenty-four thrones, and on the thrones sat twenty-four elders dressed in white clothes, with golden crowns on their heads" (4:4). Who are these elders? While scholars debate specifics, the symbolism here is rich. Twenty-four likely points to the twelve tribes of Israel and the twelve apostles — the people of God in both testaments, the complete church gathered around the throne (see Matthew 19:28; Ephesians 2:19–20). They're seated on thrones, sharing in God's rule. They're dressed in white, which signifies purity and victory. They wear golden crowns, symbols of royal authority.

This is where the redeemed end up. Not cowering in the corner or standing at a distance, but seated on thrones around the throne, clothed in righteousness, crowned with honor. What God promises His overcomers isn't just survival — it's participation in His reign, intimacy with the King, and a place within the circle of the King's own glory.

But notice their posture. They're not asserting their own authority. They're worshiping. Their crowns won't stay on their heads for long — we'll see them cast at the feet of the one on the central throne in just a few verses (4:10). Their thrones exist only because His throne exists. They rule only because He rules. Their authority flows from His throne, borrowed and held loosely, ready to be cast down in worship.

This is the picture of reality that John needs to see, that the churches need to grasp, and that we must desperately hold on to. At the center of all things is a throne, occupied by the one whose glory defines the very meaning of power. Around that throne is the sign of mercy, the rainbow promise that God keeps His word. And surrounding the throne are the redeemed, seated in honor because of grace, wearing crowns they'll gladly lay down in worship.

When you're struggling to make sense of suffering, when the world seems chaotic and God seems distant, this is the vision that reorients your entire reality. The throne is real. The one seated there is radiant with glory and ringed with mercy. And if you belong to Him, there's a throne waiting for you too — not as a rival to His authority, but as a participant in His kingdom, forever in His presence.

The beauty of the throne room isn't merely aesthetic. It's theological. It shows us who God is: sovereign yet merciful, glorious yet covenant-keeping, utterly transcendent yet making a place for His people right at the center of it all.

You might feel far from the throne today. The distance between your struggle and God's sovereignty can feel unbridgeable. Yet the rainbow encircles the throne, an eternal reminder that God remembers His promises. The elders are seated and crowned, proof that God makes a way for His people to dwell with Him forever. And the throne itself — radiant, beautiful, unmovable — is the guarantee that someone is in control, and His glory is matched only by His grace.

Prayer:

Holy God, we can barely grasp Your beauty. You are radiant beyond our ability to describe and glorious beyond our capacity to comprehend. Yet You surround Your throne with the rainbow of mercy, the sign that

You keep Your promises. Thank You for making a place for us there, for crowning us with honor we don't deserve, and for inviting us into Your presence. We worship You — radiant, sovereign, and faithful forever. Amen.

Day 15 – Lightning, Thunder, and Burning Lamps

Scripture Reading: Revelation 4:5–6a

Heart of Victory: The God whose presence thunders with holy power is also the God whose Spirit lives in us—His strength and His peace are both perfectly real.

The throne room isn't silent. It's alive with sound and movement, power barely contained. Flashes of lightning. Rumblings and peals of thunder. This is the language of Sinai, where God descended on the mountain in fire and smoke, where the people trembled at the foot of the mountain, and Moses alone could approach (Exodus 19:16–20). That same holy power, that same awesome presence, emanates from the throne.

Lightning and thunder mean something. They're not decorative. They signal the presence of the holy God, the one whose power is absolute and whose holiness can't be trifled with. When you stand before this throne, you're not standing before a kindly grandfather figure who winks at sin and pats everyone on the head. You're standing before the consuming fire, the one whose very presence shakes creation (Hebrews 12:29; see also Deuteronomy 4:24).

We've lost some of this in our casual age. We talk about God as though He's our buddy, as though intimacy with Him requires no reverence, as though grace means we can treat holiness lightly. But the throne room corrects that illusion. The God who invites us near is also the God whose presence thunders, whose holiness burns. He is approachable only because He has made a way through Christ — not because He's tame.

And yet, right before the throne, something else: "Seven fiery torches were burning before the throne, which are the seven spirits of God" (4:5). John tells us plainly what these are: the seven spirits of God, his way of speaking about the Holy Spirit in His fullness. Seven, the number of completeness and perfection. This is the Spirit in all His power and presence, the same Spirit who hovered over the waters at creation, filled the prophets with the word of God, and descended on Jesus at His baptism. He's here, before the throne, represented as fire — purifying and illuminating, the very fire that conquers and vindicates.

This is stunning when you pause to consider it. The same Spirit who burns before the throne of God — the Spirit of holiness and power, the Spirit who knows the deep things of God — dwells in you if you belong to Christ. The fire that burns in the throne room is the fire that indwells the believer. The power that radiates from God's presence is the power at work in His people.

Paul tells the Ephesians to "be filled with the Spirit" (Ephesians 5:18 ESV). We can treat that like a nice spiritual suggestion, something to add to the list of things we should probably get around to. But when you see the Spirit as He truly is — burning before the throne, full of God's own power and holiness — you realize what's actually being offered. This isn't a little boost to help you have a better day. This is the very presence and power of God, available to indwell and empower you.

Then there's the sea: "Something like a sea of glass, similar to crystal, was also before the throne" (4:6).

A sea, but not like any you've ever seen. No waves, no storm — only glassy stillness, as clear as crystal and perfectly calm. Some scholars see this as echoing the bronze sea in Solomon's temple, the basin for washing that symbolized purification (1 Kings 7:23–26). Others see it as a picture of the separation between God and creation — He is above, transcendent, and the sea reflects His purity and holiness. Either way, this sea is a portrait of victory so complete that even the waters have been stilled into crystal.

After the thunder and lightning, the sea of glass is almost jarring. The power that shakes and burns is also perfectly controlled, perfectly at peace. God's holiness doesn't make Him frantic. His power doesn't make Him erratic. There's a stillness at the center of all that might, a clarity and peace that hold everything together.

This is the God we worship. Powerful and peaceful at once. Holy yet present with us. Transcendent yet accessible through the Spirit who burns before the throne and dwells within us. When the world around you feels chaotic and your own heart is anything but calm, the throne room reminds you: God is not shaken. His purposes are not derailed. The lightning flashes, the thunder rumbles, the Spirit burns — and through it all, there is the sea of glass, perfectly still, perfectly clear.

You can't manufacture this kind of peace on your own. You can't work yourself into the calm that comes from standing before the throne. But you can receive it. You can let the Spirit who burns before God's throne fill you with the same holiness and power. You can trust that the God whose presence thunders is also the God whose purposes are irrevocable, whose control is absolute, and whose peace alone can anchor your soul when the world is in chaos.

The throne room isn't background music. It's the central reality. And when you see it — really see it — everything else shifts into perspective. The chaos is temporary. The fear is unfounded. The power of God is at work, the Spirit of God is present, and the peace of God surrounds the throne.

Prayer:

Holy Spirit, You burn before the throne of God in fullness and power, yet You condescend to dwell in us. Fill us. Purify us. Empower us with the same holiness that radiates from God's presence. When we are shaken by the world's chaos, remind us of the sea of glass — the perfect calm and clarity that surrounds Your throne. You are mighty beyond measure, and You are ours. We worship You. Amen.

Day 16 – The Living Creatures and Ceaseless Praise

Scripture Reading: Revelation 4:6b–8

Heart of Victory: The God who is utterly holy invites us into the worship that never stops—His holiness isn't a barrier but the very reason we bow in awe.

This is strange. There's no way around it. Four living creatures, covered with eyes, faces like animals, six wings each — this isn't the stuff of Sunday school felt boards. We're standing at the edge of something we can't fully grasp, seeing realities that don't fit neatly into our categories. And that's exactly the point. The victory John is about to see is far larger than the world we think we know.

These creatures are "in the middle and around the throne" (4:6) — they're as close to God as you can get, right there at the very center. They're not decorations. They're participants, essential to the worship that never stops in heaven. And they're covered with eyes — in front, in back, around, inside. Eyes everywhere. This is the picture of perfect perception, of seeing all things, of nothing hidden or missed.

The four faces — lion, ox, man, eagle — have sparked endless speculation. Do they represent the four Gospels? The four corners of creation? The fullness of created life? Maybe. However, what remains clear is that these creatures represent strength and majesty (the lion), service and sacrifice (the ox), intelligence and relationship (the man), and swiftness and transcendence (the eagle). They represent the pinnacle of creation, the best and highest of what God has made, all gathered around the throne in worship.

Six wings each. Isaiah saw seraphim with six wings: two covering their faces, two covering their feet, and two for flying (Isaiah 6:2). Even the beings closest to God veil themselves in His presence, recognizing that His holiness is too overwhelming to approach presumptuously. They fly in service, but they cover themselves in reverence.

And what do they do, these creatures who see everything and represent the fullness of created life? They worship. "Day and night they never stop, saying, 'Holy, holy, holy, Lord God, the Almighty, who was, who is, and who is to come'" (4:8).

Never stop. Not occasionally, not when the mood strikes — never. This isn't a duty they perform or an obligation they fulfill. This is what they are — worshipers of the holy God. Their entire existence is oriented toward declaring His holiness, and they never run out of reasons to praise.

"Holy, holy, holy." This is the song Isaiah heard in the temple (Isaiah 6:3), the song that shook the foundations and filled the room with smoke. Holiness repeated three times — not because once isn't enough, but because there's no superlative in Hebrew for "most holy." You say it again, and again, to pile up the emphasis, to declare that God's holiness is beyond category, beyond comparison, the kind of absolute purity that ensures His victory can never be corrupted.

Holy. Set apart. Other. Pure. The word carries weight we've mostly lost. We use "holy" for church buildings or particularly good people, but in Scripture it means radically different, utterly distinct, completely set apart from anything sinful or common. God is holy — He is not like us, not even close. His goodness is so far beyond ours that comparison fails. His purity is so complete that our best efforts look like filthy rags beside it (Isaiah 64:6). His otherness is what makes worship necessary and possible.

"Lord God, the Almighty." Not almost mighty. Not comparatively strong. Almighty. All power, all authority, all control. Nothing exists outside His sovereignty. Nothing happens that He doesn't either cause or allow. This is who the creatures worship — not a limited deity doing His best, but the Almighty, the one for whom nothing is too hard.

"Who was, who is, and who is to come." The eternal one. Not bound by time, not subject to change, not waiting to become something He isn't already. He was — before creation, before time itself. He is — present right now, sustaining all things by His powerful word (Hebrews 1:3). He is to come — the future belongs to Him, and He will consummate all things in His perfect timing.

This is the God the living creatures worship without ceasing. And here is what stops me cold: they're worshiping the same God we serve. The one whose holiness they can't stop declaring is the one who invites us to approach Him through Christ. The Almighty they praise day and night is the one who calls us His children. The eternal one they honor is the one who knows your name, numbers the hairs on your head (Luke 12:7), and has already secured your place in the song they are singing.

We tend to swing to extremes. Either God is so distant and holy that we can't imagine approaching Him, or He's so familiar and chummy that we forget He's worthy of awe. The throne room holds both truths in perfect tension. He is utterly, overwhelmingly holy — and He has made a way for us to draw near.

When was the last time your worship felt like this? When did you last consider God's holiness so fully that you couldn't stop praising? We get distracted so easily, bored so quickly. We sing a few songs on Sunday and move on with our week. But here are beings who have been worshiping for millennia and still haven't exhausted the reasons to say "Holy, holy, holy."

The call here isn't to manufacture feeling or work yourself into an emotional state. It's to see God as He truly is. Holy. Almighty. Eternal. And when you see Him — really see Him — worship becomes not a duty but a delight, not an obligation but the only reasonable response to who He is.

Prayer:

Holy, holy, holy, Lord God Almighty. We join our voices to the song that never ends. You are beyond us — utterly pure, completely other, infinitely glorious. We cannot fully comprehend who You are, but we bow in reverence for the glimpse we've been given. Guide us to worship You with the awe You deserve. You are holy, and You are ours. We will praise You forever. Amen.

Day 17 – Casting Crowns Before the Throne

Scripture Reading: Revelation 4:9–11

Heart of Victory: The crowns we cast before the throne were His gift in the first place—worship is the joyful acknowledgment that everything we have flows from the Lamb's victory.

Picture the scene. The living creatures sing their ceaseless song: "Holy, holy, holy." Each time they give glory, honor, and thanks to the one on the throne, the twenty-four elders respond. They don't merely nod in agreement or sit politely and clap. They fall down. They worship. They take the crowns from their heads and cast them at the feet of the one seated on the throne.

These are crowns they wear because God gave them. Crowns of honor, symbols of their authority and their share in God's reign. We saw them earlier, seated on thrones around the throne, dressed in white and wearing gold. They're reigning with Christ. They've overcome. They're in the place of highest honor.

And they take their crowns off and throw them down before God.

This is what worship looks like when you truly see God. It's not about holding on to what you've been given and feeling proud of it. It's recognizing that everything you have — every honor, every achievement, every bit of authority or influence — comes from Him, belongs to Him, and exists to bring Him glory (1 Corinthians 4:7). The elders don't cling to their crowns. They can't. How could they, when the one who gave those crowns is seated right there in front of them, blazing in glory?

This is the opposite of the world's instinct. The world says: take credit, build your platform, make a name for yourself, hold on to your achievements. But heaven says: cast it all down. Lay it at His feet. You have nothing He didn't give you, and even the crowns you wear are only worth something when you offer them back to Him.

"Our Lord and God, you are worthy to receive glory and honor and power" (4:11).

Worthy. Not merely powerful enough to demand worship or holy enough to deserve it, but worthy. This is a word of evaluation, of considered judgment. The elders have seen God's glory up close. They know who He is. And their verdict is unanimous: He is worthy. Worthy of all glory, all honor, all power. Not some. Not most. All.

Why? "Because you created all things, and by your will they exist and were created" (4:11).

Everything that exists does so because God willed it into being. The galaxies spinning in the void, the atoms dancing in your cells, the breath in your lungs right now — all of it exists because God spoke, because He wanted it to be. And it continues to exist because He sustains it. Creation isn't a clock God wound up and walked away from. It's an ongoing act of His will, moment by moment (Colossians 1:17; Hebrews 1:3).

This is the foundation of worship. God is Creator, and we are created. He is the source, and we are dependent. He is the origin of all things, and we exist only because He chose for us to exist. That relationship — Creator to creation — means worship is the only fitting response. We don't worship God because He needs our praise (Acts 17:25). We worship Him because acknowledging who He is and who we are is the truest thing we can do.

Here's what's remarkable. The elders aren't reluctant about this. They're not casting their crowns down in defeated resignation, wishing they could hold on to a little glory for themselves. They do it with joy and freedom, guided by the sobering yet beautiful realization that giving God all the glory is the most fulfilling act they can undertake. This isn't a loss; it's the essence of victory.

We carry crowns too, whether we realize it or not. Perhaps it's our career achievements or our standing within the community. It might be our parenting accomplishments or our spiritual credentials. Or maybe it's just the simple fact that we're managing to hold things together better than the person next to us. So we cling to these things, afraid that if we let go we'll be left with nothing.

But the throne room shows us a different reality. The crowns we cling to are nothing compared to the glory of the one on the throne. And when we finally see Him as He is, we won't want to hold on to them. We'll want to throw them down, to lay every bit of honor we've ever received at His feet, because He's the only one truly worthy.

This doesn't mean we pretend we have no gifts or that God hasn't done good things in and through us. It means we recognize where those gifts came from. It means we hold them loosely, ready to return them to the giver. It means we live in the freedom of knowing that our worth doesn't come from what we've achieved but from whose we are.

The elders cast their crowns before the throne, and in doing so, they find the joy that comes from giving God what He deserves. They don't lose themselves in worship. They find themselves. Because when you give

God all the glory, you step into the role you were made for — not the center of the story, but a worshiper of the one who is.

Prayer:

Our Lord and God, You are worthy to receive all glory and honor and power. Everything we have and everything we are comes from You. Forgive us for clinging to crowns that were never ours to keep. Teach us the joy of casting them down and giving You all the praise You deserve. You created all things by Your will, and we exist only because You chose to make us. To You alone belongs the glory, forever. Amen.

Day 18 – The Sealed Scroll in God's Hand

Scripture Reading: Revelation 5:1–4

Heart of Victory: Our unworthiness to open the scroll of God's purposes drives us to despair—but that despair prepares us to see the worthiness of the Lamb.

After all the worship and wonder of chapter 4, we might expect the vision to continue in the same triumphant key. But instead, there's a shift — sudden and sobering. John sees a scroll in the right hand of the one seated on the throne, and everything hinges on what happens next.

The scroll is written on both sides, front and back, and sealed with seven seals. In the ancient world, important documents were sealed to protect their contents. A will, a property deed, a royal decree — these would be sealed so that only the rightful person could open them (see Jeremiah 32:9–14 for a biblical example). Seven seals means this scroll is maximally protected. This isn't casual information. This is weighty, significant, maybe even dangerous. And it is held in the hand of the only One whose victory is absolute.

What's in the scroll? We're not told explicitly, but the context suggests it's the plan of God for history — the unfolding of His purposes, the consummation of all things, the judgment of the wicked and the vindication of the righteous (see Psalm 98:9; Romans 2:5–6). It's the "what must take place" that Jesus promised to show John (1:1; 4:1). Everything John is about to see in the visions of seals and trumpets and bowls — it's all contained in this scroll.

But there's a problem. "Who is worthy to open the scroll and break its seals?" (5:2)

A mighty angel proclaims this question with a loud voice. It's not a rhetorical question. It's urgent. Someone needs to open this scroll. History needs to move forward. God's plan needs to unfold. But who can do it? Who has the authority, the purity, the right to break the seals and reveal what God has decreed?

The answer comes back: no one. "No one in heaven or on earth or under the earth was able to open the scroll or even to look in it" (5:3).

No angel, no matter how powerful. No human, no matter how righteous. Nothing in all of creation has what it takes to open the scroll. The gap between the holiness required and the holiness available is infinite — the same gap Paul describes when he says "there is no one righteous, not even one" (Romans 3:10).

And John's response? "I wept and wept" (5:4).

This is worth pausing over. John doesn't just tear up. He doesn't get a little emotional. He weeps and weeps — not a passing moment of emotion but deep, sustained grief. Why? Because if no one can open the scroll, history is stuck. God's purposes are thwarted. Evil continues unchecked. The saints' suffering goes unavenged. The new creation never comes. Everything hangs in the balance, and there's no one who can move it forward.

This is the grief of realizing that humanity — on its own — cannot solve its own problem. We can't fix what's broken. We can't undo the curse (Genesis 3:14–19; Galatians 3:13). We can't atone for our sin or bridge the gap between us and God. No amount of effort, no degree of righteousness, no accumulation of good works can make us worthy to approach God's plan and execute it.

We live in a world that tells us we can be our own saviors. Work hard enough, be good enough, try hard enough, and you can earn your way. But John's weeping exposes that lie. The scroll is sealed, and we are not worthy. Not even close.

But here's the thing. John's weeping doesn't last long. In just a moment, one of the elders will tell him to stop crying because there is someone worthy. The Lion of Judah, the Root of David, has conquered. He can open the scroll. We'll get to that tomorrow. For now, we sit with the grief.

Why does John include this? Why does Revelation pause to let us feel the weight of unworthiness before introducing the solution? Because we need to understand the problem before we can grasp the magnitude of the answer. We need to feel the despair of no one being worthy so that we can fully appreciate the wonder when someone is.

If you've ever felt the weight of your own inability to fix what's wrong in your life, or looked at the brokenness of the world and realized that no human solution is adequate, then you understand John's tears. The scroll is sealed, and we can't open it. Our plans fail. Our strength runs out. Our best efforts fall short.

But that's not the end of the story. The scroll is still there, and God hasn't given up on His plan. The question "Who is worthy?" still hangs in the air. And in the throne room, an answer is coming — an answer that will turn weeping into worship and despair into hope.

For now, we sit with the reality: we are not worthy. But someone is.

Prayer:

Father, we confess that we are not worthy. We can't unlock Your purposes or execute Your plans. Left to ourselves, we would be stuck in our sin, unable to move forward, unable to fix what's broken. Thank You that our unworthiness is not the end of the story. You have provided a worthy one. We wait for Him. We trust Him. And we praise You for making a way when we had none. Amen.

Day 19 – The Lion Who Is the Lamb

Scripture Reading: Revelation 5:5–7

Heart of Victory: The Lion of Judah conquers as the slaughtered Lamb—true power is revealed not in domination but in sacrificial love.

Do not weep" (5:5).

An elder sees John's grief and speaks words of comfort. There is someone worthy. "Look," he says, and he gives John two titles: "the Lion from the tribe of Judah, the Root of David" (5:5).

Lion. The symbol of strength, majesty, and the kind of royal power that makes every other throne look like a toy. The tribe of Judah was promised the scepter, the right to rule (Genesis 49:9-10). A lion doesn't negotiate. A lion conquers. This is the image of unstoppable might, of overwhelming victory. The elder is telling John: there's a King, a warrior, someone powerful enough to break the seals and execute God's plan.

Root of David. This points to the Messiah, the promised descendant of David who would reign forever. Isaiah spoke of a shoot from the stump of Jesse, a root that would bear fruit and bring justice to the earth (Isaiah

11:1). The Root of David is the fulfillment of every promise God made to His people, the one who would establish the kingdom that never ends.

So John turns, expecting to see a lion. Expecting to see a conquering king, fierce and powerful, ready to tear open the seals with royal authority. He's expecting might and majesty.

And what does he see?

"A slaughtered lamb" (5:6).

Not a lion. A lamb. And not just any lamb — a lamb that looks like it's been slaughtered. The Greek word here is graphic. This lamb bears the marks of death, the wounds of sacrifice. John sees the risen Christ, yes, but the scars of the cross are still visible. The victory He won didn't erase the cost. The glory He wears doesn't hide the suffering He endured.

This is the central paradox of the gospel, the heart of everything Revelation wants to say: the Lion conquers as a Lamb. Victory doesn't come through brute force but through sacrifice. The one who is worthy to execute God's purposes is the one who was willing to die.

The world doesn't work this way. The world says power comes from domination — crush your enemies, take what you want by force. But heaven says power comes from laying down your life and loving your enemies, from giving yourself away. Jesus didn't win by killing His opponents. He won by letting them kill Him and rising again (1 Corinthians 15:54–57).

"Standing in the midst of the throne" (5:6). The Lamb isn't off to the side, subordinate or secondary. He's in the midst of the throne itself, sharing the very center of authority with the one who sits on the throne. The Lamb is God — the Son, equal in authority with the Father. The slaughtered one is sovereign. The crucified Christ reigns.

"He had seven horns and seven eyes" (5:6). Horns represent power and authority. Seven horns signify complete, perfect power. Eyes represent knowledge and insight. Seven eyes — actually identified as "the seven spirits of God sent into all the earth" — signify complete, perfect knowledge (5:6). The Lamb sees everything and has authority over everything. He's not just a passive sacrifice. He's the all-powerful, all-knowing God who chose to become the sacrifice.

And then the Lamb does what no one else could do: "He went and took the scroll out of the right hand of the one seated on the throne" (5:7).

The scroll that was sealed, the plan that was locked, the future that seemed stuck — the Lamb takes it. He has the authority. He has earned the right. And now history can move forward, because the worthy one has stepped into the center of the throne room and claimed what is His.

How did He earn this right? By conquering — but His conquest looked like surrender. That slaughter became the greatest triumph in history. And that willing sacrifice is what makes Him worthy to open the scroll and unfold the purposes of God.

This changes about how we understand victory. We're wired to think that winning means overpowering, that conquering means crushing. But the Lamb says otherwise. True victory comes through sacrifice. True power is revealed in love willing to suffer. True kingship looks like laying down your life for your friends (John 15:13).

And if this is how Christ won, it changes how we fight. We don't conquer by matching the world's tactics or fighting fire with fire. We conquer the same way the Lamb did — through faithfulness and love, through willing sacrifice. The world looks at that and sees weakness. Heaven looks at it and sees the only kind of strength that matters.

John expected a lion. He got a lamb. But the lamb is the lion, and the lion is the lamb, and the paradox holds together perfectly in the person of Jesus Christ. He is both — powerful beyond measure and humble beyond comprehension, reigning over all and yet bearing the marks of the cross.

When you feel weak, remember the Lamb. When you're tempted to think that power means domination, remember the slaughtered one standing in the midst of the throne. When you wonder if sacrifice is worth it, look at the one who conquered through dying and now holds the scroll in His hand.

The Lion has triumphed by becoming the Lamb. And because of that, the scroll can be opened, the seals can be broken, and the plan of God can move forward to its glorious end.

Prayer:

Lamb of God, You are worthy. You conquered not by force but by sacrifice, not by taking life but by giving Yours. We worship You — Lion and Lamb, powerful yet humble, bearing the marks of the cross while reigning over all. Teach us to follow in Your footsteps, to conquer the way You did — through faithful love and willing sacrifice. You took the scroll, and all authority is Yours. We bow before You. Amen.

Day 20 – Harps, Bowls, and a New Song

Scripture Reading: Revelation 5:8–10

Heart of Victory: Our prayers rise like incense before the throne, and our voices will join the new song of the redeemed—the Lamb has purchased us and made us a kingdom of priests.

The moment the Lamb takes the scroll, worship erupts. The four living creatures and the twenty-four elders — the ones who have been ceaselessly declaring God's holiness — now fall down before the

Lamb. They don't hesitate. They don't question. The same worship they've been giving to the one on the throne, they now give to the Lamb. This is staggering: the Lamb receives the worship that belongs to God alone, because the Lamb is God.

They have harps. Music is part of heaven's worship, and it always has been. The Psalms are full of calls to praise God with instruments, with singing, with every form of joyful noise. Heaven doesn't abandon music — it perfects it. The harps in the hands of the elders aren't background music for a corporate worship experience. They're the instruments of praise, the means by which the redeemed magnify the worthiness of the Lamb.

But then there's something unexpected: "golden bowls filled with incense, which are the prayers of the saints" (5:8).

Your prayers are in heaven. The petitions you whispered in the dark, the desperate cries you uttered when you didn't know what else to do, the halting words you offered when language failed — they're there, before the throne, held in golden bowls like precious incense rising to God. The prayers of the saints aren't lost or forgotten. They matter so much that they're represented in the throne room itself, held by the elders as part of the worship offered to the Lamb.

Incense in the Old Testament was a symbol of prayer ascending to God (Psalm 141:2). The aroma was pleasing, the smoke rising upward, carrying the petitions of the people to the presence of God. And here, in the throne room, the prayers of God's people are held in golden bowls — precious and valued. Essential to the worship that never stops.

This should change how we think about prayer. When you pray, you're not tossing words into a void, hoping they land somewhere. You're contributing to the worship of heaven. Your prayers are gathered, treasured, brought before the throne. They matter. God hears them, and they have weight in the purposes He's unfolding.

And then they sing. Not the same song the living creatures have been singing — "Holy, holy, holy" — but a new song. This is a song that couldn't be sung before, because what the Lamb has done is new. He's purchased people for God. He's accomplished redemption. And the redeemed respond with a song that declares His worthiness.

"You are worthy to take the scroll and to open its seals, because you were slaughtered" (5:9).

Worthy because of the cross. Worthy because He laid down His life. Worthy because He didn't spare Himself but gave Himself up for us (Romans 8:32). The basis of the Lamb's worthiness isn't just His divinity — it's His sacrifice. This is the heart of the victory: the King didn't win by taking lives, but by giving His own.

"You purchased people for God by your blood from every tribe and language and people and nation" (5:9).

This is breathtaking. The blood of the Lamb didn't just make forgiveness possible. It purchased us. We belonged to sin, to death, to the kingdom of darkness (Colossians 1:13). But the Lamb bought us back. He paid the price to set us free. And who did He purchase? Not just one nation or one people group, but people from every tribe, every language, every people, every nation. The scope of redemption is global, universal. No corner of the earth is excluded from the offer of the gospel.

If you're reading this, and you've trusted in Christ, you're part of this. You were purchased by the blood of the Lamb. You're no longer your own. You belong to God — not as a slave cowering in fear, but as a child welcomed into the family (Romans 8:15), as a priest given access to the throne.

"You made them a kingdom and priests to our God, and they will reign on the earth" (5:10).

There it is again — the same promise given in chapter one (1:6). The redeemed aren't just forgiven. They're given a new identity. A kingdom

— a people who belong to the King, who live under His rule, who share in His authority. And priests — people with access to God, set apart to serve Him and approach the throne without fear.

And they will reign on the earth. Not just in heaven someday, but on the earth. God's plan isn't to abandon the earth and take everyone to a disembodied spiritual realm. His plan is to transform and renew the earth — not replace it — to make all things new (21:5), and to establish His kingdom here with His redeemed people reigning alongside Him.

The new song isn't just about what Christ has done. It's about what we've become because of what He's done. Purchased, made into a kingdom, appointed as priests, and destined to reign. This is who you are if you belong to the Lamb.

Worship in heaven isn't detached from reality. It's the response to what's most real. The Lamb was slaughtered. He purchased us. He made us something new. And the only fitting response is to fall down with harps and bowls, with music and prayers, and to sing the new song that declares His worth.

Your prayers are there. Your voice will one day join the song. And the Lamb who purchased you is worthy of every note of praise you can offer.

Prayer:

Worthy Lamb, You purchased us with Your blood. We were lost, enslaved, condemned — and You bought us back. Thank You for making us a kingdom, for appointing us as priests, and for the staggering hope of reigning with You on an earth made new. Receive our prayers as incense. Receive our worship as the first fruits of the triumph You have already won. We sing the new song: You are worthy, forever and ever. Amen.

Day 21 – Myriads of Angels, Endless Praise

Scripture Reading: Revelation 5:11–14

Heart of Victory: All creation—angels beyond counting, creatures beyond measure—will one day join in declaring the Lamb's worthiness; our worship now is part of that eternal song.

The worship begins small — four living creatures, twenty-four elders. Then it expanded to include their song to the Lamb. But now it explodes outward in a cascade of praise that fills the entire universe.

John looks, and he hears the voice of many angels. Not a few. Not a choir. Countless thousands, plus thousands of thousands. The number is beyond counting, beyond imagining. These aren't the seraphim covering their faces or the cherubim singing "Holy, holy, holy." These are the hosts of heaven, the armies of angels, all gathered around the throne to add their voices to the worship of the Lamb.

And what do they sing? "Worthy is the Lamb who was slaughtered to receive power and riches and wisdom and strength and honor and glory and blessing!" (5:12).

Seven attributes. The number of perfect completeness. Not a limited list but a declaration of totality. The Lamb is worthy to receive it all: not just the important things, not just the spiritual things, but every scrap of glory in every corner of creation. Power — the authority to rule. Riches — the wealth of all creation belongs to Him. Wisdom — the knowledge and insight to govern perfectly. Strength — the might to accomplish His will. Honor — the recognition He deserves. Glory — the radiant display of His worth. Blessing — the goodness that flows from who He is.

Notice the progression. The living creatures and elders sang to the Lamb about what He has done — "You were slaughtered, and you purchased people for God." Now the angels sing about what the Lamb deserves to receive. The focus shifts from His work to His worth, from His sacrifice to His glory. Both are true. Both are essential. The Lamb is worthy because of what He did, and He is worthy to receive all things because of who He is.

But the worship doesn't stop with the angels. It keeps expanding: "I heard every creature in heaven, on earth, under the earth, on the sea, and everything in them" (5:13).

Every creature. Not just the angels or the redeemed — everything that has breath, everything that exists. The birds in the air, the fish in the sea, the beasts of the field, the creatures we've never seen. All of creation joins the song. And their declaration is stunning: "Blessing and honor and glory and power be to the one seated on the throne, and to the Lamb, forever and ever!" (5:13).

This is the destiny of all things. Not silence. Not annihilation. Not neutral existence. Worship. All creation was made to glorify God, and one day it will. The groaning of creation under the curse will give way to the singing of creation in the new heavens and new earth. The rocks that would cry out if humans stayed silent will finally get their chance to praise.

And the Lamb receives the same worship as the one seated on the throne. The distinction between the Father and the Son is maintained — they're not the same person — but the unity of their deity is absolute. To worship one is to worship the other. To honor the Lamb is to honor God. Jesus isn't a created being receiving borrowed glory. He is God, fully and completely, worthy of the same eternal worship given to the Father.

"The four living creatures said, 'Amen'" (5:14). Let it be so. We affirm this. We agree. This is true.

"And the elders fell down and worshiped." (5:14). Again. They never stop. Every time the glory of God is declared, they respond by falling down, by laying themselves prostrate before the throne, by giving themselves entirely to worship.

This is the vision John needed to see, the vision the churches needed to grasp, and the vision we desperately need to hold on to. When the world feels chaotic, when suffering seems random, and when it looks like evil has finally gained the upper hand — remember the throne room. Remember that all creation, angels beyond counting and creatures beyond numbering, is gathered around the throne in ceaseless worship of the One who sits there and the Lamb who was slain.

You might feel alone in your worship today. You might look around and see people who don't care about God, who don't acknowledge His worth, who live as though He doesn't exist. But the throne room tells you they're the minority. They're the anomaly. The true reality is a universe filled with worship, every creature declaring the Lamb's glory, every voice joining the song.

And one day, that worship won't be divided between heaven and earth. One day, the new creation will arrive, and the song that never stops in heaven will be the song that fills the earth. Every knee will bow. Every tongue will confess (Philippians 2:10–11). Every creature will join the chorus. And the Lamb who was slain will receive the glory He has always deserved.

Until then, we worship in the in-between. We're part of the redeemed, part of the kingdom of priests, part of the choir that's rehearsing for the day when all creation sings together. Our voices matter. Our worship joins with the angels and the elders and the living creatures. We're not singing alone. We're adding our small part to a song that's already shaking the foundations of heaven.

So worship. Not because you feel like it, not because the circumstances are right, but because the Lamb is worthy. Worthy was, worthy is, and worthy will be forever. And one day, you'll join the myriads of angels and every creature in heaven and on earth, and you'll sing the song that never ends.

Prayer:

Worthy is the Lamb who was slain! We join our voices with the angels, with the elders, with every creature that will one day sing Your praise. You deserve all power and riches and wisdom and strength and honor and glory and blessing. Receive our worship now as a foretaste of the day when every knee bows and every tongue confesses. To You and to the Father be glory forever and ever. Amen.

Day 22 – Living from the Throne Room

Scripture Reading: Revelation 4–5 (Summary Meditation)

Heart of Victory: The throne room isn't escapism — it's the truest reality, and when we see it clearly, we can face earthly trials with unshakable hope.

We've spent ten days in the throne room. We've seen the one seated on the throne, blazing with glory and ringed with the rainbow of mercy. We've watched lightning flash and heard thunder rumble. We've listened to the living creatures sing their ceaseless song: "Holy, holy, holy." We've seen the elders cast their crowns and angels beyond counting join the worship. We've witnessed John's weeping turn to wonder when the Lion revealed Himself as the Lamb. And we've heard all creation — every creature in heaven and on earth — declare the worthiness of the one on the throne and the Lamb who was slain.

Now we pause. Before the seals are opened and the trumpets sound, before the conflict intensifies and the judgments fall, we need to let this vision sink in. Because what John saw in chapters 4 and 5 isn't just background information. It's the lens through which everything else in Revelation must be understood.

Here's the question these chapters answer: Who's really in control?

When you look at the world from ground level, the answer seems unclear. Governments rise and fall. Empires come and go. Evil people prosper while the righteous suffer. The powers of darkness seem to have the upper hand, and God seems silent or absent or too slow to act. If you judge reality by what you can see with your eyes and measure with your hands, the conclusion is often despair.

But the throne room shows you a different reality. The throne is occupied. The one seated there is sovereign, holy, unchanging. His purposes are sealed in a scroll, and when the right time comes, they will be opened and executed. History isn't careening out of control. It's unfolding exactly as God has planned, and the Lamb holds the scroll in His hand.

This is why John needed to see the throne before he saw the seals. This is why the churches needed to grasp God's sovereignty before they faced the vision of suffering and persecution. And this is why we need to internalize the worship of heaven before we try to make sense of the trials on earth.

When you know that the throne is occupied, fear loses its grip. Not because the danger isn't real — it is. Not because the suffering won't come — it will. But because you know who's in charge, and you know that the one in charge is both mighty enough to accomplish His will and merciful enough to keep His promises.

The rainbow around the throne matters. It's not just decorative. It's the reminder that the God who judges is also the God who made a covenant, who keeps His word, who promises to preserve and redeem His people. You can trust Him. Even when you don't understand what He's doing, you can trust Him, because His character is on display in the throne room. Holy, yes. Powerful, yes. But also covenant-keeping, merciful, and faithful.

And the Lamb — this is the heart of it all. The one who is worthy to open the scroll isn't some distant, aloof deity who rules from a safe distance. He's the slaughtered Lamb, the one who bore the marks of suffering, the one who purchased us with His blood. He's been where we are. He's faced what we face. He knows the cost of faithfulness, and He paid it willingly.

That changes everything about how we endure. We're not following a God who demands suffering without understanding it. We're following the Lamb who was slain, who conquered through sacrifice, who reigns because He was willing to die. And He promises that those who follow Him in faithful suffering will share in His victory.

The prayers of the saints aren't forgotten. They're held in golden bowls, precious and valued, part of the worship that fills the throne room. Your cries for justice, your petitions for mercy, your desperate pleas when you don't know what else to do — they matter. God hears them. He treasures them. And one day, when the seals are opened and the purposes of God unfold, you'll see that your prayers were part of the story all along.

So how do we live from the throne room? How do we let this vision reshape the way we navigate life on earth?

We remember who's on the throne. When the news is overwhelming, when the powers of this world seem unstoppable and it feels like evil is winning — we remember. The throne is occupied. The one seated there is holy and sovereign, and nothing happens outside His will.

We trust the Lamb. When suffering comes and faithfulness requires sacrifice — we remember the Lamb who conquered by dying. We follow in His footsteps, trusting that His way is the way of victory, even when it looks like defeat.

We worship. Not just on Sundays, not just when we feel like it. We join the song that never stops, the worship that fills the throne room day and night. We add our voices to the angels and the elders and the living creatures, declaring that the Lamb is worthy, that God is holy, that His purposes will be accomplished.

And we wait with hope. The scroll is in the Lamb's hand. The seals will be opened. The plan will unfold. And when it does, every tear will be wiped away, every wrong will be made right, and all creation will sing the song we've been practicing: "Blessing and honor and glory and power be to the one seated on the throne, and to the Lamb, forever and ever" (5:13).

The throne room isn't escapism. It's reality. And when you see it — really see it — you can face whatever comes next, because you know who's in control and you know how the story ends.

Prayer:

Father, thank You for lifting the veil and letting us see the throne. When we're overwhelmed by what's happening around us, remind us of what's happening in heaven. The throne is occupied. The Lamb has conquered. The worship never stops. And one day, we'll join the song in person. Until then, hold us in hope. Teach us to live from the throne room, to trust Your sovereignty, to follow the Lamb's path of faithful sacrifice. To You and to the Lamb be glory forever. Amen.

PART THREE: The Seals and the Sealed

Revelation 6–7

Heart of Victory: Though seals unleash suffering and martyrs cry out for justice, God's people are sealed by His name, protected by His purposes, and certain of the great multitude's triumph before the throne.

After the worship of the throne room, after seeing the Lamb take the scroll, John watches as the seals begin to open. And what emerges is both terrible and hopeful — a vision of the age we live in right now, where suffering and security exist side by side.

The first seal opens, and a rider on a white horse goes forth, conquering. This is gospel advance, the unstoppable spread of the message that Christ is King. But the seals that follow reveal the brokenness of this in-between time: war strips away peace, famine brings scarcity, and death stalks the earth. These are not random tragedies. The Lamb is opening the seals. Even the suffering of this age is under His sovereign oversight: the Lamb has the first word in the conflict, and He will have the final word in the victory.

Then comes the fifth seal, and John sees something that stops him: the souls of martyrs under the altar, crying out, "How long, Lord?" They've paid the ultimate price for their faithfulness, and they're asking God to vindicate them. His answer is tender: white robes, rest, and the promise that justice is coming — just not yet. More martyrs will join them before the end.

The sixth seal breaks, and creation comes undone. The sun goes dark. The moon turns to blood. Stars fall like figs from a shaken tree. Mountains move from their places. Kings and slaves alike beg the rocks to crush them rather than face the wrath of the Lamb. The question hangs in the air: "Who is able to stand?"

Before the seventh seal opens, John sees the answer. Four angels hold back the winds of judgment while another angel marks God's people with a seal on their foreheads. John hears the number: 144,000 — symbolic of all God's people, complete and secure, sealed from every tribe of the true Israel. And then he looks, and he sees a multitude beyond counting from every nation, tribe, people, and language, standing before the throne in white robes, holding palm branches, declaring that salvation belongs to God and to the Lamb.

These are the same people seen from different angles — first as the complete Israel of God, then as the global harvest gathered from every corner of the earth. They've come through the great tribulation. They've washed their robes in the blood of the Lamb. And now they stand before the throne, where the Lamb will shepherd them to springs of living water and God will wipe away every tear from their eyes.

This is Part Three: suffering and security held together. The riders are real, but so is the sealing. The martyrs cry out, but they're clothed in white. The great day of wrath is coming, but God's people will stand because they bear His mark. The world is broken, but the gospel advances. Death takes many, but the multitude beyond counting gathers before the throne.

The heart of victory is seen here in the tension: we suffer and endure, yet we're sealed and not alone. We wait, yet we're assured. The Lamb who opens the seals is the same Lamb who marks His people, shepherds them through the tribulation, and brings them safely home.

The question "Who is able to stand?" has an answer: those who belong to the Lamb. Those whose robes are washed in His blood. Those who bear the seal of the living God. And when the final Day comes, they will stand — not because they were strong enough, but because He was faithful enough to keep them.

Welcome to Part Three.

Day 23 – The Rider on the White Horse

Scripture Reading: Revelation 6:1–2

Heart of Victory: The gospel rides forth conquering, unstoppable by any earthly power—and when the Lamb opens the seal, what He sets in motion cannot be undone.

You don't forget the first time you witness power being unleashed. Maybe it was watching storm clouds gather on the horizon, knowing the deluge was coming. Maybe it was the moment a judge's gavel fell and a verdict became final. There's something about watching power set in motion that makes you hold your breath.

John has been standing in the throne room, watching worship cascade from the living creatures to the elders to angels beyond counting to every creature in existence. The Lamb has taken the scroll from the hand of the one seated on the throne. The seals are about to be broken. And now, in chapter 6, the first seal is opened, and history begins to unfold.

"Then I saw the Lamb open one of the seven seals, and I heard one of the four living creatures say with a voice like thunder, 'Come!' I looked, and there was a white horse. Its rider held a bow; a crown was given to him, and he went out as a conqueror in order to conquer" (6:1–2).

The living creature doesn't whisper. It thunders: "Come!" This is a summons, a command. And in response, a rider appears on a white horse. White — the color of victory, of purity, of triumph. The rider holds a bow, wears a crown, and rides forth conquering and to conquer. This is not defeat, neither is it chaos. This is power moving forward with purpose — the unstoppable momentum of the King's own triumph.

But who is this rider? The interpretations have multiplied over the centuries. Some see Christ Himself, the victorious King riding out in conquest. Others see the Antichrist, a false Christ deceiving the world. Still others see a specific empire or military power. But if we pay attention to the context and the pattern of Revelation, a clearer picture emerges.

This is the first seal, the beginning of what unfolds when the Lamb opens the scroll. And what follows in the remaining seals is a picture of the world as we actually experience it — not a neat chronological timeline, but a symbolic portrayal of the realities the church faces in this age. War, famine, death, persecution, cosmic upheaval. These are the sufferings that mark the time between the times, the groaning of creation waiting for redemption.

But the first seal isn't suffering. It's conquest. It's the advance of something victorious. And given the context — the Lamb who was slain now opening the scroll, the living creature thundering the command — this rider on the white horse most naturally represents the advance of the gospel. The good news of Jesus Christ going forth into the world, conquering hearts, establishing the kingdom, pushing back the darkness.

The rider has a bow but no arrows mentioned. This isn't military conquest in the earthly sense. This is the victory of the word — the unstoppable power of the Gospel to pierce through darkness and lay claim to the human heart. A crown is given to him — authority from God, not seized by force. And he goes out conquering and to conquer — not with violence, but with the message that reclaims the world.

Paul writes to the Romans that he's "not ashamed of the gospel, because it is the power of God for salvation to everyone who believes" (Romans 1:16). The gospel is power. It conquers. It subdues. Not with swords and spears, but with truth and grace. It rides into the world on a mission of conquest, and nothing can stop it.

This is what the first seal reveals: the age of the church is the age of gospel advance. Yes, there will be war and famine and suffering — those seals are coming. But the first reality, the foundational reality, is that the Lamb's victory is going forth. The kingdom is advancing. The message is spreading. And no power on earth or in hell can ultimately resist it.

Think about what this means for how we understand history. When you look at the world and see conflict, injustice, and brokenness — and you will, because the other seals are real — you might be tempted to think that evil is winning or that the gospel is losing ground, fearing that the church has been forced into a permanent retreat. But the first seal tells you otherwise. The rider on the white horse is already out there, already conquering. The gospel is on the move, and it will not be stopped.

This doesn't mean the advance is always visible to us. It doesn't mean the church grows numerically in every place or that persecution disappears. But it does mean that the Lamb's purposes are being accomplished. This message is penetrating hearts, and the kingdom is breaking in even when we can't see it clearly. The rider doesn't ask permission. He goes forth because the Lamb has opened the seal, and what the Lamb sets in motion cannot be undone.

The white horse rider has been at work since Pentecost, when the Spirit fell, and the church was born. He's been at work through every missionary journey, every faithful sermon, every quiet conversation where the gospel took root. He's been at work in your life if you've come to faith — because you didn't conquer yourself. The rider came to you, and the gospel did what only the gospel can do: it brought you from death to life.

And he's still riding. Right now, in places you've never heard of, the gospel is advancing. Hearts are being conquered by grace. The kingdom is expanding, not through political power or military might, but through the unstoppable word of God carried by faithful witnesses. The first seal is open, and what it reveals is this: the Lamb's victory is on the march.

You might feel small in your witness. You might wonder if your faithfulness matters, if your prayers make a difference, if the gospel you carry has any power. But the first seal answers every one of those doubts — because the rider on the white horse is not you. He's already out there, conquering. You're just joining the campaign he's already winning.

The living creature thundered, "Come!" And the rider came. The bow is drawn and the crown is worn; the conquest is underway. And when all the seals are opened, and history reaches its consummation, we'll see that the rider never stopped, never faltered, never failed. The gospel will have done its work. The kingdom will have come. And every knee will bow to the Lamb who set it all in motion.

Prayer:

Lord Jesus, thank You that the first seal reveals not chaos but conquest — the advance of Your gospel into a broken world. When we're tempted to think the church is losing or the darkness is winning, remind us that the rider on the white horse is already out there, conquering hearts by grace. Use us in Your campaign, but help us remember that the victory is Yours, not ours. You are on the move, and nothing can stop what You've set in motion. Amen.

Day 24 – War, Scarcity, and Death

Scripture Reading: Revelation 6:3–8

Heart of Victory: The riders of war and famine and death are real, but they ride under the Lamb's authority — and the day is coming when He will call them to heel.

The second seal breaks, and peace breaks with it.

"When he opened the second seal, I heard the second living creature say, 'Come!' Then another horse went out, a red one, and its rider was allowed to take peace from the earth, so that people would slaughter one another. And a large sword was given to him" (6:3–4).

Red — the color of blood. The rider carries a sword, and his mission is to remove peace from the earth. This isn't a localized conflict or a single war. This is the reality of human violence throughout the age. War, conflict, bloodshed — these are constants in the world between Christ's ascension and His return. When the Lamb opens this seal, He's not starting the violence — He's unveiling what has always been true. The red horse images the violence that has marked humanity since Cain killed Abel—and it hasn't stopped.

Notice the passive voice: the rider "was allowed" to take peace, and a sword "was given to him." This isn't chaos. This is permission. The Lamb has opened the seal, revealing what unfolds under His sovereign control. That doesn't make war good or justify violence. But it does mean that even in the wreckage, even in the horror of human conflict, God is not absent. The Lamb is still holding the scroll.

Then the third seal: "When he opened the third seal, I heard the third living creature say, 'Come!' And I looked, and there was a black horse. Its rider held a set of scales in his hand. Then I heard something like a voice among the four living creatures say, 'A quart of wheat for a denarius, and three quarts of barley for a denarius, but do not harm the oil and the wine'" (6:5–6).

Black — the color of famine. The scales are for measuring out food carefully, rationing what's scarce. A denarius was a day's wage. And the voice announces prices that mean survival is expensive. A quart of wheat — barely enough for one person for one day — costs a full day's work. Barley, the cheaper grain, goes a little further, but not much. This is economic hardship — hunger, gnawing fear that there won't be enough.

"Do not harm the oil and the wine." Luxuries remain for those who can afford them. The rich still have their comforts while the poor scrape by. Famine doesn't hit everyone equally. It's always the vulnerable who suffer most.

And then the fourth seal, the most chilling of all: "When he opened the fourth seal, I heard the voice of the fourth living creature say, 'Come!' And I looked, and there was a pale horse. Its rider was named Death, and Hades was following after him. They were given authority over a fourth of the earth, to kill by the sword, by famine, by plague, and by the wild animals of the earth" (6:7–8).

Pale — the sickly color of a corpse. The rider's name is Death, and Hades follows behind like a shadow, swallowing up those who fall. Authority is given — again, this is permission, not randomness — to kill by sword, by famine, by plague, by wild animals. The four instruments of death that Ezekiel warned about (Ezekiel 14:21) are here, unleashed on a quarter of the earth.

This is grim. There's no sugarcoating it. War strips away peace. Famine brings hunger and inequality. Death stalks the earth, and Hades opens wide to receive the slain. If you stopped reading here, if this were the only vision John received, you'd be left in despair.

The vision is dark, but remember where we are. The Lamb is opening these seals. The living creatures — those beings who never stop declaring God's holiness — are summoning these riders. This isn't the devil running wild or the universe spinning out of control. This is the Lamb revealing what the age between His first and second coming looks like. Revelation isn't showing us a distant, seven-year window of tribulation—it's unveiling the ongoing character of this whole present age between Christ's ascension and return. It's an age marked by suffering, by violence, by scarcity, by death. And He's not pretending otherwise.

We live in this age. The horses are still riding. War hasn't ceased, famine hasn't been eradicated, and death is still at work. We don't have to read

Revelation to know these realities — we see them in the news every day. The question is: what do we do with them?

Some people look at the ruin around them and conclude that God must not exist, or if He does, He's either powerless or indifferent. But Revelation says something different. The brokenness is real, yes. The suffering is horrible, yes. But it's not outside of God's knowledge or His control. The Lamb is the one opening the seals. He sees it all. He permits it for purposes we may not fully understand. And one day, He will bring it to an end.

The fact that the riders are "given" authority and "allowed" to act tells us something crucial: there are limits. Death can kill a quarter of the earth, but not more than that. Famine can make survival hard, but oil and wine remain. The red horse can take peace, but only because the Lamb permits it. The boundaries are set by the one who holds the scroll, and when He's ready, He will call time.

This doesn't make the suffering less painful for those who experience it. It doesn't diminish the tragedy of war or the injustice of hunger or the grief of death. But it does mean that the story isn't over. The seals are opening one by one, and there are more to come. The Lamb is unfolding His purposes, and the misery we see is part of the age we're in — not the age we're heading toward.

You might be living in the path of one of these riders right now. Maybe war has touched your life, your family, your nation. Maybe economic hardship has you rationing resources, wondering how you'll make it. And maybe death has come closer than you ever expected — taking someone you love or forcing you to face your own fragile mortality. The seals are open, and the riders are real.

But here's what Revelation wants you to see: even now, even in this, the Lamb is sovereign. The riders answer to Him. The boundaries are His. And the day is coming when He will open the final seal, when He will return in glory, when war will cease and famine will end and death itself will be thrown into the lake of fire. The riders are not the end of the story. They're part of the middle — the hard, broken, groaning middle — but the end is coming, and it belongs to the Lamb.

Until then, we endure. We mourn the brokenness. We work against hunger and violence and death in whatever ways we can. We don't become resigned to the suffering or treat it as normal. But we also don't lose hope, because we know who's holding the scroll. The Lamb who was slain is also the Lamb who reigns, and when He's finished opening the seals, we'll see that the red horse, the black horse, and even the pale horse of death itself were never outside the grip of His sovereign victory.

Prayer:

Lord Jesus, this world is broken. War rages. Hunger gnaws. Death takes those we love. We don't understand why You permit the riders to go forth, but we trust that You are sovereign even over this. Give us courage to endure, strength to help those who suffer, and hope that doesn't fade even when the darkness presses close. You are the Lamb who holds the scroll, and we trust You with what we cannot control. Amen.

Day 25 – The Cry under the Altar

Scripture Reading: Revelation 6:9–11

Heart of Victory: The martyrs' cry is heard, their suffering is seen, and God's vindication is certain—justice delayed is not justice denied.

Some prayers are whispered in private. Others are shouted in public worship. But the prayers in Revelation 6 are different. They're cries — raw, unfiltered, desperate cries from people who have paid the ultimate price for their faithfulness.

"When he opened the fifth seal, I saw under the altar the souls of those who had been slaughtered because of the word of God and the testimony they had given. They cried out with a loud voice: 'Lord, the one who is holy and true, how long until you judge those who live on the earth and avenge our blood?'" (6:9–10).

The fifth seal doesn't summon another rider. It reveals something John hasn't seen before: an altar in heaven. And under that altar, the souls of martyrs. These aren't abstract symbols or poetic imagery only. These are real people who were killed for their faith — and they represent the ongoing reality of faithful believers who are slain throughout this present age. "Because of the word of God and the testimony they had given" — they spoke truth and bore witness to Jesus, and it cost them their lives.

Their location is significant. In the Old Testament sacrificial system, the blood of the sacrifice was poured out at the base of the altar. These martyrs are presented as living sacrifices, poured out for God. Their deaths weren't waste; they were worship, offered up to the one who gave His own life for them. But they're not silent. They cry out.

"How long, Lord?"

This is the prayer of the suffering church throughout history. How long until You act? How long until the wrongs are made right and the wicked are held accountable? It's not a prayer of doubt — they address God as "the one who is holy and true," affirming His character even as they ask Him to vindicate them. But it is a prayer of urgency, of longing, of deep grief over the injustice they've experienced.

And notice: they're asking God to judge and avenge. Not to forgive their killers. Not to show mercy to those who persecuted them. They want justice. They want vindication. They want God to act.

Some people are uncomfortable with this. We're taught to forgive, to love our enemies, to pray for those who persecute us. And we should. But here's what we often miss: forgiveness and justice aren't opposites.

You can forgive personally and still long for God to set things right. In fact, the martyrs' cry is an act of faith. They're entrusting vengeance to God, trusting that He will judge rightly, rather than taking matters into their own hands.

Paul writes, "Friends, do not avenge yourselves; instead, leave room for God's wrath, because it is written, 'Vengeance belongs to me; I will repay,' says the Lord" (Romans 12:19). The martyrs have indeed left room — they haven't sought their own revenge. They've died trusting God. And now they're asking Him to fulfill His promise: to repay, to judge, to make things right.

God's response is tender. "They were each given a white robe, and they were told to rest a little while longer until the number would be completed of their fellow servants and their brothers and sisters, who were going to be killed just as they had been" (6:11).

White robes. The symbol of purity, of victory, of being clothed in Christ's righteousness. The martyrs are honored. Their deaths are not forgotten. They stand vindicated in God's sight and declared righteous — welcomed into His presence where their blood no longer cries out from the dirt. And they're told to rest. Not because God is ignoring their prayer, but because the time isn't yet.

"A little while longer." God has a plan. There's a number He's appointed — more martyrs are coming, more faithful witnesses who will pay the ultimate price. This doesn't mean God is prolonging suffering for no reason. It means He's patient, giving more people the chance to repent, allowing the full number of His redeemed to come in before He closes the door.

But make no mistake: the judgment is coming. The vindication will happen. God has heard the cry of His martyrs, and He will answer. Not on their timeline, but on His. And when He acts, it will be decisive, final, and just.

If you've suffered for your faith — whether persecution, mockery, or loss — you're not alone. The martyrs under the altar know what it's like to pay a price for following Jesus. And they're interceding, crying out to God on behalf of all who suffer. Your pain is not invisible. Your faithfulness is not forgotten. And one day, God will answer the cry: "How long?"

You might be tempted to take matters into your own hands, to seek your own vengeance, or to let the poison of retaliation against those who have wronged you settle in your soul. But the fifth seal tells you to leave room for God's wrath. Entrust yourself to Him. He sees and knows, and He will act. The white robes are ready, the rest is assured, and the judgment is certain.

Until then, we wait with the martyrs. We join our voices to theirs: "How long, Lord?" And we trust that when He acts, it will be worth the wait.

Prayer:

Lord, we cry with the martyrs: how long? How long until You judge? How long until You make things right? We trust You, but the waiting is hard. The injustice is painful. The suffering of Your people feels unbearable. Clothe us in white. Give us rest. And help us to trust that Your timing is perfect, that Your justice is sure, and that when You act, every tear will be answered. We wait for You. Amen.

Day 26 – The Great Day of Wrath

Scripture Reading: Revelation 6:12–17

Heart of Victory: When the great day of wrath arrives, every false refuge will collapse—but those who belong to the Lamb will stand secure in His righteousness.

The sixth seal opens, and creation comes undone.

"Then I saw him open the sixth seal. A violent earthquake occurred; the sun turned black like coarse sackcloth made of hair; the whole moon became like blood; the stars of heaven fell to the earth as a fig tree drops its unripe figs when shaken by a high wind; the sky separated like a scroll being rolled up; and every mountain and island was moved from its place" (6:12–14).

This is cosmic collapse. The sun goes dark. The moon turns to blood. Stars fall from the sky like fruit shaken from a tree. The sky itself rolls up like a scroll. Mountains and islands — the most stable, immovable things we know — are displaced. Everything that seems solid and permanent is shaken. The universe is falling apart.

This is the language the prophets used to describe "the Day of the Lord" — that final, terrible day when God judges the earth. Isaiah saw it: "All the stars in the sky will dissolve. The sky will roll up like a scroll" (Isaiah 34:4). Joel saw it: "The sun shall be turned to darkness, and the moon to blood, before the great and terrible day of the Lord comes" (Joel 2:31 KJV). John is seeing what they saw: the end of all things as we know them.

And the response? Terror. Absolute, unmitigated terror.

"Then the kings of the earth, the nobles, the generals, the rich, the powerful, and every slave and free person hid in the caves and among the rocks of the mountains. And they said to the mountains and to the rocks, 'Fall on us and hide us from the face of the one seated on the throne and from the wrath of the Lamb, because the great day of their wrath has come! And who is able to stand?'" (6:15–17).

Look at the list. Kings, nobles, generals, the rich, the powerful — all the people who seemed untouchable in this life. All the people who wielded authority, who had wealth, who controlled others. They're hiding in caves, begging the rocks to crush them. And alongside them are slaves and free people. Everyone. High and low, powerful and powerless, all of them running from the same thing.

They're not running from a disaster. They're running from a person. "Hide us from the face of the one seated on the throne and from the wrath of the Lamb." The earthquake, the darkened sun, the falling stars — these aren't the threat. They're the prelude. What terrifies them is the prospect of facing God and the Lamb in judgment.

"The wrath of the Lamb." That's a phrase that stops you. Lambs don't have wrath. A lamb's only purpose is to be led — silent, defenseless, and ultimately sacrificed. But this Lamb — the one who was slain, the one whose blood purchased people from every tribe and tongue — this Lamb has wrath. And on the day it's unleashed, no one will be able to stand.

They'd rather die under falling rocks than face Him. That's how terrifying the prospect of judgment is for those who have rejected God. Every self-chosen shelter fails — caves can't hide you, mountains can't shield you, and neither wealth nor power can buy off or intimidate the Judge. There's nowhere to run, nowhere to hide, because the one you're running from is the one who made all things and sees all things.

And they ask the question that has no answer: "Who is able to stand?"

If this were the end of the story, the answer would be no one. No one can stand before the wrath of the Lamb. No one is righteous enough, pure enough, strong enough to endure the day of His judgment. But Revelation isn't done speaking, and neither is God. The terror of the sixth seal shows us the futility of running from Him, the collapse of every false refuge, the moment when all pretense is stripped away and we stand naked before the one who knows us completely.

> **The Same Day, Different Angle:** This vision of cosmic collapse and the great day of wrath appears again at the seventh trumpet (11:15-19) and the seventh bowl (16:17-21). Revelation shows us the same final reality from multiple angles, each time with more detail and intensity. These aren't three different Days, but three visions of the same final, glorious and terrible Day when Christ returns—each adding perspective and urgency.

This isn't the whole picture. The sixth seal shows the terror of judgment for those who have rejected God. But chapter 7 — which comes next — will show the security of those who belong to Him. The great day of wrath is real, but so is the sealing of God's people. The question "Who is able to stand?" has an answer, and we'll see it in the next passage.

For now, the sixth seal is a warning. It's a reminder that the Day is coming. God's patience has limits. His wrath is real. And when the final judgment arrives, every earthly power structure will collapse, every false refuge will fail, and every person will face the one they've been avoiding.

If you belong to Christ, this isn't a threat — it's a promise that justice will finally be done. Every wrong will be made right, and every shadow will be chased away by the brilliance of the Lamb's victory. Every oppressor will answer for their deeds. The Lamb who was slain will be vindicated, and those who mocked Him will see Him for who He truly is.

But if you've been running from God, if you've been trusting in wealth or power or your own righteousness, the sixth seal is a plea: stop running. There's nowhere to hide. But there's still time to turn around, to throw yourself on the mercy of the Lamb who was slain for sinners. The day of wrath is coming, but the door of grace is still open. Come to the Lamb while He's still offering salvation. On that Day, it will be too late.

Prayer:

Lord Jesus, we tremble at the vision of Your wrath. You are the Lamb, but You are also the Judge, and when You come, no one will be able to hide. Thank You that we don't have to run from You. Thank You that Your wrath was poured out on the cross, absorbed by Your own body for those who trust in You. We don't fear the great Day because we belong to You. Come quickly, Lord, and make all things right. Amen.

Day 27 – Sealed on Their Foreheads

Scripture Reading: Revelation 7:1–3

Heart of Victory: God seals His people before the judgment falls—we are marked, owned, and protected by the living God who will not lose what He has claimed.

The sixth seal just showed us cosmic collapse. The question hung in the air: "Who is able to stand?" And now, before the seventh seal is opened, John sees something crucial. Four angels standing at the four corners of the earth, holding back the winds of judgment. Everything is paused, and destruction is delayed. Not canceled, but delayed. And the reason is clear; God's people need to be sealed first.

Another angel appears, rising from the east — the direction of the sunrise, the place where light breaks into darkness. This angel carries the seal of the living God. Not a dead idol, not a powerless deity, but the living God — the one who is and who was and who is to come. And the angel's command is urgent: "Don't harm the earth or the sea or the trees until we seal the servants of our God on their foreheads" (7:3).

A seal in the ancient world was a mark of ownership and protection. When a king sealed a document, it meant "this is mine, and anyone who touches it answers to me." When merchants sealed their goods, it meant "this cargo is protected; don't tamper with it." A seal was visible proof that someone powerful stood behind what was sealed.

And here, God is sealing His servants. Not on their hands, where it could be hidden. On their foreheads — both visible and public. This is God's mark of ownership. These people belong to Him. They're under His protection. And when the judgment comes, when the winds are released and the earth is harmed, those who bear the seal will be kept secure.

This is the answer to the question "Who is able to stand?" Those who are sealed by God. Those who belong to Him. Not because of their own strength or righteousness, but because God has claimed them as His own and marked them with His seal.

Paul writes about this seal in Ephesians: "In him you also were sealed with the promised Holy Spirit when you heard the word of truth, the gospel of your salvation, and when you believed. The Holy Spirit is the down payment of our inheritance, until the redemption of the possession, to the praise of his glory" (Ephesians 1:13-14). The seal is the Spirit. When you come to faith in Christ, God marks you with the presence of His Spirit. It's His guarantee that you belong to Him, that you're secure, and He will finish what He started.

The seal isn't something you can see in a mirror. It's not a literal mark on your skin. But it's real. Revelation will later speak of another mark on the forehead — the beast's — but here we see the prior and greater reality: God's own claim on His people. It's the Spirit dwelling in you, bearing witness with your spirit that you are a child of God. It's God's signature on your life, His claim that you are His and no one else's.

And the seal means protection. Not that you'll escape suffering in this life — the martyrs under the altar were just as much God's own, marked by Him, and yet they died for their faith. But it means that on the day of final judgment, when the wrath of God falls on a rebellious world, you will stand. Not because you deserve it, but because you bear the mark of the Lamb who was slain.

Think about the care here. The winds are held back and judgment is delayed. Why? So that God's people can be sealed. God doesn't unleash wrath carelessly. He doesn't judge indiscriminately. Before the final judgment falls, He makes sure His own are marked — fully protected and secured. He knows who belongs to Him, and He will not let them be swept away in the flood of His righteous anger.

You might feel vulnerable. You might look at the chaos of the world and wonder if God sees you, if He remembers you, or if you'll be safe when the foundations of the world begin to crack. The seal says yes. You are seen and remembered by the One who never slumbers, who calls you by name — and you are safe. Not because the world is kind, but because you bear the mark of the living God. You're His servant, and He has claimed you. The winds are held back until the sealing is complete, and when they're released, you will not be harmed.

This should instill confidence in you. Not arrogance, like thinking, "I'm safe and everyone else is lost," but a calm, consistent trust that you belong to God and that nothing can take you away from His hand. The seal is intact, and the Spirit is the promise. When the final day arrives, you'll stand firm, not because of anything you've done, but because God has marked you as His own.

Prayer:

Living God, thank You for sealing us with Your Spirit. We belong to You, and nothing can change that. When we're afraid of what's coming, when the world feels like it's falling apart, remind us that we bear Your mark. We are Your servants. You have claimed us as Your own, and You will keep us safe. Hold back the winds of judgment until all Your people are sealed, and then bring us through to the day when we stand before You in joy. Amen.

Day 28 – The Number No One Can Break

Scripture Reading: Revelation 7:4–8

Heart of Victory: The 144,000 represents all of God's people, sealed and complete—not one missing, not one forgotten, every believer counted and kept by God Himself.

And I heard the number of those who were sealed: 144,000 sealed from every tribe of the Israelites." (Revelation 7:4)

A number. Specific and complete. And then John lists the tribes: twelve thousand from Judah, twelve thousand from Reuben, twelve thousand from Gad. He goes through all twelve tribes of Israel, and the count is the same for each one. Twelve thousand. Twelve tribes. 144,000 total.

Some have tried to take this literally. They've said the 144,000 is a special group — Jewish believers during the tribulation, or perhaps the only ones making it to heaven. But when you pay attention to how Revelation uses numbers, a different picture emerges.

Twelve is the number of God's people — twelve tribes of Israel, twelve apostles of the Lamb. It represents completeness, the fullness of God's chosen people. A thousand is the number of abundance and magnitude — it means more than you can count. Twelve times twelve times a thousand equals 144,000. This isn't a head count. It's a symbolic statement: all of God's people, from every part of His covenant community, are sealed. Not one is missing. The number is complete.

Notice how the list is arranged. It's not the exact order of the twelve tribes you'd find in the Old Testament. Dan is missing (a detail many have linked to Dan's prominent idolatry in Israel's history), and Manasseh is included separately from Ephraim. This isn't a literal genealogical registry. It's a theological statement: the true Israel, the people of God from all ages, are sealed in their entirety.

Paul writes about this in Romans: "Not all who are descended from Israel are Israel" (Romans 9:6). Physical descent doesn't make you part of God's people. Faith does. And in Christ, the dividing wall between Jew and Gentile has been torn down. All who trust in Jesus — whether from Jewish or Gentile background — are part of the true Israel, God's people who inherit the promises.

So the 144,000 represents all believers. Every single person who belongs to Christ, from every generation, from every nation, sealed by God and kept secure. Not a select few. All of them — every single one. Complete. And numbered by God Himself.

This matters because it means you're not an afterthought. If you belong to Christ, you're part of this number — not as one digit in a literal 144,000, but as someone included in the complete people of God the number represents. God didn't seal 143,999 people and then squeeze you in as a bonus. You were counted and intended from the beginning. God included you in the plan before time began. The number is precise because God knows exactly who His people are, and He will not lose a single one. Jesus said, "This is the will of him who sent me: that I should lose none of those he has given me but should raise them up on the last day" (John 6:39). The 144,000 is that promise in symbolic form. Every person the Father has given to the Son will be raised on the last day. Not 143,000. Not 145,000. The exact number God intended — complete, secure, and sealed.

Some people worry about whether they're really saved, whether they'll make it to the end. The 144,000 is God's answer to that fear. If you belong to Christ — if you've trusted in His death for your sins and His resurrection for your life — then you're sealed. You're part of the number, included in the count. And God doesn't lose what He seals.

This should also give you confidence in God's mission. The gospel isn't a desperate attempt to scrape together whatever followers Jesus can find. It's the fulfillment of a plan, the gathering of a people God has already chosen and sealed. The harvest isn't up in the air. God knows the number, and He will bring every one of them home.

But there's also humility here. You don't know who's sealed. You can't look at someone and say, "You're in" or "You're out." Only God knows the number. What you can do is proclaim the gospel, trusting that God will use your words to call His people to Himself. You're not responsible for sealing anyone — that's God's work. You're just responsible for speaking the truth and trusting Him with the results.

The number is complete. The sealing is secure. Every tribe is represented, every person God has chosen is marked, and when the final day comes, not one will be missing. The winds of judgment are held back until the last one is sealed. And when they're released, all 144,000 — symbolic of all believers — will stand, not because of their own righteousness, but because God has claimed them and will not let them go.

Prayer:

Father, thank You that the number of Your people is exact, that You know who we are and You will not lose even one of us. We're part of the 144,000 — not because we're special, but because You chose us and sealed us as Your own. Give us confidence in Your promises and humility in our witness. Finish the work You've started. Seal every last one, and bring us all home. Amen.

Day 29 – A Great Multitude from Every Nation

Scripture Reading: Revelation 7:9–12

Heart of Victory: The multitude beyond counting from every nation declares what we all know: salvation belongs to God and to the Lamb—we are here by grace alone.

The scene shifts. John just heard the number: 144,000, sealed from the tribes of Israel. And now he looks, and he sees something that can't be numbered. A vast multitude. Not twelve thousand from each tribe, but people beyond counting. And they're not from Israel alone—they're from every nation, every tribe, every people, every language. The whole world is represented. Every corner of the earth has contributed to this crowd.

They're standing before the throne and before the Lamb. Not cowering in fear like those who cried out in chapter 6, begging the rocks to crush them. These are standing in victory, clothed in white robes, holding palm branches—the ancient symbol of triumph and celebration. And they're worshiping.

"Salvation belongs to our God, who is seated on the throne, and to the Lamb!" (7:10)

This is their song. Not "We achieved salvation." Not "We earned our place here." Salvation belongs to God and to the Lamb. They're here because of what God has done, because of the Lamb who was slain. And they know it. Their white robes didn't come from their own righteousness. Their victory didn't come from their own strength. They're here by grace, purchased by blood, and they're giving all the credit where it belongs.

> **Another Angle:** Just verses earlier (7:4-8), we saw 144,000 sealed from the tribes of Israel. John hears the number, then looks, and now we see a numberless multitude from every nation. These aren't two different groups but the same people—God's complete church—pictured first as the true Israel and then as the harvest from all nations. Revelation shows us the same reality from different perspectives.

All the angels stood around the throne and the elders, surrounding the four living creatures. And they joined in the worship. "Amen! Blessing and glory and wisdom and thanksgiving and honor and power and strength be to our God forever and ever. Amen" (7:12).

Seven attributes again. Perfect worship. The angels don't say "salvation belongs to us"—that's not their song to sing. But they join in affirming that everything—blessing, glory, wisdom, thanksgiving, honor, power, strength—belongs to God forever. The throne room erupts in worship because the redeemed are finally home, because the plan has actually worked, and because the Great Commission has been transformed from a task into a sea of faces from every nation.

This is what Jesus died for. Not just a few people from one nation or one ethnic group. He died to purchase "from every tribe and language and people and nation" (5:9). And here they are. The mission is accomplished. The harvest is gathered. And they're standing before the throne, declaring that salvation belongs to God.

If you belong to Christ, you're part of this multitude. You might look around your church and see a small gathering, a handful of faithful people in a world that doesn't care. But this is the reality you're heading toward. You're not alone. You're part of a multitude beyond counting, from every tribe and tongue, all purchased by the same blood, all clothed in the same white robes, all holding the same palm branches, all singing the same song.

And notice the diversity. Every nation. Every tribe. Every people. Every language. The new humanity in Christ doesn't erase cultural distinctives. It doesn't turn everyone into clones. But it does unite people who had no business being together—people who were enemies on earth, people separated by language and custom and history—and makes them one family, one people, one worshiping multitude before the throne.

This is the gospel's power. It crosses every boundary and breaks down every wall, taking people who were alienated from God and alienated from each other and bringing them together in Christ. And in the end, the throne room will look like this: not one nation dominating, not one culture erasing the others, but every nation and tribe represented, every tongue singing, all of them declaring that salvation belongs to God and to the Lamb.

Paul writes, "There is no Jew or Greek, slave or free, male and female; since you are all one in Christ Jesus" (Galatians 3:28). The distinctions remain, but they no longer divide. In Christ, we're one. And one day, that unity will be visible for all to see—a vast multitude that no one can number, from every corner of the earth, standing together before the throne.

Your tribe is represented and your people are there among them. Your language will join the chorus. You're not an outsider or a second-class citizen in this kingdom—you're part of the multitude. Clothed in white and holding a palm branch, you'll stand before the throne to declare with everyone else that salvation belongs to our God and to the Lamb.

So when you worship now, remember: you're practicing for that Day. The song you sing on Sunday is the song you'll sing forever. And the people you worship with—different backgrounds, different stories, all woven together by grace—are a tangible foretaste of the multitude that no one can count.

Prayer:

God of all nations, thank You for the multitude You're gathering from every tribe and tongue. We're amazed that You chose us and included us, that we get to stand before the throne and worship with people from every corner of the earth. Give us a heart for the nations. Help us to see the diversity of Your people as a gift, not a threat. And prepare us for the Day when we join the multitude in singing: salvation belongs to You and to the Lamb. Amen.

Day 30 – Robes Washed in the Blood

Scripture Reading: Revelation 7:13–17

Heart of Victory: The blood of the Lamb makes us white, and the presence of God shelters us forever—every hunger satisfied, every tear wiped away by His own hand.

The elder asks John a question he can't answer: "Who are these people, and where did they come from?" (7:13) John's response is humble: "Sir, you know" (7:14). And the elder explains.

These are the ones emerging from the fire of the great tribulation—the survivors of a war already won, even though many of them died in the fight. This is not a specific seven-year period at the end of history, but the ongoing suffering and persecution that God's people have faced in every generation. From the moment Stephen was stoned to the last martyr before Christ returns, this is the great tribulation — the sustained pressure, the relentless hostility, and the quiet, daily cost of remaining faithful to a King whom the world still refuses to recognize.

And they made it through. They're standing before the throne. But how?

"They washed their robes and made them white in the blood of the Lamb"(7:14).

This is paradox at its most vivid. Blood doesn't make things white. Blood stains. Blood marks. Blood ruins white cloth. But the blood of the Lamb does the opposite. It cleanses and purifies. It makes white what was filthy, and pure what was defiled.

Isaiah saw this: "Though your sins are scarlet, they will be as white as snow; though they are crimson red, they will be like wool" (Isaiah 1:18). What seems impossible — washing away the stain of sin — is exactly what the blood of Jesus accomplishes. Not because blood has magical properties, but because the Lamb's blood represents His sacrifice. Christ is the Substitutionary King who took our place and bore the punishment we deserved.

You didn't wash your robe by being good enough. You didn't make it white by trying harder or doing better. You washed it in the blood of the Lamb. His righteousness became yours, His purity covered your filth, and His death dealt with your guilt. And now you stand clothed in white, not because of anything you did, but because of what He did for you.

The elder continues: "For this reason they are before the throne of God, and they serve him day and night in his temple. The one seated on the throne will shelter them: They will no longer hunger; they will no longer thirst; the sun will no longer strike them, nor will any scorching heat" (7:15–16).

This is the promise. Not just forgiveness, but presence. Not just pardon, but proximity. They're before the throne, serving God in His temple. And God Himself shelters them. The word there means to spread a tent over them, to dwell with them. This is intimate, protective presence. God wrapping Himself around His people like a covering.

They will no longer hunger or thirst. No more longing. Every need that once went unmet is satisfied at last. In this life, we hunger for all kinds of things — food, security, love, meaning. But in the presence of God, every hunger is satisfied. He is enough. More than enough.

The sun will no longer strike them, nor any scorching heat. No more suffering. No more pain. No more burning injustice or searing grief. The trials of this life — the great tribulation they came through — are over. And in their place, there's comfort. There's rest. There's shelter under the wings of God.

And then the most beautiful promise: "The Lamb who is at the center of the throne will shepherd them; he will guide them to springs of the waters of life, and God will wipe away every tear from their eyes" (7:17).

The Lamb will shepherd them. The one who was slain, the one whose blood washed their robes, is also the one who cares for them forever. He's not just Savior. He's Shepherd. He's not distant or detached. He's leading them, guiding them, bringing them to springs of living water. Everything they need, He provides. Every thirst, He quenches.

And God will wipe away every tear. Not just dry their eyes or tell them to stop crying. He will personally, tenderly, lovingly wipe away every tear. Every sorrow. Every grief. Every pain that brought tears in this life — He will touch those eyes and make the tears stop, because there will be nothing left to cry about.

This is what awaits those who wash their robes in the blood of the Lamb. You escape judgment, yes — but you also enter the very presence of God. You survive, but you're also sheltered and satisfied. The Lamb who died for you will shepherd you forever, and God Himself will wipe away your tears.

If you're in the middle of the great tribulation now — if following Jesus has cost you something, if you're weary and worn, if the hunger and thirst and scorching heat of this life are pressing hard — hold on. The robes are already white. The shelter is already prepared. The Lamb is already waiting to shepherd you. And the day is coming when God will wipe away every tear, and you'll wonder why you ever doubted that it was worth it.

Prayer:

Lamb of God, thank You for washing our robes in Your blood. We were filthy, and You made us white. We were guilty, and You made us pure. Thank You that Your work doesn't end with forgiveness. You shepherd us, shelter us, guide us to living water, and promise to wipe away every tear. We're tired, Lord. We hunger and thirst. The great tribulation presses hard. But we trust You. We're holding on. And we can't wait for the Day when You dry our eyes, and we stand before the throne, robed in white, forever in Your presence. Amen.

Day 31 – Tribulation and Triumph

Scripture Reading: Revelation 6–7 (Summary Meditation)

Heart of Victory: The tribulation is real, but so is the triumph—the Lamb who permits our suffering is the same Lamb who seals us, shepherds us, and will wipe away every tear.

We've watched the Lamb open six seals. We've seen riders go forth — white horse of gospel conquest, red horse of war, black horse of famine, pale horse of death. We've heard the martyrs cry out from under the altar: "How long, Lord?" We've witnessed the sky roll up like a scroll and the mountains shake from their foundations. We've watched kings and slaves alike beg the rocks to crush them rather than face the wrath of the Lamb.

And then, just when the vision seems darkest, we've seen the sealing. Four angels holding back the winds of judgment while another angel marks the servants of God on their foreheads. We've heard the number: 144,000 — symbolic of all God's people, complete and secure. We've seen the multitude beyond counting from every nation, clothed in white, holding palm branches, declaring that salvation belongs to God and to the Lamb.

This is the tension we live in — the jarring overlap of tribulation and triumph, suffering and security. It's the raw cry of 'How long?' echoing alongside the promise of white robes, and the great day of wrath outside the door while the sovereign seal keeps us safe within.

Revelation doesn't pretend the suffering isn't real. The riders are real. War is real. Famine is real. Death is real. People suffer for their faith, and some die for it. The martyrs under the altar aren't just abstract symbols — they represent actual people who paid the ultimate price for following Jesus. The great tribulation isn't a metaphor — it's the sustained hostility the church faces from the moment Christ ascended until the moment He returns.

But the seals show us that the suffering is not meaningless, nor random. It's not outside of God's control. The Lamb is the one opening the seals. The riders are given authority — by God. The martyrs are clothed in white robes — by God. The sealing happens before the final judgment falls. Every detail is under the oversight of the one who sits on the throne and the Lamb who stands in the midst of it.

This doesn't mean God causes evil. It doesn't mean He delights in suffering. But it does mean He permits it for purposes we may not fully understand, and He remains sovereign over it even when it feels like chaos. The red horse takes peace from the earth, but only because it was allowed. Death kills a fourth of the earth, but only a fourth. The boundaries are defined. The limits are real. When the moment arrives, the Lamb will bring it all to a stop.

The martyrs' cry — "How long?" — is the prayer of every believer who has ever suffered. How long until You act? How long until justice comes? How long until the wrongs are made right? And God's answer is not "Stop asking." His answer is "Wait a little while longer. Rest. You are clothed in white. The vindication is coming."

The waiting is hard. The "little while longer" can feel like an eternity when you're the one suffering. But the sealing does tell us something crucial. God knows who His people are, and He will not lose them. The winds are held back until every last one is marked. The number is exact. Not one too many, not one too few. All of God's people will be gathered, sealed, and kept.

And then there's the multitude. The vision doesn't end with suffering; it ends with worship. The great tribulation is real, but so is the great gathering. Those from every nation, tribe, people, and language — standing before the throne, robed in white, holding palm branches. They made it through. They washed their robes in the blood of the Lamb. And now they're singing: "Salvation belongs to our God and to the Lamb."

This is where we're heading. Not just escape from suffering, but entrance into the presence of God. Not just survival, but triumph. Not just relief, but joy — the kind of joy that comes when you've been through the fire and come out refined. You realize you've lost everything earthly and gained everything eternal.

The Lamb who opens the seals is also the Lamb who shepherds His people. The one who permits the tribulation is also the one who promises to wipe away every tear. He's not distant. He's not indifferent. He's sovereign over the suffering, as He's present in it. The martyrs are under the altar — right there in the throne room, in the presence of God, crying out and being heard.

So how do we live in the tension? How do we endure the tribulation while clinging to the triumph — a victory we can't yet see, but one that is already won?

We remember the throne. The Lamb is opening the seals. He's in control. The riders answer to Him.

We remember the sealing. We belong to God. We bear His mark. When the final judgment comes, we will stand.

We hold on to the multitude. We're not alone. We're part of a vast company from every nation, all heading to the same place, all washed in the same blood.

And we cling to the promise. The Lamb will shepherd us. God will wipe away every tear. The hunger and thirst and scorching heat of this life will give way to satisfaction, comfort, and rest in His presence.

And we keep crying out: "How long, Lord?" Not because we doubt His power or question His goodness, but because we long for the Day when the seals are finished, the scrolls are opened, the tribulation is over, and the triumph is complete.

Until then, we endure. We hold fast. We wash our robes in the blood of the Lamb. And we trust that suffering under His seal is never wasted, because He weaves it into our refinement and final joy. And when we stand before the throne, robed in white, we'll understand that it was worth it.

Prayer:

Lamb of God, we live in the tension. The suffering is real, the waiting is hard, and the cry of "How long?" is on our lips. But You are sovereign. You are opening the seals. You have sealed us. You will bring us through. Strengthen us to endure. Comfort us in the tribulation. And hasten the Day when we join the multitude before Your throne, robed in white, declaring that salvation belongs to You. We trust You, even when we don't understand. Hold us fast. Amen.

Day 32 – Sealed Hearts in an Unsealed World

Scripture Reading: Revelation 6–7 (Topical Meditation)

Heart of Victory: We endure not because we're strong but because we're sealed—marked by God, held by the Spirit, destined for the Day when every tear is wiped away.

The world is not sealed. It's still broken, still groaning, still waiting for redemption. The riders still go forth. War still rages, famine still gnaws, and death still takes. The powers of this age still rage against God and His people. If you're looking for safety in the world as it is, you won't find it.

But your heart is sealed. If you belong to Christ, you bear the mark of the living God. The Spirit dwells in you as God's guarantee that you are His and He will finish what He started. And that seal — that assurance of belonging, that promise of protection, that certainty of future glory — redefines every moment you live in an unsealed world.

Assurance fuels endurance. When you know you're secure, you can face what's coming without being crushed by it. When you know the outcome and that the Lamb is opening the seals while you bear His mark, you can walk through the tribulation without losing hope.

Let's be honest, endurance is hard. It's one thing to sprint through a crisis. It's another thing to keep going when the pressure doesn't let up. Suffering stretches on and the martyrs' cry — "How long?" — becomes your own. You get tired. You get discouraged. You start to wonder if it's worth it. You begin to wonder if faithfulness even matters anymore. Does God really see you.

This is where assurance makes the difference. You don't endure because you're strong. You endure because you're sealed. You don't keep going because you have endless reserves of willpower. You keep going because you know who holds you and where you're heading.

Paul writes to the Ephesians about being "sealed with the promised Holy Spirit" (Ephesians 1:13). The Spirit is the down payment, the guarantee, the first installment of everything God has promised. He doesn't just save you and send you on your way, hoping you'll make it. He seals you and marks you as His own, depositing the Spirit in you as proof that He's not letting go.

And that seal does something in you. It gives you confidence. Not arrogance — not "I'm saved and nothing I do matters" — but steady, quiet confidence that you belong to God and He will keep you. When the world feels like it's falling apart, the seal reminds you that you're held together by the one who cannot fail. When your own strength runs out, the seal says, "this isn't about your strength. It's about His."

The sealing also gives you perspective. The riders are real. The suffering is real. But they're not the end of the story. The Lamb is opening the seals. God is holding back the winds until every last one of His people is marked. The multitude beyond counting is already gathering. You're not watching chaos unfold — you're watching a plan executed. And you're part of it.

This changes how you respond to suffering. You don't deny it or minimize it. You don't pretend it doesn't hurt. But you also don't let it have the final word. The martyrs under the altar are suffering, yes. But they're also clothed in white robes, waiting for vindication, secure in God's presence. The great tribulation is real, but so is the great gathering. You can grieve without despairing. You can lament without losing hope because YOU ARE sealed.

Here's what this can look like in practice: You face opposition at work for your faith. It costs you a promotion, maybe even your job. The world says you're a fool for holding the line. But you know, so you remind yourself, "I'm sealed. I belong to God. He sees this. And He will vindicate me, if not now, then on the Day when every wrong is made right."

You watch someone you love suffer. Maybe it's illness or injustice. Perhaps even persecution. You cry out, "How long, Lord?" You don't understand why He's allowing it. But you know: they're sealed. If they belong to Christ, they bear His mark. The Lamb is their Shepherd. And one day, God will wipe away every tear from their eyes.

You look at the state of the world — there's violence and brokenness — and you feel small and powerless. And yet you know, you remember: the riders answer to the Lamb. The boundaries are set. The number is complete. God is gathering His people from every nation, and when the last one is sealed, He will act. Your faithfulness isn't futile. The gospel is advancing. The white horse rider is still conquering.

Assurance doesn't remove the struggle. It reframes it. The struggle is real, but it's not meaningless. The suffering is hard, but it's not outside God's control. The waiting is long, but it's not endless. You're sealed, and that seal guarantees your future: standing before the throne, robed in white, joining the multitude in worship, shepherded by the Lamb, sheltered by God Himself, every hunger satisfied, every tear, FINALLY, wiped away!

So how do you endure? You remember the seal. When fear creeps in, you remember: "I bear the mark of the living God." When discouragement weighs you down, you remember: "the Spirit in me is God's guarantee." When suffering feels unbearable, YOU still remember: "I'm sealed for a Day when suffering will be no more." And you PRAISE GOD! THANK YOU LORD! AMEN and AMEN and AMEN!!!

And you live in light of that Day. You don't hoard comfort or cling to safety. You don't protect yourself at all costs. You're willing to suffer and to sacrifice, to lose what this world values, because you know: "the world is not sealed, but my heart is. And what I lose here, I'll gain back a hundredfold there."

The unsealed world is passing away. The riders will be called to heel and the seals will all be opened. The scroll will be unrolled completely. And when it is, those who bear the seal of God will stand — not because they were strong enough, but because they were marked by the one who is.

You're sealed. Live like it. Endure because of it. Hope in it. And when the Day comes, you'll join the multitude beyond counting, and you'll know that every moment of endurance, every single act of faithfulness, every tear shed in this unsealed world was worth it.

Prayer:

Father, thank You for sealing us with Your Spirit. In an unsealed world, that makes all the difference. When we're tired, when the suffering is long, when we don't understand why You're allowing what You're allowing — remind us of the seal. We belong to You. You will keep us. You will finish what You started. And one day, we'll stand before Your throne, and this will all make sense. Until then, hold us. Fuel our endurance with Your assurance. We are Yours. Amen.

PART FOUR: Trumpets, Prayers, and Witness

Revelation 8–11

Heart of Victory: The prayers of the saints rise like incense before God's throne, His witnesses testify with power even unto death, and the seventh trumpet declares what has always been true—the kingdom belongs to our Lord and His Christ forever.

The throne room fades from view, but its reality doesn't. We've seen God enthroned in majesty and the Lamb holding the scroll of history. Now we watch as that scroll opens further, as the seventh seal gives way to seven trumpets, and as heaven's warnings sound across the earth.

This is where Revelation gets loud. Silence gives way to thunder, and creation itself shudders under the weight of God's judgments. But these aren't random disasters or cosmic accidents. These are measured warnings — partial judgments designed to shake the world awake, to call people to repentance before the final trumpet sounds. And woven through these sobering visions is something startling: the prayers of the saints matter. For they are the hidden weaponry of God's victory. The incense rises, the angel throws fire from the altar to the earth, and heaven breaks its silence to respond to the cries of a people who thought they were forgotten. Prayer isn't wishful thinking. It's the fuel for God's action in history.

Then come the witnesses — two prophets who speak truth in a world that hates them, who are killed and raised, who testify that the gospel cannot be silenced. Their story is the church's story. And when the seventh trumpet finally sounds, the kingdom is declared: "The kingdom of the world has become the kingdom of our Lord and of his Christ" (11:15).

Part Four is about warnings and witness. It's about the power of prayer and the inevitability of judgment. A God who doesn't destroy without warning, and who treasures the prayers of His people, and ensures that His truth is proclaimed even when it costs His witnesses everything.

The trumpets are sounding and the witnesses are testifying. The kingdom is being declared.

Welcome to Part Four.

Day 33 – Silence in Heaven

Scripture Reading: Revelation 8:1

Heart of Victory: Even heaven falls silent before the judgment of God—sometimes reverence requires us to stop speaking and simply stand in awe.

Silence.

After all the worship — after the living creatures singing ceaselessly, after the elders casting their crowns, after angels beyond counting declaring the Lamb's worthiness, after the great multitude from every nation crying out with loud voices — silence.

For about half an hour.

Silence in heaven is stunning. Heaven is the place where worship never stops. "Holy, holy, holy" echoes continuously. Praise rises like incense before the throne. But when the seventh seal is opened, all of that stops. The singing ceases and the declarations pause. Even the ceaseless worship of the living creatures falls quiet.

Why?

The seventh seal is different from the six that came before it. The first six revealed specific visions — riders going forth. Martyrs under the altar and cosmic collapse. But the seventh seal doesn't immediately show another vision. Instead, it opens into the seven trumpets, which will unfold God's judgments in a new cycle. The silence marks a transition, a pause before the storm intensifies.

But it's more than that. The silence is reverence. It's the hush that falls when something holy and terrible is about to happen, the catch in your breath before the verdict is read. The moment when words fail and all you can do is wait in awe.

In the Old Testament, silence often accompanies God's presence or His impending judgment. The prophet Habakkuk declares, "The LORD is in his holy temple; let the whole earth be silent in his presence" (Habakkuk 2:20). Zephaniah warns, "Be silent in the presence of the Lord GOD, for the day of the LORD is near" (Zephaniah 1:7). Silence isn't absence. It's awareness — the recognition that you're standing before something so holy and so weighty that speech is inadequate.

The silence in heaven signals that what's coming next is serious. The seals have shown us the realities of the age we live in — gospel advance, war, famine, death, the cry of the martyrs, cosmic upheaval, and the sealing of God's people. But now the trumpets are about to sound, and they'll reveal God's judgments with increasing intensity. Before they do, heaven falls silent.

This is the silence of anticipation — silence before lightning strikes, before the dam breaks. Heaven knows what's coming, and even the angels stop singing to take it in.

We're not comfortable with silence. We fill every moment with noise — music, podcasts, conversations, screens. Silence feels awkward. Empty. Even unsettling. But sometimes silence is exactly what we need. Sometimes we need to stop talking and filling the space with our words, and simply wait in the presence of God.

Silence can be a form of worship. It's saying, "You are so great, so far beyond me that I have no words." It's the recognition that God doesn't need our commentary or our attempts to make sense of everything. He is God, and sometimes the most appropriate response is to be still and know that He is God.

The silence also reminds us that judgment is not casual. God doesn't unleash wrath carelessly or flippantly. There's gravity here. The angels stop praising not because God isn't worthy, but because what's about to unfold demands a different posture — one of reverent silence before the Judge of all the earth.

Half an hour might not seem long. But in heaven, where worship is ceaseless, half an hour of silence is an eternity. It's enough time to feel the weight of what's coming and absorb the magnitude of God's holiness and justice. Enough time to realize that the trumpets about to sound are not background music — they're a warning and a call, a declaration that God will not let evil go unanswered forever.

When you're overwhelmed by the noise of the world, maybe what you need is to join the silence. Not because you have nothing to say, but because there are moments when the only appropriate response to God is stillness. Moments when the best thing you can do is stop, breathe, and wait in His presence.

The seventh seal is open. The silence won't last forever. The trumpets are about to sound. But for now, for this moment, heaven is still. And in that stillness, there's a reverence that speaks louder than any song.

Prayer:

Lord, teach us the silence of reverence. We're so used to filling every space with words, with noise, our own thoughts. But You are holy. You are the Judge. And sometimes the most faithful response is to be still and know that You are God. As the trumpets prepare to sound, help us to hear what You're saying in the silence. We wait and we listen. We worship in awe. Amen.

Day 34 – Fire from the Altar and Our Prayers

Scripture Reading: Revelation 8:2–5

Heart of Victory: Our prayers are not whispers in the dark—they rise like incense before God, and He responds with fire from the altar, unleashing His purposes on the earth.

The silence breaks. Seven angels step forward, and seven trumpets are placed in their hands. But before they sound, another angel appears. He has a golden incense burner, and he stands at the altar. He's given a large amount of incense to offer along with something precious: the prayers of all the saints.

We saw these prayers before, held in golden bowls as part of the worship offered to the Lamb (5:8). Now they're being offered again, this time with incense at the altar. And the smoke of the incense, carrying the prayers of God's people, rises in the presence of God. He sees it and smells it. He receives it.

Your prayers are not lost. They're not shouted into a void. They rise like incense before the throne of God. Every desperate cry, every whispered plea — even the groaning that can't be put into words — God receives them all. They matter to Him and reach Him. And He responds.

Watch what happens next. The angel takes the incense burner, fills it with fire from the altar, and hurls it to the earth. Immediately, there are peals of thunder, rumblings, flashes of lightning, and an earthquake. The prayers of the saints have been taken up into what God is now doing. He is responding. Not with silence. Not with indifference. With action — powerful, unmistakable action.

This is one of the most important truths in Revelation: prayer is not passive. It's not a spiritual exercise we do to make ourselves feel better while we wait for God to act on His own. Prayer is participation in God's work, aligning ourselves with His purposes and asking Him to do what He's promised to do — then watching Him do it.

The martyrs under the altar cried out, "How long, Lord?" (6:10). The prayers of all the saints rise before God. And now, fire from the altar is hurled to the earth. The trumpets are about to sound. God is answering. Not always in the way we expect or on the timeline we'd choose, but He is answering. The prayers are fuel for the fire of God's own holy response.

This should change how we pray. You're not just sharing your thoughts with God, hoping He's listening. You're participating in a cosmic reality. Your prayers rise before the throne, mingled with incense, received by God, and they have consequences. They move things. They're part of how God brings about His purposes in the world.

James writes, "The prayer of a righteous person is very powerful in its effect" (James 5:16). Powerful. Not weak or futile, and certainly not meaningless. But powerful. Your prayers have weight. They have impact. When you pray for God's kingdom to come, for His will to be done, for justice to rush down like water — you're not just expressing a wish. You're asking God to act, and He will.

We also need to see that the fire from the altar represents a sobering judgment. The prayers rising before God are heavy with the cries for vindication and the deep, raw pleas for justice — the visceral longing for God to finally make things right. And when He responds, it isn't always with a whisper. Thunder, lightning, and earthquakes are the signatures of a victory being unleashed upon a rebellious world.

This is why prayer is serious. When you pray "Your kingdom come," you're asking for everything opposed to that kingdom to be swept away. When you pray for justice, you're asking God to judge — and when you pray for His will to be done, you're asking for resistance to be broken. And God hears those prayers. And He acts.

Some people are uncomfortable with the idea of praying for judgment. They want to pray for mercy and grace. And those are good prayers. But Revelation shows us that there's also a place for praying, "How long, Lord?" for asking God to vindicate the oppressed and judge the wicked, to make things right. The martyrs aren't rebuked for their prayer. Their prayers are received and mingled with incense, then offered before God. And fire falls.

So pray. Pray boldly and persistently. Pray for God's kingdom, for His will and His justice. Your prayers matter more than you realize. They rise before the throne. They're received by God. And when the time is right, He responds — with thunder and lightning, power and authority, and with the unmistakable demonstration that He hears His people and will not ignore their cries forever.

The incense burner is filled with fire from the altar. The prayers are offered. The response is on the way. The trumpets are about to sound. And in this vision, the trumpet judgments are unleashed as the prayers of the saints rise before God.

Prayer:

Father, thank You for receiving our prayers. We confess that we often pray timidly, doubting whether our words reach You or matter to You. But You've shown us that they rise like incense, that they're mingled with worship, and that You respond. Hear our cries for justice and our pleas for mercy. Hear our longing for Your kingdom to come and Your will to be done. Respond, Lord. Send fire from the altar. Act in power. We're asking and trusting that You hear us. Amen.

Day 35 – The First Four Trumpets

Scripture Reading: Revelation 8:6–12

Heart of Victory: The Lamb who opened the seals now sends the trumpets—creation shakes at His command, and every warning is both a display of His sovereign power and an act of patient mercy.

"The seven angels who had the seven trumpets prepared to blow them" (8:6).

The silence is over. The prayers have risen. The fire has been hurled to the earth. Now the angels lift their trumpets, and one by one, they sound. And when they do, creation itself convulses in response.

The first angel blows his trumpet, and hail and fire mixed with blood are hurled to the earth. A third of the earth is burned up, a third of the trees, all the green grass. The second trumpet sounds, and something like a great mountain ablaze with fire is hurled into the sea. A third of the sea becomes blood, a third of the living creatures in the sea die, and a third of the ships are destroyed. The third trumpet brings a great star blazing like a torch, falling on a third of the rivers and springs. The star's name is Wormwood, and a third of the waters become wormwood — bitter, poisonous, deadly. The fourth trumpet strikes the sun, moon, and stars, and a third of them are darkened. A third of the day loses its light, and the night as well.

These are not gentle warnings. Creation is being hit hard. Earth, sea, fresh water, celestial bodies — all of them are struck. A third is affected each time. Not everything, but enough to be catastrophic. Enough to get attention. To make people stop and ask, "what's happening?"

The trumpets echo the plagues of Egypt. God struck Pharaoh's kingdom with hail and fire, the Nile was full with blood, utter darkness blanketing the land. Those plagues were warnings. They were demonstrations of God's power, calling for Pharaoh to relent and let God's people go. But Pharaoh hardened his heart. Plague after plague, refusing to submit. And eventually, judgment fell in full force.

> **Same Ground, Different Angle:** The trumpet judgments may sound familiar—and they should. The seven seals showed us the realities of life between Christ's ascension and His return: conquest, war, famine, death, martyrdom, cosmic upheaval. Now the trumpets show us the same period from a different angle. Where the seals revealed what the church endures, the trumpets reveal how God responds — shaking creation itself as a warning to those who refuse to repent. The pattern will intensify again when we reach the seven bowls. Revelation doesn't march forward in a straight line. It circles back, showing the same realities with increasing urgency and detail.

The trumpets work the same way. They're warnings. God is shaking creation to wake people up and get their attention, to call them to repentance before it's too late. The fact that only a third is affected shows restraint. God isn't annihilating the earth yet. He's giving space for people to turn and recognize what's happening, to cry out for mercy.

In later chapters we'll see the tragedy that people don't repent. They experience the judgments, they see the signs, and they refuse to turn to God. Their hearts grow harder, not softer. The warnings don't produce the response God desires.

This is the mystery of human stubbornness. God can shake the earth and darken the sun, turn water to blood, and people will still refuse to acknowledge Him. They'll blame nature and circumstances, blame anything but their own rebellion against the Creator. And so the warnings escalate. The trumpets grow louder and judgments intensify. Not because God delights in destruction, but because people won't listen to anything less.

Notice that the judgment strikes at the very foundations of our self-sufficiency — the things we have learned to depend on more than God. Earth, where we grow our food. Trees, which give us shelter and oxygen, our essential resources. Sea, which provides fish and trade routes, sustaining life. Fresh water, which we need to survive. Sun, moon, stars, which give us light and mark time, orienting us in the world. God is touching the things we take for granted, the systems and structures that keep life functioning. And He's saying, "All of this is fragile. All of this depends on Me. You think you're self-sufficient? Watch what happens when I shake just a third of what you depend on."

These judgments should drive us to humility and repentance, to recognition that we are not the masters of our own fate. We're creatures dependent on a Creator. And when He shakes creation, we should fall to our knees and cry out for mercy.

But the trumpets aren't just warnings to unbelievers. They're also reassurance to believers. God sees the brokenness and injustice. He sees the suffering of His people. And He is not passive. He's acting. The prayers have risen, and the fire has fallen. The trumpets are sounding. Judgment is beginning. Not the final judgment — that's still to come — but a preview and foretaste, a warning that the Day is approaching.

If you've been crying out, "How long, Lord?" — this is part of the answer. God is moving. He's shaking things and warning people. He's demonstrating His power. And while it may not look like the final victory yet, it's a sign that He has not forgotten or abandoned His purposes, He has not left evil unchecked.

Creation groans, Paul tells us, waiting for redemption (Romans 8:22). The trumpets are part of that groaning. They're the sound of a world under judgment, a creation crying out for its Creator to set things right. And one day, He will. The trumpets will give way to the final consummation, when every wrong is made right, and the new creation comes, when there are no more tears or pain or death.

But for now, the trumpets sound. A third of the earth is struck. The warnings intensify. And the question hangs in the air: will people listen? Will they repent? Or will they harden their hearts until the day when mercy gives way to judgment, and there's no more time to turn?

Prayer:

Creator God, You hold all things together by Your word. When You shake the earth and darken the sun, when You turn water bitter, You're reminding us that we are not in control — You are. Forgive us for taking Your gifts for granted, for living as though we're self-sufficient. Open our eyes to see these warnings for what they are. Mercy and patience, a call to turn back to You before it's too late. Sound the trumpets, Lord, and shake what needs to be shaken. Bring Your people safely through. Amen.

Day 36 – Woe, Woe, Woe

Scripture Reading: Revelation 8:13

Heart of Victory: The eagle's cry of woe is itself a mercy—the God who could judge without warning instead sends notice, because His victory includes every possible chance for repentance.

Four trumpets have sounded. Creation has been struck — earth, sea, fresh water, the heavenly lights. It's been catastrophic. A third of everything has been affected. You'd think that would be enough. But it's not. There's more coming. And before the next trumpet sounds, an eagle appears, flying high overhead, crying out a warning: "Woe! Woe! Woe!" (8:13)

Three woes. One for each of the remaining trumpets. The fifth, sixth, and seventh trumpets are going to be different from the first four —

worse and more terrible, more direct in their assault. The first four struck creation; the next three will strike humanity itself. And the eagle's cry is an alarm: brace yourselves. What's coming is going to be harder than what you've already seen.

The word "woe" is strong. It's not just a prediction of trouble. It's a lament, a cry of grief over impending disaster. When Jesus said "woe to you" to the Pharisees, He wasn't just pronouncing judgment — He was grieving over their hardness of heart and refusal to see the truth, the tragedy of what was coming upon them because they wouldn't repent. The eagle's cry carries that same weight. This isn't celebration. This is sorrow over what's about to happen.

"Woe to those who live on the earth" (8:13). That phrase, "those who live on the earth," appears repeatedly in Revelation. It doesn't just mean "people who exist on the planet." It's a way of describing those whose allegiance and hope are in this world and earthly things, whose loyalty is not to God but to the systems and powers that oppose Him. These are the people who refused the warnings of the first four trumpets, who hardened their hearts, who chose to trust in their own strength rather than turn to God.

And now the eagle cries out to warn us that more is coming. The judgments will intensify and the woes will fall. Those who refuse to listen will experience the full weight of what it means to stand against God.

We need to hear the mercy hidden within the warning itself. God doesn't have to send an eagle flying overhead, crying out to alert people to what's coming. He could just let the next trumpet sound without warning. But He doesn't. He gives notice and sounds the alarm. He says, "This is your chance. Turn now, while there's still time. The woes are coming, but you don't have to face them if you'll only repent."

This is who God is. Even in judgment, He's merciful. Even as He shakes the earth and darkens the sun, He's giving space for people to respond.

The eagle's cry is an invitation: hear the warning and take it seriously, then turn back before it's too late.

But the eagle also speaks to us, to those who belong to God. The woes are coming for "those who live on the earth" — those whose allegiance is to the world. If you're sealed by God and your hope is in Christ, if your citizenship is in heaven, the woes are not against you. You're protected and secure. The judgments will fall, but they will not destroy you. The eagle's cry is a reminder to stay faithful and keep your eyes on Christ, to not let the chaos around you pull your allegiance away from the one who holds you.

In a moment like this, we are forced to look at the foundation of our own allegiance. Am I living for this world and investing in what's temporary, building my life on what will one day be shaken? Or am I living for the kingdom that cannot be shaken, trusting in the King who reigns forever?

The eagle flies overhead, crying out. It's not too late to listen. It's not too late to turn. But the time is short. The remaining trumpets are about to sound. The woes are coming. And those who refuse to heed the warning will face the consequences.

If you hear the eagle's cry and feel fear, good. That fear can drive you to the right place — to your knees and to repentance, to the mercy of God that's still available. But if you hear it and shrug, if you think "I'll be fine, I don't need God and can handle whatever comes," then you're not listening. The woes are not hypothetical. They're real. And they're coming for those who refuse to acknowledge the one who made them.

The first four trumpets were warnings. The next three will be woes. The alarm has been sounded. The eagle has cried out. The question is, will you heed the warning and turn? Or will you harden your heart and face the woes that are coming for those who live on the earth?

Prayer:

Lord, we hear the eagle's cry. Woe, woe, woe. It's a terrifying warning, and we don't take it lightly. Thank You for not leaving us in the dark, for sounding the alarm and giving us time to turn. Search our hearts. Show us where our allegiance is divided, where we're living for this world instead of Your kingdom. Drive us to repentance. Keep us faithful through what's coming. And protect us, for we belong to You. Amen.

Day 37 – The Locusts from the Pit

Scripture Reading: Revelation 9:1–12

Heart of Victory: The locusts torment those who reject God's seal—but those marked by Christ are protected, secure under the hand of the one who holds the key to the abyss.

The fifth angel blew his trumpet, and I saw a star that had fallen from heaven to earth. The key for the shaft to the abyss was given to him. He opened the shaft to the abyss, and smoke came up out of the shaft like smoke from a great furnace so that the sun and the air were darkened by the smoke from the shaft. Then locusts came out of the smoke on to the earth, and power was given to them like the power that scorpions have on the earth." (9:1–3)

This is dark. The first four trumpets struck creation. The eagle warned of three woes. Now the fifth trumpet sounds, and what emerges is nightmarish. A star falls from heaven — likely an angel, given authority to open the shaft to the abyss. Smoke pours out, darkening the sun. And from the smoke come locusts, but not ordinary locusts. These are creatures of torment, given power like scorpions to sting.

They're told what not to harm: "They were told not to harm the grass of the earth, or any green plant, or any tree, but only those people who do not have God's seal on their foreheads" (9:4). The sealed are protected. The ones who belong to God are off-limits. But those without the seal — those who have rejected God, who have hardened their hearts against Him — they're the target.

And the torment is specific: "They were not permitted to kill them but were to torment them for five months; their torment is like the torment caused by a scorpion when it stings someone. In those days people will seek death and will not find it; they will long to die, but death will flee from them" (9:5–6).

Five months of agony. Pain so intense that people want to die but can't. They seek death as a relief, but even that escape is denied them. This is torment of the deepest kind — not physical death, but something worse. A suffering that makes you long for death but doesn't grant it.

The description of the locusts is bizarre and terrifying. They look like horses prepared for battle, with faces like human faces, hair like women's hair, teeth like lions' teeth, chests like iron breastplates, wings that sound like chariots rushing into battle, tails with stingers like scorpions. And their king is the angel of the abyss, named Abaddon in Hebrew or Apollyon in Greek — both names mean Destroyer.

This imagery is symbolic, not literal. John is trying to describe spiritual realities using physical images, and the result is a vision of demonic power unleashed on those who refuse God. These locusts represent the torment that comes when people reject the truth and harden their hearts against the light, choosing darkness over the one who offers life.

It is a heavy truth to realize that this is not arbitrary punishment, but the consequence God sovereignly permits when people reject His light. If we refuse the light, we eventually find ourselves in darkness; if we push away the truth, we are left only with the lies that torment us. To reject the One who offers life is to be left with a kind of living death — a haunting torment where people long for the grave, but the grave refuses to answer.

Paul describes this dynamic in Romans: "God delivered them over" (Romans 1:24, 26, 28). When people persistently reject God, He eventually gives them what they want — life without Him. And life without God is not freedom. It's torment. It's being handed over to the powers of darkness that you've chosen instead of Him.

The locusts are allowed to torment, but only for a limited time. Five months. Not forever, not yet. Even in judgment, there are boundaries. God is still restraining the full force of what sin deserves. But the time is coming when the restraint will be lifted completely, when those who have rejected God will face the full weight of that choice.

But notice again the sealed are protected. "Only those people who do not have God's seal on their foreheads" are tormented. If you belong to Christ, you're not the target. The locusts can't touch you. You're under God's protection, marked by His Spirit and completely secure in His hand. The demonic powers that torment the unbelieving world have no claim on you.

This should drive us to two responses. First, gratitude. You're sealed. You're protected. You belong to God, and the torment that falls on those who reject Him will not fall on you. Not because you're better, but because you've trusted in Christ, and His seal is on you.

Second, urgency. People without the seal are heading toward this. They're walking into a torment they can't imagine, a suffering that will make them long for death. And the only thing that can save them is the gospel, the message that there's a Lamb who was slain, who offers forgiveness and sealing to all who will trust Him. We need to tell them. We need to warn them. The locusts are coming, but the seal is still available.

The fifth trumpet has sounded, unleashing the first woe. The abyss has been opened. And the choice is clear: be sealed by God, or face the torment of rejecting Him.

Prayer:

Lord Jesus, this is a terrifying vision. We don't want to face what comes to those who reject You. Thank You for sealing us and marking us as Yours, for protecting us from the torment that falls on those without Your seal. Give us urgency to share the gospel with those who are heading toward this judgment. They don't know what's coming. Help us to warn them and plead with them, to tell them there's still time to turn. You are the only refuge. Seal more people, Lord. Bring them to safety before it's too late. Amen.

Day 38 – Hardened Hearts and the Sixth Trumpet

Scripture Reading: Revelation 9:13–21

Heart of Victory: Human rebellion cannot derail God's purposes—even when hearts refuse to turn, the Lamb's victory stands unshaken and His call to repentance still echoes with patient authority.

The sixth trumpet sounds, and the second woe falls. Four angels are released from the Euphrates River—ancient enemies from the east, symbols of invasion and terror for Israel. These angels have been bound and held back, waiting for this precise moment. Not just any moment, but the moment: "the hour, day, month, and year." God's timing is exact. Nothing happens by accident. These angels are released because the appointed time has come.

And what they do is devastating: they kill a third of mankind. Not torment, like the locusts. Kill. A third of humanity dies. The scale of this judgment is staggering. After all the warnings — the seals and the first four trumpets, the locusts from the pit — now comes massive loss of life.

The army that follows is described in numbers and imagery that defy literal interpretation: two hundred million mounted troops. Riders with breastplates of fiery red, hyacinth blue, and sulfur yellow. Horses with heads like lions, breathing fire and smoke and sulfur from their mouths. Tails like serpents with heads that inflict injury. This is not a literal army from a specific nation. This is a vision of judgment unleashed, of demonic power given permission to execute God's wrath on a scale that leaves a third of the world dead.

You'd think this would finally break through. You'd think that after losing a third of humanity, people would fall to their knees and cry out to God for mercy. But watch what happens:

"The rest of the people, who were not killed by these plagues, did not repent of the works of their hands, so that they would not worship demons and idols of gold, silver, bronze, stone, and wood, which cannot see, hear, or walk. And they did not repent of their murders, their sorceries, their sexual immorality, or their thefts" (9:20–21).

They didn't repent. Even after all this — the darkness, the torment, the death — they didn't repent. They kept worshiping demons and trusting in idols made of gold, silver, bronze, stone, and wood. They kept murdering, practicing sorcery, committing sexual immorality, stealing. The judgments didn't change their hearts. They hardened even further.

This is the tragedy of persistent rebellion. God can shake the earth, darken the sun, unleash torment and death, and people will still refuse to acknowledge Him. They'll blame anything — nature, fate, bad luck, other people — but they won't turn to the one who made them. The plagues of Egypt didn't soften Pharaoh's heart until it was too late. The trumpets of Revelation don't soften the hearts of those who have set themselves against God.

It is striking to see exactly what they refuse to repent of, which is the suffocating grip of their own idolatry. They are found worshiping demons and bowing before silent statues that can neither hear nor walk — yet we know an idol is rarely just a statue. It is any shadow we trust more than the Substance: wealth, reputation, or the hollow promise of power. This misplaced worship inevitably spirals into deeper darkness, manifesting as murder, immorality, and theft. When we deify anything other than God, we inevitably end up dehumanizing the people around us, treating them as objects to be used rather than souls to be loved.

But here's the mercy hidden in this dark passage: God is still giving them time. The plagues haven't killed everyone. The judgments are still partial. A third is killed, but two-thirds remain. God is restraining the full force of His wrath, still allowing space for repentance. Even now, even after all this, there's room to turn. But they won't.

This is a warning for us. Sin hardens the heart. Every time you say no to God and choose your way over His, every time you suppress the truth you know deep down — your heart gets a little harder. And if you keep going, if you keep refusing, there comes a point where the warnings don't register anymore. The judgments don't move you. You're so committed to your idols, so invested in your sin, that even catastrophic loss doesn't shake you awake.

Paul describes this process in Romans 1. People suppress the truth and exchange the glory of God for images, worshiping created things instead of the Creator. And God gives them over to their choices (Romans 1:18–25). He lets them have what they want — life without Him. And that life spirals into darkness and destructive behaviors, into hardness that can't be penetrated.

But if you're reading this and your heart is stirring, or if you feel the weight of this warning and are troubled by your own hardness — that's grace. That stirring is the Spirit. You're not beyond reach yet. The door is still open. The call to repent is still sounding. Don't wait for a trumpet to blow or a plague to fall. Turn now. Confess your idolatry and acknowledge the sin. Come to the Lamb who was slain, who offers mercy to all who will receive it.

The sixth trumpet has sounded. A third of mankind is dead. And the rest still won't repent. It's one of the most tragic verses in all of Scripture. But it doesn't have to be your story. You can be different. You can hear the warning and respond. You can soften while others harden. You can turn while others refuse.

Prayer:

Lord, soften our hearts. We don't want to be like those who refuse to repent even after seeing Your judgments. Show us our idols — the things we trust more than You and the sins we cling to, the ways we've hardened ourselves against Your truth. Break through our resistance. Give us tender hearts that hear Your warnings and respond. We don't want to be counted among those who refuse until it's too late. We repent now and turn to You. Forgive us and make us new. Amen.

Day 39 – The Mighty Angel and the Little Scroll

Scripture Reading: Revelation 10:1–7

Heart of Victory: The delay is ending—God's mystery is about to be completed, and every promise He made will be fulfilled when the seventh trumpet sounds.

Between the sixth and seventh trumpets, there's an interlude. John sees a mighty angel descending from heaven, wrapped in a cloud, wearing a rainbow like a crown. His face shines like the sun, his legs are like pillars of fire. This is a figure of overwhelming authority and power. And he's holding a little scroll, already opened.

The angel plants one foot on the sea and one foot on the land — a posture of absolute dominion. All creation is under his feet. And when he shouts, his voice sounds like a roaring lion. Seven thunders respond, speaking in voices John can hear. But then something unexpected happens: "When the seven thunders spoke, I was about to write, but I heard a voice from heaven, saying, 'Seal up what the seven thunders said, and do not write it down'" (10:4).

John is told not to record what the seven thunders said. There's something God has revealed that He's choosing not to share with us. We don't get to know everything. There are mysteries that remain sealed, truths that God keeps to Himself. And that should humble us. We have what we need in Scripture, but we don't have everything. There are things God knows that He hasn't told us, and we have to be okay with that.

The angel raises his right hand toward heaven and swears by the one who lives forever and ever, who created heaven and earth and sea and everything in them. And he makes a solemn declaration: "There will no longer be a delay, but in the days when the seventh angel will blow his trumpet, the mystery of God will be completed, as he announced to his servants the prophets" (10:6–7).

No more delay. The time has come. God's mystery — His redemptive plan, final judgment, and restoration—is about to be completed. The prophets foretold it, and the seals and trumpets have been revealing it. When the seventh trumpet sounds, the mystery will be finished. The wait will be over. God's purposes will be accomplished.

"No longer be a delay." This echoes the cry of the martyrs under the altar: "How long, Lord?" (6:10). They wanted to know when God would act and justice would come, when the suffering would end. And the answer has been "wait a little longer." But now the angel swears: the delay is ending. The seventh trumpet is about to sound. And when it does, everything God promised will come to pass.

This should fill us with both anticipation and urgency. Anticipation because the day we've been waiting for is near. The mystery of God — all the ways His plan has seemed confusing or delayed or unclear — is about to be revealed in full. Every promise He made will be kept. Every prophecy will be fulfilled. The wait is almost over.

But also urgency because if the mystery is about to be completed, then time is running out. The opportunity to turn, to repent, to come to Christ while the door is still open — that opportunity won't last forever. The angel's declaration is both comfort and warning. Comfort for those who belong to God: your vindication is coming and your hope is secure — the Day is near. Warning for those who don't: you're running out of time. Turn now, while there's still space to turn.

The little scroll in the angel's hand is opened. Unlike the big scroll with seven seals that only the Lamb could open, this scroll is already accessible. The message is clear. There's no mystery about what God is doing. He's announced it to the prophets. He's revealed it in Scripture. The question isn't whether God's plan is knowable — it's whether we're listening.

We live in the time of "there will no longer be a delay." The seventh trumpet hasn't sounded yet, but it's about to. The mystery of God is reaching its completion. The purposes He set in motion before the foundation of the world are converging on their fulfillment.

And when the trumpet sounds and the mystery is complete, there will be no more waiting or wondering, no more asking "How long?" Until then, we hold to the promises and trust the plan, waiting with a kind of patient urgency. We are patient because we know God's timing is perfect, yet we are urgent because we feel the weight of a clock that is running out. The angel has already sworn by the One who lives forever, and the declaration is fixed: the seventh trumpet is coming. And when it finally sounds, the old world will dissolve to make room for a victory that has no end.

Prayer:

Eternal God, You have sworn by Your own name that there will be no more delay. The mystery You set in motion is reaching its completion. We've been waiting, asking "How long?" — and now You tell us: not much longer. The seventh trumpet is coming. Give us patience to wait and urgency to act. Help us to trust Your timing, to hold on to Your promises, and to live as people who know the Day is near. Complete Your mystery, Lord. Finish what You started. We're watching. We're ready. Come quickly. Amen.

Day 40 – Bitter and Sweet: Eating the Scroll

Scripture Reading: Revelation 10:8–11

Heart of Victory: The scroll that tastes sweet and turns bitter is God's authoritative word entrusted to His people—we proclaim victory and judgment together because both flow from the Lamb's completed work.

John is told to take the scroll from the angel's hand. Not just to read it. To eat it. Ezekiel had a similar experience — God told him to eat a scroll before he went to prophesy to Israel (Ezekiel 3:1-3). Eating the scroll is a way of internalizing God's word and making it part of you, of consuming it so completely that it becomes the message you carry.

The angel warns John: "It will be bitter in your stomach, but it will be as sweet as honey in your mouth" (10:9). Sweet to taste, bitter in the stomach. And that's exactly what happens. John eats it, and it's sweet going down — like honey, delicious and satisfying. But once it's in his stomach, it turns bitter.

This is the paradox of bearing God's word. On one level, God's word is sweet. It's truth. It's good news, and the message of the Lamb who was slain — offering salvation to all who believe. It heralds the coming kingdom and the dawn of the new creation. When you first experience the gospel, it feels incredibly sweet; nothing compares to knowing you're forgiven, loved, sealed by God, and headed for glory.

On another level, God's word carries a bitter flavor because it encompasses judgment, the call to repent, and warnings about what awaits those who refuse. It confronts the harsh truth that not everyone will be saved, and some will harden their hearts to face the wrath they've chosen. When you've internalized God's word and ingested the scroll, that bitterness becomes a weight in your stomach, difficult to ignore.

This is what it means to be a faithful witness. You carry both the sweetness and the bitterness. You proclaim the good news, but you also warn of the bad news. You tell people about the Lamb who offers life, but you also tell them about the judgment that awaits those who reject Him. And that's hard. The sweetness of the gospel is easy to share. The bitterness of judgment is harder. It costs you something to carry it.

John is then told: "You must prophesy again about many peoples, nations, languages, and kings" (10:11). After he eats the scroll, after he internalizes the message — sweet and bitter together — he's commissioned to speak. The message isn't just for him. It's for many peoples, nations, languages, and kings. It's a global word. And John has to deliver it, even when it's bitter in his stomach.

This is the calling of every believer. We've tasted the sweetness of the gospel and eaten the scroll. We know the truth. And now we're sent to prophesy — to speak God's word to a world that desperately needs to hear it, even when that word includes warnings they don't want to accept.

You know the sweetness. You've experienced the joy of knowing Christ and being forgiven, of having hope in the midst of a broken world. But do you also feel the bitterness and carry the weight of knowing that people you love are heading toward judgment? Do you grieve over the hardness of hearts and refusal to repent, the tragedy of what's coming for those who reject God?

If the gospel is only sweet to you, you might not have internalized it fully. The scroll is both. And those who bear God's word faithfully carry both the joy of salvation and the sorrow of judgment. Paul described this tension when he wrote about being the "fragrance of Christ" to God among those being saved and those perishing — "to some we are an aroma of death leading to death, but to others, an aroma of life leading to life" (2 Corinthians 2:15-16). Sweet to some, bitter to others. And we carry both.

We need to remember that bitterness doesn't cancel out the sweetness. The warnings of judgment don't erase the beauty of the gospel. They're part of the same message. And we share them both because we love people and warn them because we don't want them to face what's coming. We tell them the hard truth because the alternative — staying silent and letting them walk blindly into destruction — would be far worse.

John ate the scroll. It was sweet, then bitter. And then he was sent to prophesy. That's the pattern. Taste the sweetness of knowing God and feel the bitterness of what's at stake. Then go speak — to people, nations, languages, and kings. Tell them about the Lamb and about the judgment. Tell them there's still time to turn. The scroll is open, the message is clear, and the choice is theirs.

Prayer:

Lord, we've tasted the sweetness of Your word. The gospel is honey to us — forgiveness, life, hope, joy. But we also feel the bitterness. We grieve over those who refuse and harden their hearts, who walk toward judgment. Give us the courage to speak both the sweetness and the bitterness, and don't let us soften the warnings or hold back the hard truths. But also, don't let us lose the joy. Send us out to prophesy to peoples and nations, carrying the scroll You've given us and proclaiming the message You've entrusted to us. It's sweet and bitter. It's true. Help us to speak it well. Amen.

Day 41 – Measuring the Temple

Scripture Reading: Revelation 11:1–2

Heart of Victory: God measures and protects what matters most—the inner temple of our souls—while allowing outer suffering that cannot touch our standing before Him.

John is given a measuring reed and told to measure the temple of God, the altar, and those who worship there. But he's specifically told not to measure the outer courtyard. That part is given to the nations, who will trample the holy city for forty-two months — three and a half years, or 1,260 days. John uses this number throughout Revelation as a broken seven: a period of real but limited suffering, intense yet bounded by God's sovereign control.

This vision is packed with symbolism. There's no physical temple standing in John's day — the Romans destroyed it in AD 70. So this isn't about measuring a literal building. It's about God's people, the church. Paul tells us that we are the temple of God, that the Spirit dwells in us (1 Corinthians 3:16). We're the place where God's presence resides, where true worship happens.

The measuring is an act of marking and defining boundaries, of claiming ownership. When God measures something, He's saying, "This is Mine. I know its dimensions. I know who belongs here. And I will protect it." The temple, the altar, the worshipers — all of it is measured, marked, and protected by God.

But notice that the outer courtyard is not measured. It's given to the nations. They will trample it. This is the outward, visible part of the church's existence in the world. The nations will attack, oppress, persecute, and trample. For forty-two months — the entire time between Christ's ascension and return — the church will experience suffering from a hostile world.

In this tension God protects what matters most while allowing outer suffering. The inner temple — your relationship with God and identity as His child, your standing before Him — is measured and secure, untouchable by the enemies of God. But the outer courtyard — your physical life and reputation, your comfort in this world — is not guaranteed protection. It can be trampled. And often is.

This is what Jesus meant when He told His disciples, "Don't fear those who kill the body but are not able to kill the soul; rather, fear him who is able to destroy both soul and body in hell" (Matthew 10:28). The nations can trample the outer courtyard. They can harm your body, take your possessions, ruin your reputation, even kill you. But they cannot touch what's measured. They cannot reach the inner temple where God dwells in you and they cannot snatch you out of the Father's hand.

The forty-two months echo Daniel's prophecy about "a time, times, and half a time" (Daniel 7:25; 12:7) — a period of persecution and testing. It's not a literal three and a half years. It's the age we're in now, the time when the church endures suffering while awaiting Christ's return. The outer courtyard is given to the nations. The trampling is real, but it's limited. God has set boundaries so nations can only go so far. And when the time is up, that trampling will end.

This should shape how we think about suffering. If you're being trampled, if you're facing persecution and hardship and loss because of your faith, this passage tells you two things. First, the trampling is real. God isn't pretending you're not suffering. He acknowledges it. The outer courtyard is given to the nations. You're experiencing what God said you would experience. Second, the trampling is limited. It has a time frame: forty-two months. Not forever. Not unending. God has measured the suffering just as He's measured the temple. And when the time is up, the trampling stops.

But the inner temple is secure. Your soul is measured, your worship counted. Your relationship with God is protected. The nations cannot reach it. They can harm your body, but they cannot touch your spirit. They can trample the courtyard, but they cannot destroy the temple.

Paul writes, "Therefore we do not give up. Even though our outer person is being destroyed, our inner person is being renewed day by day" (2 Corinthians 4:16). The outer courtyard is being trampled. The outer person is being destroyed. But the inner temple is being renewed. God is at work in the part that matters most, even when the visible part is under assault.

So when you face suffering, and the nations are trampling, when the cost of following Jesus feels heavy — remember the measuring reed. God has measured you and knows exactly who you are. He's marked you as His own. The inner temple is secure. The trampling of the outer courtyard is temporary. When the forty-two months are complete and the time of suffering ends, the measuring will matter more than the trampling ever did.

Prayer:

Lord, thank You for measuring us, marking us as Yours, and protecting what truly matters. The outer courtyard is being trampled. We feel it. We see it. The nations rage, and the cost of following You is real. Yet You've measured the inner temple. You've secured our souls. You've set boundaries on our suffering. Help us endure the trampling, knowing it's temporary, that it cannot touch what You've protected, and that when the forty-two months are finished, we will stand before You — measured, secure, and whole. Amen.

Day 42 – Two Witnesses, One Lord

Scripture Reading: Revelation 11:3–14

Heart of Victory: The witnesses may be killed, but they will rise—our testimony is never in vain, and resurrection follows every martyrdom in Christ's name.

Two witnesses. God doesn't leave Himself without testimony in the world. During the same forty-two months when the nations are trampling the outer courtyard, God sends two witnesses to prophesy. They're dressed in sackcloth — the clothing of mourning and repentance. Their message is somber, yet urgent. It's a call for people to turn back to God before it's too late.

Why two? Because under God's own law, the testimony of a single witness was never enough. Two or three witnesses were required for testimony to be established as true (Deuteronomy 19:15). God isn't just sending a message to the world — He's sending a message that meets His own standard of proof. The testimony is legally valid, binding, and beyond dispute.

The imagery draws from the Old Testament. Zechariah saw two olive trees standing beside a lampstand, representing the anointed ones who stand before the Lord (Zechariah 4:3, 11-14). These two witnesses represent the church's prophetic testimony during the age between Christ's ascension and return. These are not two end-time celebrity prophets standing on a Jerusalem street, but the church as a whole in its Spirit-empowered testimony throughout this age — God's people speaking truth to a world that doesn't want to hear it.

And they have power: "If anyone wants to harm them, fire comes from their mouths and consumes their enemies. If anyone wants to harm them, he must be killed in this way. They have authority to close up the sky so that it does not rain during the days of their prophecy. They also have power over the waters to turn them into blood and to strike the earth with every plague whenever they want" (11:5–6).

These witnesses are protected from being silenced before the time — their testimony continues until God's purposes are fulfilled. Fire from their mouths —the word of God, which judges and purifies. Authority to stop the rain — like Elijah, who prayed and the heavens were shut for three and a half years. Power to turn water to blood and strike with plagues—like Moses, confronting Pharaoh. The witnesses carry the authority of the prophets, speaking God's word with power. And that pairing is no accident. Moses and Elijah represent the Law and the Prophets—the two great pillars of Old Testament revelation. These are the same two who appeared with Jesus on the Mount of Transfiguration, confirming His identity and mission (Matthew 17:1–8). The church's witness carries the full weight of everything God has spoken.

But then comes the turning point: "When they finish their testimony, the beast that comes up out of the abyss will make war on them, conquer them, and kill them" (11:7).

After they finish their testimony and have completed what God sent them to do — the beast is allowed to conquer them. They're killed. Their bodies lie in the street of "the great city, which figuratively is called Sodom and Egypt, where also their Lord was crucified" (11:8). This is best read as Jerusalem functioning symbolically for the world system that opposes God — the place where prophets are killed, where Jesus Himself was crucified. John even tells us the name is figurative: Sodom and Egypt.

And the world celebrates: "Those who live on the earth will gloat over them and celebrate and send gifts to one another, because these two prophets had tormented those who live on the earth" (11:10). The witnesses are silenced. The testimony is over. And people rejoice because the voice that convicted them and called them to repent, who reminded them of their sin — that voice is finally quiet.

But the silence doesn't last. "After three and a half days the breath of life from God entered them, and they stood on their feet. Great fear fell on those who saw them. Then they heard a loud voice from heaven saying to them, 'Come up here.' They went up to heaven in a cloud, while their enemies watched them" (11:11–12).

Three and a half days. John uses "three and a half" throughout Revelation—forty-two months, 1,260 days, time, times, and half a time — always as a broken seven, a period of real but limited suffering that falls short of completeness. Here the period is compressed to days rather than years, shorter than Jesus' three days in the tomb, but long enough for everyone to be sure they're dead. And then God breathes life into them and they stand up. And the people who celebrated their death now watch in terror as the witnesses ascend to heaven. The apparent defeat was not the end. Resurrection follows martyrdom and vindication follows suffering. God has the final word.

This is the pattern of the church's witness throughout history. We prophesy, speaking truth. We're protected while our testimony continues. But then comes persecution, even martyrdom. The beast makes war on us and seems to win. The world celebrates when our voice is silenced. But the silence is temporary. Resurrection is coming. Vindication is certain. And those who thought they'd defeated us will watch in terror as we rise.

Immediately after the witnesses ascend, "a violent earthquake took place, a tenth of the city fell, and seven thousand people were killed in the earthquake. The survivors were terrified and gave glory to the God of heaven" (11:13). Judgment falls, but also—finally — repentance. Some survivors turn and give glory to God. The testimony that seemed to fail produces fruit after the resurrection.

The second woe has passed. The witnesses have testified, died, risen, and ascended. And now: "The third woe is coming soon" (11:14). The seventh trumpet is about to sound. Everything is converging on the final consummation.

What does this mean for us? We're the witnesses. We speak truth in a world that doesn't want to hear it. We're protected while our testimony continues, but we're not promised escape from suffering or even death. The beast will make war on us. The world will celebrate when we're silenced. But that's not the end. Resurrection is coming. Vindication is certain. And when God breathes life back into us and calls us up to heaven, those who thought they had defeated us will know they were wrong.

So keep witnessing and keep speaking. Keep prophesying. Your testimony matters. Even if it costs you everything, even if you're killed for it, you will rise. God will have the final word.

Prayer:

Lord, make us faithful witnesses. Give us courage to speak truth even when it costs us. Protect us while our testimony continues, and if the beast is allowed to conquer us, if we're called to give our lives for Your name — remind us that death is not the end. You will breathe life into us and call us up. You will vindicate us. The world may celebrate when we're silenced, but You will have the final word. Keep us faithful. We're Your witnesses. Use our voices. And when the time comes, raise us up. Amen.

Day 43 – The Seventh Trumpet Sounds

Scripture Reading: Revelation 11:15–19

Heart of Victory: The seventh trumpet declares what has always been true—the kingdom belongs to our Lord and His Christ, and He will reign forever and ever.

The seventh trumpet sounds. And immediately, heaven erupts in worship. Loud voices declare what has always been true but is now fully manifest: "The kingdom of the world has become the kingdom of our Lord and of his Christ" (11:15).

This is the declaration we've been waiting for. The kingdoms of this world — all the empires and rulers that have set themselves against God, all the systems that thought they were in charge and opposed the Creator — they're finished. The pretense is over. The rebellion has failed. The world belongs to God and to His Christ, and He will reign forever and ever.

Notice the weight of the tense here — it says the kingdom 'has become' the Lord's. This isn't a distant hope or a 'someday' promise; it is a present-tense reality. Right now, as the seventh trumpet sounds, the kingdom is declared. This is the moment when what has been true in heaven becomes undeniable on earth. The Lamb who was slain has taken His authority, and with the scroll now wide open, the mystery of God is finally complete. And the kingdoms of this world are now — fully, finally, irrevocably — the kingdom of our Lord.

The twenty-four elders fall on their faces and worship: "We give you thanks, Lord God, the Almighty, who is and who was, because you have taken your great power and have begun to reign" (11:17). God has always been sovereign. But now He's taken it up publicly to begin His reign in a way that silences every objection and rebellion, every claim to rival authority.

And the elders continue: "The nations were angry, but your wrath has come. The time has come for the dead to be judged and to give the reward to your servants the prophets, to the saints, and to those who fear your name, both small and great, and the time has come to destroy those who destroy the earth" (11:18).

This is the final judgment where the dead are judged, and the servants of God are rewarded. Those who destroy the earth are themselves destroyed. Everything comes to a head here. The wicked don't get away with it, and the faithful aren't forgotten. Justice is done and rewards are given. Wrath is poured out. And when it's over, God's kingdom stands alone.

> **Parallel Scene:** This vision of the kingdom declared and final judgment executed appears again at the seventh bowl (16:17-21) and the great white throne (20:11-15). Like the sixth seal before it (6:12-17), these aren't separate events but the same glorious consummation shown from different angles. Revelation spirals toward the end, returning again and again to the certainty of Christ's coming and the finality of His judgment.

Then God's temple in heaven is opened, and the ark of His covenant appears. There are flashes of lightning, rumblings of thunder, an earthquake, and severe hail. The signs of God's presence and power, the markers of His holiness and judgment, all converge in this moment. The temple is opened because the time of separation is over. God's people have full access. The covenant is revealed. And the power of God is unleashed on a world that refused to acknowledge Him.

This is where all the trumpets have been leading. The first four struck creation. The fifth and sixth brought torment and death. And now the seventh declares: it's over. The kingdom has come and the reign has begun. The judgment is here. And those who belong to God will be rewarded while those who opposed Him will be destroyed. What we see is that the seventh trumpet doesn't describe prolonged events. It declares a reality. The kingdom has become the Lord's. The time has come. This is announcement, not process. The trumpets have been warnings, calls to repent, and opportunities to turn. But when the seventh sounds, the warnings are over and the verdict is in. The kingdom is established and there is nothing that can change it.

If you're reading this and you belong to Christ, this is your hope. The day is coming when the trumpet sounds and the kingdom is declared, when every power that opposes God is swept away. The saints are rewarded and the wicked are judged. You're on the winning side. Not because you're strong, but because you belong to the King whose kingdom will never end.

But if you're reading this and you haven't turned to Christ, the seventh trumpet is a warning. The time is coming when it will be too late, when the opportunity to repent will be gone and the nations' anger will be met with God's wrath. Turn now. Bow before the King while there's still time. The trumpet is about to sound. Don't wait until the kingdom is declared to acknowledge what's always been true: He is Lord, and He will reign forever.

The seventh trumpet has sounded in John's vision. In our experience, it hasn't sounded yet. But it will. And when it does, every knee will bow and every tongue will confess that Jesus Christ is Lord. The question is whether you'll bow willingly now or unwillingly then.

Prayer:

Lord God Almighty, we give You thanks. You have taken Your great power and begun to reign. The kingdoms of this world are Yours. Every rival authority will bow, and every rebellious power will fall. We long for the day when the trumpet sounds, when the kingdom is declared, when the dead are judged and the faithful are rewarded. Hasten that Day. Come quickly. Until then, keep us faithful and watching, keep us ready. The kingdom is Yours. It has always been Yours. One day, everyone will know it. We worship You now. We'll worship You then. Forever and ever. Amen.

PART FIVE: The Dragon, the Beasts, and the Lamb

Revelation 12–14

Heart of Victory: The dragon rages and the beasts deceive, but the Lamb stands on Mount Zion with His people sealed and singing —because the accuser has been thrown down and those who follow the Lamb have already overcome by His blood.

The curtain pulls back, and we see what's really happening. Behind every earthly conflict, beneath every political struggle, there's a cosmic war — a dragon raging against a woman and her child, beasts rising to demand allegiance, and a Lamb standing victorious with His sealed people.

This is where Revelation gets intense. The dragon has been thrown down from heaven, defeated but not yet destroyed. He knows his time is short, and that makes him desperate. He pursues the church into the wilderness. He empowers beasts from the sea and the earth to wage war on the saints. He demands visible worship through the mark that determines who can buy and sell, participate in society, and who will survive.

But this isn't merely ancient history or distant prophecy. This pattern repeats in every age. The dragon always pursues and the beasts always demand worship. The mark always forces allegiance into the open. And God's people always face the same choice: take the mark and survive, or bear the Lamb's name and endure.

Part Five is about spiritual warfare made visible. It's about the accuser, who was thrown down but still accuses, and counterfeit powers that mimic the Lamb's authority. It's about the pressure to compromise, the cost of refusal, and the promise that those who endure will stand with the Lamb on Mount Zion.

The dragon rages because he's lost. The beasts demand worship because they're doomed. And the Lamb stands with the 144,000 — the complete number of the redeemed — ready to gather His harvest and welcome His faithful home.

This is the unseen war, and this is what's really at stake. This is why every ordinary choice about worship, allegiance, and faithfulness matters more than we might think.

The question isn't whether you're in the battle. The question is whose mark you'll bear.

Welcome to Part Five.

Day 44 – A Woman, a Child, and a Dragon

Scripture Reading: Revelation 12:1–6

Heart of Victory: The dragon's rage against the church is proof of his defeat—the child has ascended to the throne, and no power in heaven or on earth can undo what Christ has accomplished.

There are moments when the veil between heaven and earth grows thin, when you catch a glimpse of what's really happening behind the scenes of history. Revelation 12 is one of those moments. John sees a sign in heaven — a woman clothed with the sun, with the moon under her feet and a crown of twelve stars on her head. She's pregnant, crying out in labor pain. And then we see another sign appear. An enormous red dragon with seven heads and ten horns, wearing seven crowns. The dragon's tail sweeps a third of the stars from the sky and hurls them to earth. And the dragon stands before the woman, ready to devour her child the moment it's born.

Nothing here is random. This is the story you've been living in all along.

Why the Story Rewinds: If the seventh trumpet just declared "The kingdom of the world has become the kingdom of our Lord" (11:15), why does Revelation suddenly take us back to a pregnant woman and a dragon? Because Revelation doesn't tell one story from beginning to end—it tells the same story from multiple angles. Chapters 1–11 traced the church age through seals, trumpets, and the testimony of God's people. Now chapters 12–14 rewind to the birth of Christ and retell the whole drama as cosmic warfare between the dragon and the Lamb. You're not reading a new chapter of history. You're seeing the same battle from behind the curtain.

The woman represents God's people — first Israel, then the church. She's clothed with the sun because she reflects God's glory. The moon is under her feet because she stands on the promises of the old covenant. The crown of twelve stars points to the twelve tribes of Israel, the foundation of God's chosen people. She's laboring because she's bringing forth the Messiah, and that labor involves suffering and hope long deferred.

The child she bears is clear: "She gave birth to a Son, a male child, who is to rule all nations with an iron rod" (12:5). This is Jesus. The language echoes Psalm 2, where the Messiah is promised dominion over the nations (Psalm 2:8–9). The woman's child is the One all of history has been waiting for — the King who will crush His enemies and establish His kingdom forever.

But there's a dragon — enormous and red, the color of bloodshed and violence. Seven heads, representing completeness in evil, a parody of God's perfect wisdom. Ten horns, symbolizing earthly power and authority. And seven crowns, because this dragon has claimed dominion over the nations. His tail sweeps a third of the stars from the sky — fallen angels who followed him in his rebellion. He stands in front of the woman, poised to devour the child as soon as He's born.

This dragon is Satan. The same ancient serpent from Eden. The accuser of God's people and the prince of this world. He's been waiting for this moment because if he can destroy the child, he can thwart God's plan of salvation. If the Messiah never lives, He never dies and rises — and all the promises of God fall with Him. This also means that all God's promises fail. The kingdom doesn't come. And the dragon wins.

And so the dragon waits. He watched as Pharaoh tried to slaughter Israel's male children in Egypt. He watched as Herod ordered the massacre of the innocents in Bethlehem. He watched as religious leaders plotted to kill Jesus. He was there at the cross, thinking he had won. This isn't a story told in abstract, mythical terms. This is the real battle that played out in real history, with real stakes.

But the woman gave birth, and despite the dragon's fury, the child lived. "Her child was caught up to God and to his throne" (12:5). This is the ascension — Jesus rising to the right hand of the Father after His resurrection, beyond the reach of the dragon's rage. The Messiah didn't just survive — He conquered and ascended, taking His seat at the throne where He now reigns.

The dragon didn't devour the child. The child devoured death.

But the battle isn't over. The woman — God's people — flees into the wilderness, where God has prepared a place for her. She's protected for 1,260 days — that same broken seven, a period of real suffering but sovereign protection. The wilderness is the place of testing, of apparent vulnerability and dependence on God's provision. Israel wandered there for forty years. Jesus was tempted there. And the church lives there now — in the world but not of it, pursued by the dragon but sustained by God.

The dragon couldn't destroy the child, so now he turns his rage toward the woman. He pursues the church. He seeks to devour those who belong to the Messiah. But this vision reveals that the dragon's pursuit is not a sign of his power. It's a sign of his defeat. He's raging because he's lost while the child has been caught up to the throne. The kingdom is secure. And the woman, though pursued, is protected.

This is the story of salvation seen as cosmic conflict. The birth of Christ wasn't just a historical event. It was the decisive moment in the war between God and Satan, the clash of light against darkness. And the outcome was never in doubt. The dragon tried to devour, but the child was caught up to God and the woman was preserved. And the story continues, with the dragon still raging but already defeated, while the church lives in the wilderness under God's protection.

If you're reading this and you feel the weight of spiritual opposition and the exhaustion of enduring in a world that hates Christ, you're not imagining it. The dragon is real. The pursuit is real. But so is the child on the throne and the place God has prepared for you. And so is the 1,260 days that will come to an end when Christ returns.

The dragon couldn't stop the birth or the ascension, and he won't stop the return. The woman will be vindicated when the child comes back, and the dragon will be cast down. That's not wishful thinking. That's the story Revelation 12 reveals. And you're part of it.

Prayer:

Lord Jesus, You are the child born to rule the nations. The dragon tried to destroy You, but You conquered death and rose victorious, ascending to Your throne in glory. We praise You for Your victory. And we ask You to sustain us in the wilderness. The enemy still rages, but You have prepared a place for us. Keep us safe. Keep us faithful. And remind us every day that the dragon's fury is the fury of one who has already lost. We belong to the child on the throne. Hold us fast. Amen.

Day 45 – War in Heaven and a Defeated Accuser

Scripture Reading: Revelation 12:7–12

Heart of Victory: The accuser has been thrown down by the blood of the Lamb, and we overcome not by our strength but by trusting in His finished work and testifying to His name, even unto death.

There's a war in heaven. Not a future war. Not a war that might happen if things go badly. A war that has already been fought and won. "Then war broke out in heaven: Michael and his angels fought against the dragon. The dragon and his angels also fought, but he could not prevail, and there was no place for them in heaven any longer" (12:7-8).

This is the cosmic background to everything you've experienced as a follower of Jesus. The dragon — Satan, the ancient serpent, the devil, the accuser — has been thrown down. He lost. The war is over. And what looks like ongoing spiritual conflict on earth is actually the death throes of an enemy who has already been defeated.

Michael the archangel leads the battle. He's the defender of God's people, the one who stands guard over Israel in Daniel's visions. But this isn't Michael's victory — this is the victory of the Lamb, and the timing makes that clear. The dragon is thrown down after the child is caught up to God's throne. The cross and resurrection seal Satan's defeat, and Christ's ascension to God's throne makes that victory complete. When Jesus died and rose again, "He disarmed the rulers and authorities and disgraced them publicly; He triumphed over them in him (Colossians 2:15)." The war in heaven is the heavenly reality of what happened at Calvary.

When the dragon falls, a voice in heaven declares: "The salvation and the power and the kingdom of our God and the authority of his Christ have come, because the accuser of our brothers and sisters, who accuses them before our God day and night, has been thrown down" (12:10).

The accuser. That's who Satan is. He stands before God day and night, pointing out every failure and weakness of God's people, cataloging their sins. He's the prosecutor in the cosmic courtroom, demanding judgment, insisting on condemnation. But the cross has silenced him and he's been thrown down. His accusations have no power anymore because the blood of the Lamb has answered every charge.

Think about what this means for you. When you feel the weight of guilt or hear that voice in your head whispering that you'll never be good enough, it can be easy to wonder if God could possibly forgive you again. That is the voice of the accuser who's been thrown down, stripped of his voice, and permanently silenced by the victory won at the cross. As the writer of Hebrews says, the blood speaks a better word (Hebrews 12:24) than the voice of accusation, and that word is "forgiven." Which means you have been justified and declared righteous — accepted in the Beloved by a victory that the accuser is now powerless to contest.

But here's the other side of the victory: "They conquered him by the blood of the Lamb and by the word of their testimony; for they did not love their lives to the point of death" (12:11).

The saints overcome. Not by their own strength or moral perfection. They overcome by the blood of the Lamb—the finished work of Christ on the cross, which has already defeated the accuser and secured their salvation. That's the foundation. Without the blood, there's no overcoming. But the blood isn't just a past event. It's an ongoing reality that we lay hold of, trust in, and testify to.

"The word of their testimony." The saints overcome by speaking the truth about Jesus. They tell the story of what He's done. They bear witness to His death and resurrection, proclaiming His lordship. They don't hide their faith or soften the gospel to avoid offense. They testify, knowing that the gospel is the power of God for salvation, and that testimony is itself an act of spiritual warfare.

And they "did not love their lives to the point of death." This is the cost of overcoming. The saints are willing to die rather than deny Christ. They value Jesus more than their own safety, their own comfort, even their own survival. They're not reckless or suicidal — they treasure life as a gift from God. But when the choice comes down to allegiance to the Lamb or preservation of their own lives, they choose the Lamb. And in choosing Him, they conquer.

This is the upside-down victory of the kingdom. You overcome by dying and conquer by surrendering, winning by losing your life for the sake of Christ. The dragon can't understand this. He deals in power and coercion, wielding fear as his weapon. But the saints overcome by a different power — the power of sacrificial love, faithful witness, and confident trust in the blood that has already won the war.

Then the voice in heaven says, "Therefore rejoice, you heavens, and you who dwell in them!" (12:12). Heaven is celebrating. The accuser is gone. The saints are conquering. The kingdom has come. But the voice also issues a warning: "Woe to the earth and the sea, because the devil has come down to you with great fury, because he knows his time is short" (12:12).

The dragon has been thrown down to earth. He's lost the war, but he's not done fighting. He knows his time is short, and that makes him even more dangerous. He can't win, but he can still cause suffering and destruction. He rages because he's desperate. He attacks because he's doomed. And the church, living in the time between the dragon's defeat and his final destruction, bears the brunt of his fury.

You live right here in the time when the war has been won but the defeated enemy still rages. The accuser has been thrown down, yet his accusations still echo. And the saints overcome by the blood of the Lamb — sometimes that overcoming looks like suffering and even death.

As Christians, this is what we hold on to. The dragon's fury is proof of his defeat. If he had won, he wouldn't be raging. If he had any real power, he wouldn't be desperate. His short time is running out. And when it's over, the victory that was secured at the cross will be fully realized, the accuser will be silenced forever, and the saints who overcame by the blood of the Lamb will reign with Christ in glory.

Prayer:

Lord Jesus, thank You for defeating the accuser. His voice no longer condemns us because Your blood has spoken a better word. Help us to overcome by trusting in what You've done and by bearing witness to Your name. When the dragon rages, remind us that his fury is proof of his defeat. When we're tempted to save our lives, give us the courage to lose them for Your sake. You have won the war. Hold us steady until the victory is fully revealed. Amen.

Day 46 – Pursuit in the Wilderness

Scripture Reading: Revelation 12:13–17

Heart of Victory: The dragon's pursuit drives us into the wilderness, but the wilderness is where God nourishes and protects His people—even the dragon's fury cannot destroy those whom God has promised to preserve.

The dragon has been thrown down to earth. He couldn't devour the child, so now he turns his fury on the woman — God's people. "When the dragon saw that he had been thrown down to the earth, he persecuted the woman who had given birth to the male child" (12:13).

This is the reality we live in right now. The dragon pursues and rages, persecuting God's people who live in the wilderness — a place that looks exposed and desolate. But the wilderness is really the place where God protects His own.

"The woman was given two wings of a great eagle, so that she could fly from the serpent's presence to her place in the wilderness, where she was nourished for a time, times, and half a time" (12:14). Two wings of a great eagle. This is the language of Exodus, where God tells Israel, "You have seen what I did to the Egyptians and how I carried you on eagles' wings and brought you to myself" (Exodus 19:4). The same God who delivered Israel from Pharaoh delivers the church from the dragon. And the same God who led His people through the wilderness sustains them now.

The wilderness is not abandonment. It's refuge. God prepares a place for His people, a place where they're nourished for "a time, times, and half a time" — a period of real hardship but certain protection, bounded by God's sovereign hand. The wilderness is where we live now. Not in the comfort of Eden, not yet in the glory of the New Jerusalem, but in the in-between, where we're sustained by God's provision and protected by His power.

But the dragon doesn't stop. "From his mouth the serpent spewed water like a river flowing after the woman, to sweep her away with the flood" (12:15). The dragon spews a flood, trying to drown the woman and overwhelm her. This is spiritual warfare. The flood represents lies and accusations — a torrent of deceptive opposition meant to destroy the church. The dragon uses propaganda, persecution, cultural pressure, and internal division to sweep away God's people.

But the earth helps the woman. "The earth opened its mouth and swallowed up the river that the dragon had spewed from his mouth" (12:16). Even creation itself works to protect the church. God uses means the dragon never anticipated — even the structures of this fallen world — to preserve His people when the flood threatens to overwhelm them. The dragon's schemes fail. The flood is swallowed up and the woman remains safe in the wilderness.

This doesn't mean the church never suffers. It means that when the church suffers, it's not because God has lost control or because the dragon has won. The woman is protected, even in the wilderness. She's nourished, even in apparent vulnerability. And the dragon's fury, no matter how intense, cannot destroy what God has promised to preserve.

Then the dragon, enraged by his failure to destroy the woman, "went off to wage war against the rest of her offspring — those who keep the commands of God and hold firmly to the testimony of Jesus" (12:17). The dragon shifts tactics. If he can't destroy the church as a whole, he'll attack individual believers. He wages war against those who keep God's commands and testify to Jesus. This is where persecution becomes personal and the cost of discipleship becomes real.

But also notice what defines the dragon's targets. They keep the commands of God, and they hold firmly to the testimony of Jesus. The dragon attacks those who remain faithful. He goes after those who won't compromise or be silent, who won't abandon Christ under pressure. The fact that you're being attacked is not a sign that you've done something wrong. It's often a sign that you're doing something right. The dragon reserves his fury and rages against those who still stand.

So what does this mean for you?

It means the wilderness is not a mistake. You're not in the wilderness because God has forgotten you or because you've somehow failed. You're in the wilderness because this is where the church lives between Christ's first and second comings. And in the wilderness, God provides. He nourishes. He protects. The dragon may pursue, but he can't overcome.

It means the flood will come. The dragon will spew lies and accusations as opposition mounts. He'll try to overwhelm you with doubt and despair, drowning you in cultural pressure. But the flood doesn't get the last word. God has ways of swallowing up the dragon's schemes, and preserving His people even when destruction seems certain.

And it means you may be personally targeted. If you keep God's commands and hold firmly to the testimony of Jesus, you're in the dragon's sights. He'll wage war against you. But his fury is proof of his defeat. He wouldn't be raging if he'd won. He wouldn't be attacking if you weren't a threat to his kingdom.

The wilderness is where you are. But the wilderness is also where God is with you, the place where He carries you on eagles' wings, and nourishes and protects you. The dragon pursues, but he cannot prevail. You're safe in the place that looks most vulnerable, held by the God who never lets His people go.

Prayer:

Father, we live in the wilderness, pursued by the dragon, targeted by his rage. But You have carried us on eagles' wings. You have prepared a place for us. You nourish us even in this in-between time. When the flood comes, help us trust that You will swallow it up. When we're attacked for keeping Your commands and testifying to Jesus, remind us that the dragon's fury is proof that we belong to You. Hold us fast in the wilderness. We're safe in Your hands. Amen.

Day 47 – The Beast from the Sea

Scripture Reading: Revelation 13:1–10

Heart of Victory: The beast may conquer our bodies, but it cannot claim our worship—endurance and faithfulness to the Lamb is our victory, even when that faithfulness costs us everything.

John stands on the sand of the sea and watches something rise from the water. "I saw a beast coming up out of the sea. It had ten horns and seven heads. On its horns were ten crowns, and on its heads were blasphemous names" (13:1). This is the beast — terrifying and powerful, utterly opposed to God.

The imagery draws on Daniel's visions, in which beasts symbolize oppressive kingdoms that oppose God's people (Daniel 7:1–8). However, it's not tied to a single empire. Instead, it reflects a recurring pattern of beastly power throughout history — political systems and cultural forces that claim what is God's alone. The beast represents Rome and Babylon, as well as any totalitarian ideology that declares, "Worship and obey me, or be destroyed."

The dragon gives the beast its power. "The dragon gave the beast his power, his throne, and great authority" (13:2). Behind every beastly system stands the dragon. Satan doesn't always work directly. He empowers human systems, co-opts political structures, and animates cultural forces to do his work. The beast is the dragon's agent, carrying out his rage against God's people.

And one of the beast's heads appears to have been fatally wounded, but the wound is healed. "The whole earth was amazed and followed the beast" (13:3). This is a parody of Christ's death and resurrection. The beast mimics the Lamb while pretending to have overcome death. It offers a false salvation, a counterfeit hope. And the world, desperate for something to worship, falls at its feet.

They worship the dragon and the beast, saying, "Who is like the beast? Who is able to wage war against it?" (13:4). This is what beastly power does — it presents itself as invincible and unstoppable. It says, "Resistance is futile. You have no choice but to bow." And when a system convinces you that opposition is impossible, it has already defeated you in your mind before it ever touches your body.

The beast is given a mouth to speak boasts and blasphemies. "And it was permitted to wage war against the saints and to conquer them" (13:7). Notice that word: "allowed." The beast operates under God's sovereignty. It doesn't act outside God's control. God permits the beast to rage and blaspheme, making war on the saints. This doesn't mean God approves of the beast's actions. It means that even the beast's fury serves God's purposes, refining the saints' faith and revealing who truly belongs to the Lamb.

"If anyone is to be taken captive, into captivity he goes. If anyone is to be killed with a sword, with a sword he will be killed" (13:10). This is a word of both warning and comfort. The saints won't escape suffering. Some will be captured. Some will be killed. The beast does conquer, in the sense that it ends the earthly lives of those who refuse to worship it. But this isn't defeat. This is martyrdom. This is faithfulness unto death. And the reward isn't escape from suffering — it's the crown of life.

Then comes the call: "This calls for the endurance and faithfulness of the saints." (13:10). Not heroism or spectacular resistance — just endurance. Holding on. Staying faithful when the beast demands your worship and threatens your life. But how do you overcome the beast? Not by fighting it on its own terms, but by refusing to give it what it wants. The beast craves worship—you worship the Lamb instead. It demands allegiance and threatens death, but you pledge yourself to Christ and choose faithfulness unto death, knowing that the Lamb who was slain has already defeated death.

The beast is real. You live in a world where political powers and social structures press you to bow. They may not look like literal beasts, but they operate the same way. Demanding total allegiance while punishing dissent. The form changes — Rome, medieval Christendom, fascism, communism, consumer capitalism, authoritarian regimes — but the pattern remains. The beast always says, "Worship me or suffer."

So what does this mean for you today?

It means the beast's power comes from the dragon. When you're facing beastly power, you're not just facing human systems. You're facing spiritual opposition. The battle isn't ultimately against flesh and blood. It's against the dragon who animates the beast, who gives it power and authority to wage war on the saints.

And it means endurance is your victory. You're not called to overthrow the beast through political revolution or violent resistance. You're called to endure and to remain faithful, while refusing to worship. When the beast conquers your body, it doesn't conquer your soul. When it takes your life, it proves that you didn't love your life more than you loved Christ. Martyrdom isn't defeat. It's the ultimate act of worship.

The beast is terrifying. It looks invincible. It seems unstoppable. But this is what we must not miss. The beast was given a mouth. He was allowed to make war. The beast operates within the boundaries God has set. And the beast, for all its fury and power, cannot touch those whose names are written in the Lamb's book of life. You may suffer. You may be captured or killed. But you remain the Lamb's, and the Lamb remains victorious.

This is the call for the endurance and faithfulness of the saints. Not because endurance comes easily, but because the Lamb who was slain is worth it. The beast rages for a time, but the Lamb reigns forever.

Prayer:

Lord Jesus, the beast is real and terrifying, demanding worship we will not give and threatening suffering we cannot avoid. But You are the Lamb who was slain, and You have overcome. Give us endurance as the pressure mounts. Give us faithfulness when the cost is high. Remind us that the beast operates under Your sovereignty, that our suffering is not outside Your control, and that our names are written in Your book of life. We will not bow to the beast. We bow to You alone. Hold us fast. Amen.

Day 48 – The Beast from the Earth

Scripture Reading: Revelation 13:11–18

Heart of Victory: The mark of the beast reveals visible allegiance, but those who belong to the Lamb already bear His name—no pressure, deception, or threat can erase the mark of our true King.

Another beast rises, this one from the earth. "It had two horns like a lamb, but it spoke like a dragon" (13:11). This second beast doesn't come with obvious horror. It looks harmless, even religious. It has the appearance of a lamb — gentle and non-threatening, safe. But when it speaks, you hear the dragon's voice. This is deception at its most dangerous: evil that wears the mask of good.

This beast exercises all the authority of the first beast. It makes the earth and its inhabitants worship the first beast. And it performs great signs, even making fire come down from heaven. "It deceives those who live on the earth because of the signs that it is permitted to perform in the presence of the beast" (13:14).

Power doesn't always look like brute force; sometimes it looks like miracles. The second beast doesn't coerce, it deceives. It doesn't threaten, it persuades. It uses signs and wonders to make people believe that the first beast deserves their worship. And the world, dazzled by the spectacle, bows down.

This is how false religion works. It doesn't announce itself as evil. It presents itself as enlightened and spiritually mature. It performs wonders that make people say, "This must be from God." But underneath the lamb-like appearance is the voice of the dragon, leading people away from the true Lamb who was slain.

The second beast commands the people to make an image of the first beast and give it breath so that it can speak. Then comes the ultimatum: "Whoever does not worship the image of the beast will be killed" (13:15). This is the point of decision. Worship the beast or die. There's no middle ground, no compromise position. The pressure is total, and the stakes are life itself.

And then the mark: "It also forced all people — small and great, rich and poor, free and slave — to receive a mark on their right hand or on their forehead, so that no one could buy or sell unless he had the mark, the beast's name, or the number of its name" (13:16-17).

The mark isn't just a symbol. It's a sign of allegiance. Those who take the mark can participate in the economy, can buy and sell, can function in society. Those who refuse are shut out — excluded from commerce, unable to provide for their families, marked for persecution. The mark makes allegiance visible and economic survival dependent on worship.

The mark of the beast is less about a specific technology or literal tattoo and more about visible allegiance. Throughout history, beastly systems have required public displays of loyalty — sacrificing to Caesar, party membership cards, ideological oaths, and so forth. The form changes, but the function remains, "Show us you belong to the beast, or you can't participate."

This is spiritual warfare at the level of everyday decisions. Do you take the mark and survive, or do you refuse and suffer? Do you go along with the system that provides for you, or do you stand apart and face the consequences? The mark forces you to choose publicly whose you are.

And notice this contrast that those who belong to the Lamb also have a mark—His name on their foreheads. The question isn't whether you're marked. The question is whose mark you bear. The beast marks his own. The Lamb marks His own. And the mark you bear reveals who you worship.

The number 666 is the number of a man, a human number. It's the number of incompleteness, falling short of seven — the number of perfection — at every turn. The beast, for all its power and deception, is merely human. It reaches for divinity but never attains it. It mimics the Lamb but falls eternally short. And those who bear its mark share in its incompleteness, its failure to be what it claims.

This deception is more dangerous than persecution. The second beast doesn't threaten — it deceives. It doesn't force — it persuades. In a world full of false prophets and false signs, you need discernment. When someone performs wonders but speaks with the dragon's voice, don't be dazzled by the spectacle. Listen to the voice. There will come moments when allegiance becomes visible. The mark isn't always a literal mark. It's the moment when you have to choose publicly. Will you conform to what the system demands, or will you bear the cost of refusal? Will you take what's offered to ensure your survival, or will you trust the Lamb to provide even when it looks like you'll be shut out?

And it means the Lamb's mark is already on you. You don't need to fear being accidentally marked by the beast. You belong to Christ. His name is written on your forehead. And no matter what pressures come, no matter what the cost of refusal, you remain His. The mark has already been given. The question is whether you'll live in the reality of whose you are.

Prayer:

Lord Jesus, the second beast may look harmless but speaks the dragon's lies. Give us eyes to see through deception and ears to hear Your voice above the noise. When the choice comes between survival and allegiance, when we're pressed to take the mark or face exclusion, remind us that we already bear Your name. We belong to You. We will not bow to counterfeits. We will not worship images. Keep us faithful when the cost is high. You are our true King. Amen.

Day 49 – The Lamb and the 144,000

Scripture Reading: Revelation 14:1–5

Heart of Victory: Those who bear the Lamb's name and follow Him through suffering will stand with Him on Mount Zion, singing the song of the redeemed that only those who endured can learn.

After all the darkness — the dragon's pursuit, the beasts' blasphemy, the mark of allegiance — here's a vision of hope. The Lamb stands on Mount Zion, and with Him stand His people, marked not with the beast's number but with the Lamb's name. This is the church triumphant. The redeemed who endured, the saints who refused to worship the beast and lived to stand with the Lamb.

> **Another Angle on God's People:** We saw the 144,000 earlier in Revelation 7:4-8, sealed from the twelve tribes of Israel. There they represented the complete people of God, perfectly protected. Here in chapter 14, the same 144,000 stand with the Lamb on Mount Zion. This isn't a different group — it's the same people seen from another perspective, now glorified and vindicated. The sealed become the standing. Those who endured with the Lamb's name on their foreheads now stand victorious with the Lamb Himself.

The 144,000 isn't a literal count. It's twelve thousand from each of the twelve tribes — a number that speaks of completeness, perfection, the fullness of God's redeemed people. This is everyone who belongs to the Lamb, everyone whose name is written in the book of life, everyone who refused the beast's mark and bore the Lamb's name instead. You're part of this number if you belong to Christ. The count is symbolic, but your inclusion is real.

And they sing a new song before the throne, a song that only they can learn. "No one could learn the song except the 144,000 who had been redeemed from the earth" (14:3). This is the song of the redeemed — the song of those who know what it cost to follow the Lamb, who understand the price of refusal, who have tasted both suffering and salvation. You can't sing this song unless you've walked the path — you can't learn it by observation alone. You have to live it.

Then John describes them: "These are the ones who have not defiled themselves with women, since they have kept their virginity" (14:4). This isn't about literal celibacy or physical virginity. This is about spiritual purity, faithfulness to the Lamb, refusal to commit spiritual adultery by worshiping the beast. Throughout Scripture, idolatry is described as adultery — turning away from God to chase other lovers. These 144,000 have remained faithful. They haven't defiled themselves by bowing to false gods or compromising with beastly systems.

They follow the Lamb wherever He goes. That's the mark of true discipleship — not spectacular displays of power, but simple, daily following. Where the Lamb leads, they go, and when the Lamb calls, they answer. When the Lamb suffers, they suffer with Him. And when the Lamb stands on Mount Zion in victory, they stand with Him.

"They were redeemed from humanity as the firstfruits for God and the Lamb" (14:4). Firstfruits. This is harvest language — the first portion of the crop, dedicated to God, a promise that more is coming. The 144,000 aren't the only ones who will be saved. They're the firstfruits, the guarantee that the full harvest is on its way. If these have been redeemed, more will follow. The ingathering has begun.

And then the final description: "No lie was found in their mouths; they are blameless" (14:5). They spoke truth in a world full of lies. They testified to the Lamb when the beast demanded allegiance. They didn't compromise, didn't hedge, didn't say what was convenient or safe. They spoke truth, and their testimony was without deceit.

Blameless. Not sinless — these are redeemed people, not perfect people. But blameless because they're clothed in the Lamb's righteousness and washed in His blood. They stand before God not on the basis of their own purity but on the basis of the Lamb's.

If you are a believer, you're part of the 144,000. If you belong to Christ, if you bear His name, if you've refused the beast and pledged allegiance to the Lamb, you're part of this complete number. You're sealed and protected and counted among the redeemed. The number is symbolic, but your inclusion is personal.

It means faithfulness is the path to standing with the Lamb. These 144,000 didn't get there by power or influence. They got there by following the Lamb wherever He went, by refusing to defile themselves with false worship, by speaking truth when lies were easier. The path to Mount Zion runs through the wilderness. The path to glory runs through suffering. But the Lamb walks that path with you, and one day you'll stand with Him.

This means you're learning the song now. Every act of obedience, every refusal to compromise, and every single testimony you give — you're learning the song of the redeemed. You can't learn it in theory. You learn it by living it, following, and enduring it. And when you stand on Mount Zion with the Lamb, you'll sing it perfectly, because you'll have lived it fully.

Prayer:

Lord Jesus, You stand on Mount Zion, and with You stand Your redeemed people. We bear Your name. We refuse the beast's mark. We follow You wherever You go, even when the path leads through suffering. Teach us the song of the redeemed. Keep us faithful, pure in our allegiance, truthful in our testimony. And bring us to the day when we stand with You on Mount Zion, clothed in Your righteousness, counted among the 144,000 who endured. Hold us and keep us. Amen.

Day 50 – The Everlasting Gospel and Three Angels

Scripture Reading: Revelation 14:6–13

Heart of Victory: The eternal gospel still calls us to worship God alone, Babylon is already falling, and those who endure in faith will find rest and reward even if endurance costs them their lives.

After the vision of the Lamb and the 144,000, three angels appear. Each one carries a message of proclamation and warning. These aren't isolated announcements. They're the core of what the church needs to hear in the face of beastly opposition. The gospel is being preached, and those who endure will be blessed.

The first angel flies in mid-heaven with the eternal gospel to proclaim to those who live on the earth — to every nation, tribe, language, and people. "Fear God and give him glory," the angel says, "because the hour of his judgment has come. Worship the one who made heaven and earth, the sea and the springs of water" (14:7).

This is the everlasting gospel, the good news that doesn't change, no matter what empires rise or beasts rage. At its heart is a call: fear God and give Him glory. Not the beast, not the dragon, not the systems that demand your loyalty — worship the Creator alone, the one who made everything and to whom all worship rightly belongs.

The hour of judgment has come — a moment that carries both a sobering warning and a staggering hope. While judgment is a terror for those who worship the beast, it is the ultimate vindication for those who worship God. The gospel declares that God is finally moving to reconcile every injustice, the wicked will not escape, and faithfulness will not go unrewarded. The very message that sounds the alarm for the world is the same one that anchors the believer in comfort.

Then a second angel follows, proclaiming, "It has fallen, Babylon the Great has fallen. She made all the nations drink the wine of her sexual immorality, which brings wrath" (14:8).

Babylon represents the seductive worldly system — wealth, power, pleasure, all the things that promise satisfaction but lead to ruin. And Babylon, for all its apparent strength, has fallen. The announcement is in the past tense, as if it's already done. In one sense, Babylon's fall is future — we're still waiting for the final collapse. But in another sense, Babylon's fall is certain. It's as good as done. You can bank on it with absolute certainty.

This is a lifeline for anyone currently refusing the intoxicating wine of Babylon — those who have been shut out of the markets because they refused the beast's mark. While Babylon still looks invincible from the outside, the truth is she has already fallen. There is no reason to be seduced by a world that is in the middle of a collapse or to chase a future that is already doomed.

Then the third angel speaks, and this message is the most urgent: "If anyone worships the beast and its image and receives a mark on his forehead or on his hand, he will also drink the wine of God's wrath, which is poured full strength into the cup of his anger" (14:9-10). There's no middle ground here. Worship the beast, and you share in the coming wrath. Take the mark, and you align yourself with what God will judge. This is the clearest warning Revelation gives. Don't bow to the beast. Don't take the mark. The cost of allegiance to the beast is eternal.

But notice what follows: "This calls for endurance from the saints, who keep God's commands and hold firmly to faith in Jesus" (14:12). The call isn't to fight the beast with political power or violent resistance. The call is to endure—to keep God's commands, and to hold firmly to faith in Jesus, refusing the mark no matter the cost.

And then the blessing: "Blessed are the dead who die in the Lord from now on. Yes, says the Spirit, so they may rest from their labors, since their works follow them" (14:13).

This is for the martyrs, for those who die rather than worship the beast. They are blessed. Not cursed, nor defeated, but blessed. They rest from their labors, but the weight of their works follows them. Every word of testimony they spoke and every quiet act of faithfulness they kept is written into the King's own memory, ensuring that nothing is lost and nothing goes unrewarded. For those who die in the Lord, death isn't the end of the story — it's the triumphant entrance into a rest that no enemy can ever disturb.

The gospel is still being proclaimed. Even when it looks like the beast has won, even when Babylon seduces and the dragon rages, the eternal gospel is being announced to every nation, tribe, language, and people. The gospel isn't silenced. The call to worship God hasn't been withdrawn. And that call reaches you today, "fear God and give Him glory."

Babylon itself is falling. Don't be fooled by appearances. The systems that look permanent and the wealth that looks secure are both temporary. The power that looks invincible is already doomed. Don't invest your life in what's collapsing.

You're not promised escape from suffering or exemption from pressure. You're promised that if you endure, if you keep God's commands and hold firmly to faith in Jesus, you'll be blessed, and if you die in the Lord, your death is not defeat. It's an entrance into rest, where your works follow you and your testimony stands forever.

Prayer:

Father, the gospel is eternal. It doesn't change with the times or bend to the beast. Help us fear You and give You glory, refusing to bow to any system that demands what belongs to You alone. Babylon is falling — keep us from being seduced by her charms. And when the cost of endurance is high, when faithfulness leads to suffering or even death, remind us that those who die in the Lord are blessed. Hold us steady. We're Yours. Amen.

Day 51 – The Harvest of the Earth

Scripture Reading: Revelation 14:14–20

Heart of Victory: The Son of Man who already reigns on the clouds will gather His own to safety—the harvest is as certain as the throne He already occupies.

This is harvest time, and it is Jesus Himself — the Son of Man — who holds the sickle. The hour has finally arrived for the earth to be reaped and for a definitive separation to be made, signaling the moment when the final judgment falls. There is no longer any room for delay or lingering opportunities for repentance. The harvest is here.

An angel comes from the temple and calls out, "Use your sickle and reap, for the time to reap has come, since the harvest of the earth is ripe" (14:15). The harvest is ripe and the time has come. And the one like the Son of Man swings His sickle over the earth, and the earth is harvested.

This is the great ingathering of God's people, a moment where Jesus Himself handles the reaping. He moves across the earth to gather His own, finally bringing them safely home to the place He prepared. This is the long-awaited payoff for the martyrs and the specific purpose for which the sealed were preserved: to see the harvest of the righteous finally gathered into the presence of the Lord.

But then another angel appears, this one with a sharp sickle as well. And another angel comes from the altar — the same altar where the prayers of the saints have been offered and the cries of the martyrs have ascended. This angel calls out: "Use your sharp sickle and gather the clusters of grapes from the vineyard of the earth, because its grapes have ripened" (14:18).

This is the harvest of judgment. The grapes are gathered and thrown into the great winepress of God's wrath. "The press was trampled outside the city, and blood flowed out of the press up to the horses' bridles for about 180 miles" (14:20).

The imagery here is unapologetically stark — blood flowing like a river in a judgment so overwhelming that it reaches the horses' bridles. We aren't looking at a map of literal geography, but at the symbolic weight of the totality of God's wrath. It is the final reckoning for those who worshiped the beast and persecuted the saints — those who looked at the offer of mercy and chose to refuse it. The winepress is judgment in its most final and absolute form.

These two harvests stand side by side. The Son of Man gathers His people while the angel of judgment gathers the wicked. And the separation is absolute. There's no middle ground, no neutral category. You're either gathered to the Lord or cast into the winepress. Either wheat or tares, grain or grapes destined for wrath.

This is the moment all of history has been moving toward. Every choice you've made about worship and allegiance, every stand you've taken or compromise you've made—it all leads here. To the harvest and separation. To the final accounting.

It is crucial to notice that the harvest takes place outside the city, leaving the New Jerusalem — the fortress and dwelling place of God's people — entirely secure. Within those walls, we find the fullness of life and safety in the unbroken fellowship of God. Beyond the gates, however, lies the reality of judgment and wrath — a final, sober separation from God. The line between inside and outside is clear. And once the harvest comes, that boundary becomes permanent.

The harvest is coming. The time of decision won't last forever. The door won't always be open. There will come a day when the Son of Man swings His sickle, when the separation is made, the saved are gathered and the wicked are judged. That day is appointed. It's certain. And it's closer now than it's ever been.

Your allegiance determines your harvest. If you belong to Christ and His name is on your forehead, if you've refused the beast and worshiped the Lamb, you'll be gathered to Him. You're the wheat, the fruit of His redemption. The Son of Man Himself will gather you home. But if you've worshiped the beast and taken the mark, if you've persecuted the saints or compromised with Babylon, you're destined for the winepress. The same God who gathers His own in mercy pours out wrath on those who oppose Him. The harvest separates. And the separation is final.

Take heart, for there is still good news! There's still time today. The sickle hasn't swung yet. The harvest hasn't come. You can still turn, still bow to the Lamb, still refuse the beast, but you can't wait forever. The grapes are ripening. The time is drawing near. And when the harvest comes, the time for decision will be past.

The Son of Man holds the sickle. The harvest is ripe, and the question for you is simple: When He reaps, where will you be? Gathered to Him in safety, or cast into the winepress of wrath? Your allegiance today determines your harvest tomorrow.

Prayer:

Lord Jesus, You hold the sickle, and the harvest is coming. We long for that day when You gather Your people, when the separation is made, when the wicked are judged and the righteous are brought safely home. But we also tremble at the finality of it. Help us choose rightly today.

Help us worship You alone, refuse the beast's mark, and bear Your name faithfully. When the harvest comes, gather us to You. Amen.

Day 52 – Overcoming the Dragon's Rage

Scripture Reading: Revelation 12–14 (Summary Meditation)

Heart of Victory: The dragon has thrown everything at the church—persecution, deception, economic pressure—and the church still stands, because the Lamb's victory cannot be undone by the dragon's rage.

We've walked through three chapters of cosmic conflict. The dragon has raged, the beasts have risen, and the pressure on God's people has intensified. This isn't background information. This is the reality you live in every day, the unseen war that shapes everything you experience as a follower of Jesus.

The dragon couldn't destroy the child, so he pursues the woman. He can't win, so he rages. And his rage targets those who keep God's commands and hold firmly to the testimony of Jesus. If you belong to Christ, you're in the dragon's sights. The pursuit is real. The opposition is fierce. But the outcome is already decided.

The beasts rise from the sea and the earth, empowered by the dragon, demanding worship and enforcing allegiance through the mark. They look invincible and demand unconditional surrender. They make it seem like you have no choice but to bow. But these chapters reveal the beasts operate under God's sovereignty, the mark is the beast's demand for visible allegiance, and faithfulness is the path to victory.

Then the Lamb appears on Mount Zion with the 144,000 — the complete number of the redeemed. We see them standing with their King and singing the song only they can learn. This is where the story ends for those who endure. Not with defeat or death, but with standing victorious beside the Lamb.

And finally, the harvest. The Son of Man gathers His own while judgment falls on the wicked. The separation is made. The accounting is final. And those who refused the beast's mark are gathered safely home.

So what does all of this mean when you put it together?

It means you're living in the middle of a war. The dragon has been defeated, but he hasn't been destroyed yet. He rages because his time is short, and he knows it. The beasts rise because the dragon empowers them. The mark is pressed upon people because the dragon demands visible allegiance. And the church lives in this tension — already victorious in Christ, not yet experiencing the fullness of that victory.

It means the pressure to compromise is real. The beast doesn't just threaten — it seduces. It offers security, prosperity, participation in society. All you have to do is take the mark, make the compromise, worship what everyone else worships. The cost of refusal is exclusion, suffering, possibly death. The temptation isn't to embrace obvious evil. It's to make small compromises that seem reasonable, to go along with systems that promise safety if you'll just bow a little.

But it also means faithfulness is victory. You overcome the dragon the same way the martyrs did — by the blood of the Lamb and the word of your testimony, not loving your life even unto death. You conquer the beasts not by fighting them on their terms, but by refusing to give them what they demand: your worship. You endure not by your own strength, but by trusting the Lamb who has already won. And it means the dragon's fury is proof of his defeat. If he had won, he wouldn't be raging. If he had any real power, he wouldn't be desperate. If the battle were still in doubt, he wouldn't be so frantic to destroy the woman's offspring. His rage is the death throes of a defeated enemy, lashing out because he knows his time is short.

The question these chapters force you to answer is this: Whose mark will you bear? The beast offers his mark — participation, security, survival. The Lamb offers His name — suffering, exclusion, possibly death. But the beast's mark leads to the winepress of wrath. The Lamb's name leads to standing on Mount Zion.

You can't have both. You can't take the mark and bear the name. You can't worship the beast and follow the Lamb. The choice is stark, the stakes are ultimate, and the time to choose is now.

So where does this leave you?

It leaves you in the wilderness, pursued by the dragon but nourished by God. It leaves you facing the beasts' demands, called to endure and remain faithful. It leaves you longing for the harvest, for the day when the Son of Man swings His sickle and gathers His own.

But it also leaves you with hope. The dragon is defeated. The beasts are doomed. Babylon is falling. And the Lamb stands on Mount Zion, waiting to welcome His 144,000 home. You're part of that number. Your name is written in the book of life. And when the harvest comes, you'll stand with the Lamb and sing the song of the redeemed.

The dragon rages. The beasts demand. But the Lamb has conquered them. And those who follow Him will conquer with Him.

Prayer:

Lord Jesus, we live in the dragon's time of rage, facing the beasts' demands, tempted to take the mark to survive. But You have conquered. You stand on Mount Zion, and one day we'll stand with You. Keep us faithful when the pressure mounts. Help us refuse the compromises that seem small but lead to destruction. And bring us safely through to the harvest, when You gather Your own and we join the 144,000 singing Your praise. Hold us fast. Amen.

Day 53 – Worship, Allegiance, and Everyday Decisions

Scripture Reading: Topical Reflection from Revelation 13–14

Heart of Victory: Every ordinary choice is an act of worship that reveals our allegiance—choosing the Lamb over the beast in daily decisions is how we refuse the mark and prepare to stand with Him on Mount Zion.

The beast demands worship. The Lamb calls for allegiance. And in between stands you, making choices every single day about where you'll place your trust, your hope, your worship and your ultimate loyalty. These chapters of Revelation aren't just about dramatic end-times scenarios. They're about the daily decisions that reveal whose you are.

Worship isn't just what happens on Sunday morning. Worship is what you organize your life around, what you sacrifice for. You can't imagine living without worship. The beast knows this. That's why it doesn't just threaten — it offers. It promises security and prosperity, offering you belonging. It says, "Give me your allegiance, and I'll give you everything you need."

The mark of the beast isn't primarily a technology or a literal tattoo. It's the visible expression of invisible allegiance. It's the moment when you have to declare publicly whose you are. And throughout history, that moment has come in different forms — sacrificing to Caesar, joining the party, signing the oath, going along with the system to keep your job or your reputation or your life.

The question these chapters ask is simple: What are you willing to sacrifice to survive? What compromises will you make to participate? What allegiances will you accept to belong? Because here's the reality.

The beast's system always demands something. It might be small at first — a little compromise here, a quiet participation there. But it builds. The mark isn't given all at once. It's accumulated through a thousand small decisions, each one moving you closer to the point where you can't imagine saying no.

And the tragedy is that many people take the mark without even realizing it. They don't think they're worshiping the beast. They just think they're being practical and making smart decisions. But worship isn't always conscious. Sometimes worship is just what you do without thinking. These patterns you just fall into and the systems you serve without questioning.

So how do you know if you're worshiping the Lamb or the beast? Look at your ordinary decisions.

When the culture around you demands conformity, do you bend or stand firm? When your job asks you to compromise your integrity, do you comply or refuse? When participating in the system requires you to be silent about Christ, do you go quiet or speak up? These aren't hypothetical questions. These are the daily choices that reveal your allegiance.

The Lamb asks for everything. He doesn't promise comfort or security or ease. He promises His presence with you in the wilderness and a place He has prepared. He calls you to follow Him wherever He goes, even when that path leads through suffering. And He says that if you refuse to take the beast's mark, you'll be excluded — unable to buy or sell, shut out from the system, possibly killed.

But here's what the Lamb also promises. If you bear His name, you will stand with Him on the heights of Mount Zion. For everyone who refused the mark and endured the wilderness, the harvest is coming — a final gathering where you will join the chorus to sing the song of the redeemed. The beast offers survival now. The Lamb offers life forever.

This is where everyday decisions become acts of worship. When you refuse the compromise everyone else is making, you're worshiping the Lamb. When you speak truth in a world full of lies, you're testifying to His name. When you choose integrity over profit and faithfulness over safety, when you choose Christ over comfort, you're refusing the beast's mark. And when you make those choices, you're not alone. The dragon rages, the beasts demand, but the Lamb stands with you. His name is on your forehead, and you are sealed and protected among the 144,000. And every choice you make for Him is preparing you to sing the song that only the redeemed can learn.

So today, look at your choices. Where are you being pressed to compromise? What allegiance are you being asked to express? What mark are you being offered? And then ask: Whose mark will I bear? The beast's or the Lamb's? Whose song will I sing? The world's or the redeemed? Whose name will define me? The system's or Christ's? Worship isn't just what you do in church. Worship is what you do at work, in your home, with your money, in your relationships, when no one is watching. Every choice is a declaration of allegiance. Every decision reveals whom you worship.

The beast is crafty. He makes worship look like wisdom. He makes compromise look like survival. But the Lamb sees through it all. And He calls you to something different: faithful endurance, visible allegiance, daily worship expressed through the ordinary choices that add up to a life spent following Him.

The mark you bear matters. The song you sing matters. Choose the Lamb and bear His name. And when the harvest comes, you'll stand on Mount Zion with all the redeemed, singing the song that your faithfulness has taught you to sing.

Prayer:

Lord Jesus, our daily choices matter. Help us see that every decision is an act of worship, every compromise a step toward the mark we refuse to take. When the pressure comes to conform, to be silent, to go along with systems that oppose You, give us courage to stand. We choose to bear Your name. We refuse the beast's mark. We worship You in the small decisions and the large ones. Make us faithful in the ordinary moments, because we know they're preparing us for the extraordinary day when we stand with You on Mount Zion. Amen.

Part Six: Bowls, Babylon, and the Coming King

Revelation 15–19

Heart of Victory: The bowls of wrath prove God's justice cannot be mocked, Babylon's collapse shows earthly power is temporary, and the Bride's readiness is the victory of grace—the King who died as a Lamb now prepares to return as a Lion.

The final judgments fall. The seven bowls of God's wrath are poured out on those who have taken the mark of the beast — severe and irreversible. But even under these plagues, hearts remain hard. People curse God rather than repent, choosing defiance over surrender. The sanctuary fills with smoke, and no one can enter. The time for intercession has passed. God's patience, which held back judgment to give people time to turn, has reached its appointed end.

Then Babylon appears — not as a single city but as the embodiment of every worldly system that seduces people away from God. She sits on the beast, dressed in luxury, holding a golden cup filled with abominations. She has corrupted the earth with her lies, enriched the merchants with her wealth, and killed the saints with her violence. The kings of the earth have committed adultery with her, and the nations have drunk deeply from her cup. But her fall is sudden and absolute. In a single hour, her smoke rises forever. Heaven erupts in praise—not because destruction is good, but because justice has been done. The blood of the martyrs has been avenged.

And then, with Babylon gone, the wedding can begin. The Bride has been made ready, clothed in fine linen that represents the righteous acts of the saints. The marriage supper of the Lamb is announced, and heaven shouts, "Hallelujah!" But before the feast, there is one more battle to be won. Heaven opens, and the Rider on the white horse appears. His name is Faithful and True. His eyes blaze like fire. His robe is dipped in blood. And on His thigh is written: King of Kings and Lord of Lords.

The beast and the false prophet gather the kings of the earth for war, but there is no battle. The Rider speaks, and they fall. The beast and the false prophet are thrown alive into the lake of fire. The armies are slain by the sword that comes from His mouth. Every counterfeit authority is finished, and every enemy is defeated. The stage is set for the final consummation — the end of death, the renewal of creation, and the unveiling of the New Jerusalem.

Part Six is the hinge on which Revelation turns. The judgments are complete, the seductions are exposed, and the enemies are defeated. The Lamb's victory, won at Calvary, is about to be fully consummated. What began with a slain Lamb ends with a conquering King. And the church — His Bride — will stand beside Him, clothed in righteousness, witnessing the fulfillment of every promise God has ever made.

Welcome to Part Six.

Day 54 – The Sea of Glass and the Song of the Lamb

Scripture Reading: Revelation 15:1–4

Heart of Victory: Worship declares that God's ways are just—and those who sing the Lamb's song know the ending even while the bowls are still being poured.

There are times in life when words fall short, and the only suitable response is song. A bride, filled with joy, walking down the aisle. A prisoner, emerging free after years of darkness. Song conveys what plain speech cannot — emotion that transcends ordinary language and truths too profound for simple explanation. It gives wings to what the heart struggles to express.

This is the point where Revelation 15 begins. John describes "something like a sea of glass mixed with fire," and beside it, those "who had won the victory over the beast, its image, and the number of its name" (15:2). These individuals are active participants, not mere spectators. They are victors, those who endured, rejected the mark, and held firm under intense pressure. Now, they stand on heaven's shore with harps, prepared to sing.

But notice what they sing before the final judgments fall. They don't sing about themselves. They don't celebrate their own courage or recount their own endurance. They sing the song of Moses, the servant of God, and the song of the Lamb. This is worship that looks backward to the Exodus and forward to the cross, acknowledging that every victory belongs to God alone.

The song itself is stunning in its focus: "Great and awe-inspiring are your works, Lord God, the Almighty; just and true are your ways, King of the nations. Lord, who will not fear and glorify your name? For you alone are holy. All the nations will come and worship before you because your righteous acts have been revealed" (15:3–4). Every line declares something about God — His works are great and His ways are just, and He alone is holy. The nations will worship Him. The song doesn't merely celebrate that judgment is coming; it celebrates the character of the One who judges.

This song of Moses echoes the worship Israel expressed after crossing the Red Sea. When Pharaoh's army was lost and God's people stood on the distant shore, they didn't praise their courage in entering the water. Instead, they sang about the Lord who "has thrown into the sea the horse and his rider" (Exodus 15:1, ESV). Their salvation was not their own accomplishment but God's righteous deed. And now, centuries later, on another shore—this one glassy and mingled with fire — another generation of God's people sings the same kind of song. They have been delivered not from Egypt but from the beast. Not from chariots but from the seductions of counterfeit worship. And they give glory to the same God who saves.

But this is also the song of the Lamb. The Exodus foreshadowed a greater deliverance — one achieved not through vanquishing an army, but through Jesus's blood. The Lamb who was slain has redeemed people from every tribe, and they now stand as living evidence that His victory is total. Although the beast demanded worship, it could not keep them. The dragon raged, but it could not destroy them. They conquered "by the blood of the Lamb and by the word of their testimony" (12:11), and now they sing because the One who redeemed them is about to finish what He started.

There's something deeply important about the timing here. John witnesses a vision of worship just before the seven bowls are poured out. The final judgments are imminent — swift, harsh, and unchangeable. Yet, before the first bowl is poured, heaven halts to sing. Why? Because judgment is purposeful, not random. It is neither vindictive nor capricious but stems from the character of a just and true God. The bowls are not the result of an angry deity losing control;

instead, they represent the righteous acts of the Holy One, finally revealed in all their dreadful clarity.

Notice what the song also anticipates: "All the nations will come and worship before you" (15:4). Even amid looming judgment, the vision isn't one of utter destruction but of worldwide worship. God's judgments align with His purpose, which has always been to gather a people from every nation to worship Him in spirit and truth. The bowls that are poured out are not the conclusion but a part of the larger narrative — how God removes every barrier to His glory, dismantles all rival thrones, and opens a path for all nations to return home.

For us, standing on this side of the vision, there's comfort and challenge here. The comfort is that our God is not arbitrary. His ways are just. His works are great. When we don't understand what He's doing — when life feels chaotic and evil seems to triumph, when suffering stretches on — we can trust that His righteous acts will be revealed. One day we will see clearly what we now see only dimly. One day the justice of His ways will be undeniable. And on that day, we will sing.

The challenge is to start singing now. Not because everything makes sense, but because we know the One to whom the song is sung. The victors in Revelation 15 didn't wait until all their questions were answered. They sang because they knew who God is and because they had been delivered. They sang because worship was the only fitting response to the One who alone is holy.

You might be in the middle of your own struggle with the beast right now — facing pressure to compromise, to blend in, to bow down to what everyone else is bowing to. You might feel worn out by the fight. But Revelation 15 tells you where this is going. You will stand on the sea of glass. You will hold the harp. You will sing the song. Not because you were strong enough, but because the Lamb is faithful. His righteous acts will be revealed, and you will worship Him with a joy too big for words — so you'll sing instead.

Prayer:

Lord God Almighty, Your works are great and awe-inspiring. We may not always understand what You're doing, but we trust that Your ways are just and true. Teach us to sing Your song now, even as we're still in the fight. Give us faith to believe that Your righteous acts will be revealed and that one day every nation will come to worship before You. Until then, keep us faithful. You alone are holy. Amen.

Day 55 – The Sanctuary Filled with Smoke

Scripture Reading: Revelation 15:5–8

Heart of Victory: The sanctuary fills with smoke because God's glory will not be interrupted—when His justice falls, it falls completely, and nothing can enter His presence until His purposes are fulfilled.

There's a stillness that comes before something irreversible happens. The quiet before the surgeon makes the first incision. The moment when everyone knows there's no going back, and when the point of no return has already passed. Revelation 15 gives us one of those moments — a pause heavy with the weight of what's about to unfold.

John sees the heavenly sanctuary open, and out of it come seven angels dressed in pure, bright linen with golden sashes around their chests. These aren't messengers bringing comfort or reassurance. They're carrying something final: "the seven last plagues, for with them God's wrath will be completed" (15:1). The word "completed" should arrest us. This isn't the beginning of judgment; this is the end of it. These seven bowls represent the fullness and the finality of God's response to unrepentant evil.

One of the four living creatures — those beings who never stop worshiping God's holiness — gives each angel a golden bowl "filled with the wrath of God who lives forever and ever" (15:7). And then something stunning happens: "The temple was filled with smoke from the glory of God and from his power, and no one could enter the temple until the seven plagues of the seven angels were completed" (15:8).

Smoke filling the sanctuary is not a new image. When God descended on Mount Sinai, the mountain was wrapped in smoke "because the LORD came down on it in fire" (Exodus 19:18, ESV). When Solomon dedicated the temple, "the glory of the LORD filled the LORD's temple" so completely that the priests couldn't even enter to perform their service (1 Kings 8:10–11). The smoke signifies the overwhelming presence of God — His glory, His holiness, and His power too intense for human approach.

But here in Revelation 15, the smoke also means something else: no intercession. No one can enter the temple. No prayers are being offered. The time for mercy has passed. The bowls are ready, and nothing will stop them from being poured out. This is a terrifying reality. God is patient beyond measure, but His patience has a purpose — to lead people to repentance. When that patience is continually spurned, when hearts grow harder instead of softer, there comes a moment when the sanctuary fills with smoke and the bowls are handed out.

We need to sit with this. Our culture resists the very idea of divine wrath. We're more comfortable with a God who overlooks sin and shrugs at evil. A god who never draws a line in the sand. But that's not the God of Scripture. The God who is love is also the God who is holy. And holiness cannot coexist with unrepentant wickedness forever. The wrath of God isn't a character flaw or a loss of control. It's the necessary response of perfect justice to real evil. It's what happens when mercy is continually rejected.

The fact that God "lives forever and ever" makes His wrath both sobering and inevitable. He doesn't grow tired or forget. He doesn't change His mind about what is right. The same God who has patiently endured blasphemy, idolatry, violence, and rebellion will one day say, "Enough." And when He does, the smoke will fill the temple, and the bowls will fall.

For those who have refused the mark and endured the beast's rage, and clung to the testimony of Jesus, this scene is not a threat — it's a vindication. God sees what has happened, and He will act in justice. The martyrs under the altar asked, "How long, Sovereign Lord, holy and true, until you judge the inhabitants of the earth and avenge our blood?" (6:10). Revelation 15 is the answer. Not much longer. The angels are dressed. The bowls are filled. The sanctuary is filled with smoke. Justice is coming.

But even here, even at the threshold of final judgment, we see the majesty of God's glory. The smoke isn't just about wrath. It's about the blinding, breathtaking, unapproachable holiness of the One who sits on the throne. He is glorious in power and glorious in justice, refusing to let evil have the last word. The angels come from His presence, clothed in purity, and the bowls they carry are not arbitrary punishments. They are filled with the wrath of the God who lives forever — the God whose character never changes, and a justice that never wavers.

For us today, this passage is both warning and comfort. The warning is clear. Don't presume on God's patience. The fact that judgment hasn't fallen yet doesn't mean it never will. The sanctuary will fill with smoke. The bowls will be poured. Repent now, while the door is still open. Turn to the Lamb, who bore God's wrath in your place and invites you to wash your robes in His blood and stand among the redeemed.

The comfort is equally clear. God will not let evil go unpunished forever. If you're suffering under the weight of injustice, and have watched wickedness triumph while righteousness is mocked, take heart. The angels are already holding the bowls. The smoke is already gathering. The God who lives forever and ever will complete His wrath against all that has wounded His people and defied His glory. And when He does, you will see that His ways are just and true.

Prayer:

Holy God, we tremble before Your glory and bow before Your justice. Thank You for Your patience with us, for holding back wrath so that we might repent and be saved. We confess that we've taken Your kindness for granted, assuming You would overlook what You cannot overlook. Forgive us. Clothe us in the righteousness of the Lamb, so that when the sanctuary fills with smoke, we will not fear. Give us courage to stand for You now, knowing that You will stand for us then. Amen.

Day 56 – The First Four Bowls

Scripture Reading: Revelation 16:1–9

Heart of Victory: The bowls reveal that God's justice is as certain as His patience—and the same hand that pours judgment is the hand that shelters those who belong to the Lamb.

If you've ever watched someone self-destruct — someone who keeps making the same destructive choices over and over, rejecting every offer of help, every warning, every lifeline — you know how heartbreaking it is. You see the path they're on. You see where it's headed. And you watch, helpless, as they double down and keep walking toward the cliff. That's the tragedy at the heart of Revelation 16. The bowls fall, one after another, and instead of turning to God in repentance, people curse His name and refuse to change.

John hears a loud voice from the temple commanding the seven angels: "Go and pour out the seven bowls of God's wrath on the earth" (16:1). What follows is swift and unrelenting. The first angel pours his bowl on the earth, and "severely painful sores broke out on the people who had the mark of the beast and who worshiped its image" (16:2). The second angel pours his bowl into the sea, and it becomes "like the blood of a dead person," killing everything in it (16:3). The third angel pours his bowl into the rivers and springs, and they too become blood (16:4). The fourth angel pours his bowl on the sun, and it's given power "to burn people with fire" (16:8).

These judgments echo the plagues of Egypt — water turned to blood, painful sores, scorching heat. But while the plagues in Exodus were designed to break Pharaoh's grip on Israel and reveal God's supremacy over Egypt's gods, the bowls in Revelation fall on a world that has already chosen its allegiance. These are not warnings. They are the completion of wrath on those who have decisively rejected the Lamb.

The Pattern Completed: This is the third time Revelation has shown us God's judgments falling on the earth—first the seals (chapters 6–7), then the trumpets (chapters 8–9), now the bowls. Each cycle covers the same period but escalates in intensity. The seals struck a fourth of the earth; the trumpets struck a third; now the bowls strike everything, with no restraint remaining. The warnings have ended. Where the seals revealed what the church endures and the trumpets called for repentance, the bowls pour out the final, unrestrained consequence of rejecting the Lamb. Same ground. Same period. But now the mercy that held back full judgment has given way to its completion.

And here's the heartbreak. Even in the face of these judgments, people do not repent. After the fourth bowl, when the sun scorches them with fire, the text says they "blasphemed the name of God, who has the authority over these plagues, and they did not repent and give him glory" (16:9). That phrase, "they did not repent," should make us pause. These are not people who don't know what's happening. They recognize that God has authority over the plagues. They know where the judgment is coming from. And still they refuse to turn. They curse Him instead.

This is the ultimate hardness of heart. It's not ignorance or confusion — it's deliberate defiance. The beast promised them prosperity, power, and security. They believed the lie, bowed to the image, and now they're reaping what they sowed. But instead of acknowledging their mistake, and crying out to the God who still has the power to save, they shake their fists at heaven and blaspheme His name.

That kind of hardness doesn't happen overnight. It's the result of years — maybe a lifetime — of small refusals. We brush off conviction and justify what we know is wrong. We choose comfort over obedience. Each refusal trains our hearts to resist God a little more. And if we keep it up long enough, we can reach a point where even catastrophic judgment won't move us. We'll blame God for the consequences of our own rebellion and dig in deeper rather than repent.

But there's also something profoundly just about these bowls. They fall specifically on "the people who had the mark of the beast and who worshiped its image" (16:2). This is not random destruction. It's targeted judgment on those who chose to align themselves with the beast's authority and defy the Lamb. They wanted the beast's protection and prosperity and approval. Now they're learning that the beast can't protect them from the wrath of the One who sits on the throne.

And notice the testimony of the angel in charge of the waters: "You are just, the Holy One, who is and who was, because you have passed judgment on these things. Because they poured out the blood of the saints and the prophets, you have given them blood to drink; they deserve it" (16:5–6). The judgments are not random. They fit the crime. Those who shed the blood of God's people are given blood to drink. Those who worshiped the beast's image receive the consequences of that worship. God's justice is precise.

For those of us who belong to Christ, this passage is both sobering and clarifying. It's sobering because it reminds us how dangerous it is to harden our hearts against God. We can get so used to resisting the Spirit's conviction that we stop hearing His voice altogether. We can become so invested in our own way that even disaster won't make us change course. The cure for that hardness is vigilance — daily repentance and surrender, daily prayer for soft hearts that respond quickly to God's prompting.

But this passage also clarifies that judgment is not the enemy of justice—it's the fulfillment of it. The bowls fall on those who persecuted the church and killed the faithful. These people chose the beast over the Lamb. And while that judgment is severe, it's also right. God is just. He doesn't overlook the blood of the martyrs. He doesn't shrug at the arrogance of those who mocked His name. One day — whether in history or at the end of history—He will pour out the bowls, and every debt will be either paid in Christ or borne in judgment.

So receive this as both warning and mercy. If your heart has grown hard, and you've been resisting God's voice, flirting with the mark of compromise — stop. Repent now, while there's still time. Don't wait for the bowls to fall. Run to the Lamb, who bore the wrath you deserve so that you can receive the mercy you don't. His blood is better than anything the beast could ever offer.

Prayer:

Father, we confess that our hearts are prone to wander and resist Your voice. Forgive us for ignoring Your warnings and justifying our disobedience. Keep our hearts tender toward You. Give us grace to repent quickly, to turn from sin before it takes root, and to worship the Lamb rather than the beast. We do not want to be among those who blaspheme Your name when judgment falls, but among those who sing Your praise. Amen.

Day 57 – Darkness, Deceit, and Gathering for Battle

Scripture Reading: Revelation 16:10–16

Heart of Victory: The world gathers for a battle it cannot win; we watch for a Bridegroom we cannot miss.

Darkness often makes us stumble. When the power goes out at night, you reach for walls that aren't where you thought they were. You trip over furniture you could easily see in the light. The world stays the same, but you just can't see it. That's when accidents happen, people get hurt, and simple things become confusing and risky.

The fifth bowl brings a darkness like that. The angel pours his bowl "on the throne of the beast, and its kingdom was plunged into darkness" (16:10). This isn't just a lack of light; it's a judgment that shows the emptiness of the beast's power. The kingdom that once promised strength and safety is now lost in shadow. In that darkness, people "gnawed their tongues because of their pain and blasphemed the God of heaven because of their pains and their sores, but they did not repent of their actions" (16:10–11).

Still, there is no repentance. The curses keep coming. The pattern continues: judgment comes, pain grows, and people's hearts become harder. But in this darkness, something even more troubling happens. John sees "three unclean spirits like frogs coming from the mouth of the dragon, from the mouth of the beast, and from the mouth of the false prophet" (16:13). These spirits are demons, performing convincing signs to deceive. Their goal is clear: they go out "to the kings of the whole world, to gather them for the battle on the great day of God, the Almighty" (16:14).

Let that sink in. Even while God's anger is being poured out and the beast's kingdom is falling into darkness, the dragon, beast, and false prophet send out lying spirits to gather opposition. They bring the kings of the earth to a place called "Armageddon" in Hebrew (16:16), assembling for war against God Himself. It's madness and completely hopeless. Still, this is what happens when people are so deceived that they would rather fight God than surrender to Him. But their anger cannot change His victory.

This gathering for battle isn't just about one military conflict in the Middle East. It's really about the final showdown between God's kingdom and the kingdoms of this world. Throughout history, whenever human power joins with spiritual rebellion or political leaders join with idolatry to resist God, the pattern is to gather forces and fight against heaven. Every time, the result is the same. The nations get angry, but the One on the throne in heaven laughs (Psalm 2:4). The battle is finished before it starts, because no group of earthly power can stand against the Lamb.

But notice the method of deception here. The spirits do signs that look real. They seem believable. The kings of the earth don't know they're being tricked. They think they're protecting their power and looking out for their kingdoms. They don't see the dragon controlling them, pulling them into his last desperate plan. That's how deception works. It doesn't show itself. It hides as strength and wisdom, pretending to be the smart thing to do.

This is why Jesus steps in with a warning: "Look, I am coming like a thief. Blessed is the one who is awake and clothed so that he does not go around naked and people see his shame" (16:15). In the middle of this dark vision of armies gathering, Jesus tells His people to stay awake and ready, dressed in the righteousness He gives. The world is getting ready for war, but the church is called to be alert and holy, to watch and walk in the light. While the nations head toward Armageddon, we are to watch for the Bridegroom.

That difference means everything. The beast's followers gather for a battle they cannot win, while the Lamb's followers wait for a wedding they cannot miss. The beast's kingdom is lost in darkness, but the Lamb's people are covered in light. The dragon's spirits trick people, but the Spirit of God brings truth. And when everything is over, only one side will remain.

"For us, this passage is a strong reminder that deception is real and powerful. We live in a world where lies often look like the truth. We need to be wise and test every spirit, measuring every message against the Word of God. The dragon is still sending out his frogs and spreading his lies, still gathering people to fight a war they should avoid."

But we also have hope. The darkness will not last. The beast's throne is falling apart. The kings who gather at Armageddon will run when the Rider on the white horse appears. Those of us who stay awake, dressed in Christ, and refuse to be fooled will not be put to shame. We will stand on the sea of glass and sing the song of the Lamb, celebrating a victory that was always certain.

So stay alert. Don't let the world's promises make you careless. Don't be fooled by signs that look amazing but serve the dragon. Don't join the crowd at Armageddon; instead, wait for the Bridegroom. Stay awake and stay dressed. Keep your eyes on Jesus, not on the armies. He is coming like a thief — suddenly, unexpectedly, and in glory. When He comes, you want to be ready.

Prayer:

Lord Jesus, keep us awake. Keep us clothed in Your righteousness. Guard us from the lying spirits that whisper in the dark. We know the beast's kingdom is crumbling, even when it looks strong. We know the dragon's gathering is futile, even when it looks intimidating. Give us eyes to see through the deception and courage to stand firm while others march toward Armageddon. You are coming, and we want to be ready. Come quickly, Lord. Amen.

Day 58 – "It Is Done" – The Seventh Bowl

Scripture Reading: Revelation 16:17–21

Heart of Victory: When Christ said "It is finished," He completed our redemption; when God says "It is done," He completes His justice.

Some words, once spoken, cannot be taken back. Saying 'I do' seals a marriage, while 'It's over' ends one. These statements close one chapter and open another, carrying weight long after they're spoken. In Revelation 16, God speaks such a word: 'It is done!' (16:17).

The seventh angel pours his bowl into the air, and a loud voice from the throne in the temple announces the end: "It is done." The Greek word is gegonen, which means "It has happened." Everything is finished. All the bowls of wrath have been poured out. There is no judgment left to hold back, nothing left to delay. The final judgment has come.

What happens next is catastrophic. Lightning flashes, rumblings shake the air, and thunder crashes — these are familiar signs of God's presence in judgment. Then there is, "A violent earthquake occurred — the greatest since humanity has been on the earth, so great was that earthquake" (16:18). The great city splits into three parts. The cities of the nations fall. Babylon the Great is "remembered before God" and given the cup filled with His fierce anger (16:19). Islands vanish. Mountains disappear. Then, as if that were not enough, "enormous hailstones, each weighing about a hundred pounds, fell from the sky on people" (16:21). And still, people blasphemed God because the plague of hail was so severe.

This is complete and unstoppable judgment. When God says, "It is done," He means it. The earth shakes so much that even the land changes. Cities that once seemed permanent fall apart. Babylon, which stands for worldly power, wealth, and temptation, finally gets what she deserves. The cup she filled with violence and idolatry is now full, and God makes her drink every last drop.

Yet even here mercy is embedded in these terrifying images. The fact that seven bowls fall — seven distinct, sequential judgments — means God is deliberate. He is patient. Even in wrath, He is measured. Each bowl is an opportunity to see where this is headed, a warning that the end is coming. And even now, at the seventh bowl, when the voice says, "It is done," God's justice is not capricious. It's precise. Babylon is remembered. She is given exactly what her deeds deserve. This is not vengeance out of control. This is righteousness fulfilled.

The declaration 'It is done' also reminds us of another moment in Scripture. On the cross, just before He died, Jesus cried out, 'It is finished' (John 19:30). Both are perfect tense declarations — completed, irreversible, final. On the cross, Jesus announced that redemption was accomplished, the debt paid in full. Here, God announces that judgment is complete. The wrath He held back from His people — because it fell on His Son — now comes to those who refused His Son. "It is done."

This is the final vindication. Every martyr who asked, "How long, O Lord?" now gets an answer. Not much longer. In fact, it is done. Every act of injustice and violence against God's people, every lie — none of it has been forgotten. Babylon is remembered, and she will drink the cup.

> **Echoes of Final Judgment:** This is not the first time Revelation shows us the end. The sixth seal revealed cosmic upheaval—the sky rolled up, mountains moved, and everyone hid from the wrath of the Lamb (6:12–17). The seventh trumpet announced that the kingdom of the world had become the kingdom of our Lord (11:15–19), accompanied by lightning, thunder, and an earthquake. Later, the great white throne will reveal the final judgment of every soul (20:11–15). These are not separate events at different times. They are different angles on the same reality—the moment when God's patience ends and His justice is fully shown. Each vision adds detail, each emphasizes a different aspect, but they all point to the same climactic truth: one day, God will say, "It is done," and every wrong will be made right.

For those who belong to Christ, "It is done" is not a threat but a promise. It means suffering will end and lies will be exposed. It means the systems that oppressed us will fall, and Babylon — whatever form she takes in your life, your city, or your world — will be brought down. It also means that the God who has been patient, holding back His wrath to give people time to repent, will finally act. His justice will be complete. His holiness will be proven. And those who trusted Him and endured, who refused the mark, will see it happen.

But for those who have aligned themselves with Babylon, who have taken the beast's mark, and blasphemed God even under judgment —

"It is done" is terrifying. There is no more time, and the door is closed. The wrath is complete. As severe as the seventh bowl is, it is only a preview of what is to come. Babylon may have fallen many times in history, but the final fall — the one John will soon describe in detail — is coming. When it happens, there will be no recovery and no way to rebuild what has fallen.

So where do you stand? Have you aligned yourself with the beast, chasing the security, wealth, and approval that Babylon offers? Or have you chosen the Lamb, trusting His blood to cover you, His righteousness to clothe you, and His victory to defend you? One day, maybe sooner than we expect, the voice will sound from the throne, and the words will shake the earth: "It is done." Make sure you are standing with the One who already said, "It is finished."

Prayer:

Father, we tremble before the finality of Your justice. You are patient beyond measure, but Your patience serves a purpose. When You say, "It is done," nothing can reverse it. Thank You for the cross, where Jesus said, "It is finished," and took the wrath we deserved. Clothe us in His righteousness so that when the seventh bowl falls, we will stand in awe rather than terror. We trust You, Lord. Your ways are just and your judgments are true. Finish Your work. Make all things right. Amen.

Day 59 – The Great Prostitute and the Beast

Scripture Reading: Revelation 17:1–6

Heart of Victory: Babylon's golden cup is filled with poison; the Lamb's wedding feast is filled with joy.

Seduction is dangerous because it never seems dangerous at first. It feels exciting and full of promise, as if it holds everything you've been missing. An affair doesn't start with betrayal. It starts with attention and flattery, with the quiet lie that you deserve more than what you have. By the time you realize the truth, you're already caught. That's how sin works. That's how Babylon works.

In Revelation 17, one of the seven angels with the bowls invites John to see "the judgment of the notorious prostitute who is seated on many waters" (17:1). This isn't a real woman, but a symbol — a vivid and unsettling picture of a worldly system that draws people away from God. She is called Babylon the Great, and she sits on many waters, which John explains means "peoples, multitudes, nations, and languages" (17:15). Her influence is worldwide, her reach vast, and her method is seduction.

The angel tells John, "the kings of the earth committed sexual immorality with her, and those who live on the earth became drunk with the wine of her sexual immorality" (17:2). This is the language of adultery — covenant-breaking, giving yourself to what you don't belong to, trading faithfulness for the lie that you deserve more. The kings of the earth — those with power and influence — have been drawn in by her promises. They have drunk her wine and become drunk, losing their ability to see clearly. They have traded faithfulness for pleasure, truth for lies, and the worship of God for the worship of wealth and self.

John is carried away in the Spirit to a wilderness, where he sees a woman sitting on a scarlet beast "that was covered with blasphemous names and had seven heads and ten horns" (17:3). This is the same beast from Revelation 13, the one the world worshiped and whose image demanded loyalty. Now, in Revelation 17, the prostitute is riding the beast. She is joined with it, using its power to spread her influence. This shows the partnership between worldly religion and political power, between spiritual seduction and beastly coercion. Together, they form a system that seems impossible to resist or defeat.

The woman is dressed in luxury: "purple and scarlet, adorned with gold, jewels, and pearls" (17:4). She holds a golden cup, but it is not filled with wine. Instead, it holds "detestable things and the impurities of her prostitution" (17:4). She looks beautiful on the outside. The appearance is impressive, but what is inside is disgusting. That is Babylon's oldest lie. It promises satisfaction but gives poison. It promises life but brings death. People drink from her cup because they only see the gold.

On her forehead is a name: "Babylon the Great, the Mother of Prostitutes and of the Detestable Things of the Earth" (17:5). She represents the ancient city that defied God at Babel and led Israel into exile. Babylon has returned — not as a single city, but as a spirit, a system, and a tempting way of life that makes the world seem irresistible and God easy to forget.

She is called a mother because she multiplies. Every age grows its own Babylon. Every culture fills its own cup, and people eagerly drink from it.

Then John sees something that shocks him: the woman is "drunk with the blood of the saints and with the blood of the witnesses of Jesus" (17:6). She is not only seductive, but also violent. She does not just tempt people away from God; she kills those who refuse to follow her. The same system that promises pleasure and success also demands total loyalty. If you refuse to give in and stay true to Jesus, she turns against you. She is drunk on the blood of martyrs, and she still wants more.

John is "greatly astonished" when he sees her (17:6). Why? Maybe because the image is so shocking — beauty mixed with violence, temptation mixed with destruction, all in one disturbing figure. Or maybe because he recognizes her. He sees the pattern. He knows this is not just about Rome or some future empire. It is about every system that offers the world's approval if you turn away from Christ. Every culture promises fulfillment if you give up your faithfulness. This is the tempting lie that you can have both the wealth of Babylon and God's blessing, both the prostitute's cup and the Lord's.

But you can't do both. You can't ride the beast and follow the Lamb, or drink from Babylon's cup and eat at the Lord's table. You can't be seduced by the prostitute and remain faithful to the Bridegroom. The choice is clear, and it always has been.

For us, living in a world filled with Babylon's influence, this vision is both a warning and a call to be wise. The prostitute is still riding the beast. She is still dressed in luxury, still extending her golden cup. She is still drunk on the blood of those who refuse her. She promises safety through wealth and meaning through success, happiness through indulgence. Millions are drinking deeply, believing her lies, and losing sight of the poison in her cup.

But the angel did not show John the prostitute to frighten him. He wanted John to understand her and to know that her judgment is coming. Babylon will fall, the prostitute will be destroyed, and the beast she rides will turn against her. Those who refused her cup and stayed pure for the Lamb, who faced her violence instead of giving up their witness, will be proven right.

So stay alert. Don't let yourself be drawn in. Don't drink the wine of Babylon's immorality. Don't give up your faithfulness for her short-lived pleasures. She may look beautiful, but she is deadly. She promises life, but brings death. One day soon, her cup will be empty, her beast will turn on her, and her rule will end. Hold on to the Lamb. He is preparing a wedding feast, and the wine at His table is pure.

Prayer:

Father, open our eyes to see Babylon for what she is — seductive but deadly, beautiful but full of poison. Keep us from being drunk on the world's wine and keep us from compromising our witness for the sake of comfort or approval. We want to be faithful to You, even when it costs us everything. Clothe us in purity, guard our hearts from adultery, and when the prostitute's judgment comes, let us be standing with the Lamb, sober and undefiled. Amen.

Day 60 – The Mystery of the Woman and the Beast

Scripture Reading: Revelation 17:7–18

Heart of Victory: The beast's power is fleeting, but the Lamb's reign is eternal—and we belong to Him.

Some mysteries are meant to remain mysterious — the depths of God's love, the wonder of the incarnation. But other mysteries are meant to be explained, unpacked, and understood. When the angel sees John's astonishment at the vision of the prostitute and the beast, he doesn't leave him in confusion. He says, "Why are you astonished? I will explain to you the mystery of the woman and of the beast, with the seven heads and the ten horns, that carries her" (17:7). What follows is one of the most complex passages in Revelation, full of symbols and layers, but the core message is clear: every power that sets itself against God will rise for a season and then fall forever.

The angel begins by describing the beast: "The beast that you saw was, and is not, and is about to come up from the abyss and go to destruction" (17:8). This is a parody of God Himself, who is described as "the one who is, who was, and who is to come" (1:4). The beast mimics God's eternality, but it's a cheap imitation. It "was" — it had power once. It "is not" — its power is temporary, illusory. And it will "go to destruction" — its end is certain. No matter how impressive it looks and no matter how invincible it seems, the beast is headed for the abyss.

The seven heads are explained as "seven mountains" on which the woman is seated, and also as "seven kings" (17:9–10). Five have fallen, one is reigning, and one is yet to come. Scholars debate the specific historical referents, but the point isn't to decode exactly which Roman emperors these were. The point is that empires rise and fall, kings come and go, and powers that seem permanent crumble. The seven heads represent the pattern of human authority throughout history — they are temporary and doomed to pass away.

And then there's the eighth king, who "belongs to the seven" and is "going to destruction" (17:11). This suggests a pattern that repeats, a cycle of beastly power that keeps manifesting in new forms but always ends the same way — in destruction. The beast is not one specific empire or ruler. It's the recurring pattern of worldly power that blasphemes God and demands worship, persecuting His people throughout history. Rome was a beast, other empires have been beasts, and there will be more beasts until the final beast is thrown into the lake of fire.

The ten horns are "ten kings who have not yet received a kingdom, but they will receive authority as kings for one hour with the beast" (17:12). One hour. That's how long their power lasts — a brief moment in the scope of eternity. They give their power and authority to the beast, uniting in their opposition to God. "These will make war against the Lamb," the angel says, "but the Lamb will conquer them because he is Lord of lords and King of kings" (17:14). The outcome is never in doubt. The Lamb wins. The beast loses. The kings who threw in their lot with the beast will share in its destruction.

But here's where the vision takes a stunning turn. The angel tells John that the beast and the ten horns "will hate the prostitute" and will "make her desolate and naked, devour her flesh, and burn her up with fire" (17:16). The very powers that carried her and benefited from her seduction, that used her influence — they turn on her. The alliance between political power and spiritual seduction collapses. The beast destroys Babylon. The system devours itself.

Why? Because "God has put it into their hearts to carry out his plan by having one purpose and to give their kingdom to the beast until the words of God are fulfilled" (17:17). Even in their rebellion and hatred — right in the middle of their violence — they're still fulfilling God's purposes. They think they're acting on their own, asserting their independence, but they're instruments in God's hands. The beast that carried Babylon will be the agent of her destruction. And God will use their wickedness to accomplish His justice.

This is where confidence takes root. No matter how chaotic the world looks, no matter how much it seems like evil is winning, God is still sovereign. The kings rage, but they're doing exactly what God has determined they would do. The beast destroys Babylon, thinking it's asserting its power, but it's actually fulfilling the words of God. Every rebellion and act of defiance, and every attempt to overthrow God's rule — all of it serves His purposes in the end.

For the church living under the shadow of the beast, this is more than comfort — it's strategy. We don't have to fear the beast's power or envy Babylon's wealth because both are doomed. We don't have to compromise our witness to survive because the Lamb has already conquered. The mystery is explained. The beast was, and is not, and is going to destruction. Babylon rides high for a moment, then falls to ruin. The kings have power for one hour, then vanish.

But the Lamb? He is Lord of lords and King of kings. His authority never ends and His kingdom cannot fall. The victory is already His. And those who are with Him — "called, chosen, and faithful" (17:14) — will share in His triumph.

So don't be dazzled by the beast or seduced by Babylon. Don't be intimidated by the kings who seem so powerful. They're all on borrowed time, their hour is brief, and their end is certain destruction. But the Lamb reigns forever, and those who follow Him will reign with Him. The mystery has been explained. The outcome is certain. Stay faithful.

Prayer:

Lord Jesus, Lamb of God and King of kings, thank You for revealing the mystery of the beast and the prostitute. We see their power, and sometimes we're tempted to fear or compromise. But You've shown us their end — they're going to destruction. Give us eyes to see past the illusion of their strength and to trust in Your eternal authority. Keep us called, chosen, and faithful. We don't need to fear what is temporary. We belong to the One who reigns forever. Amen.

Day 61 – Fallen, Fallen Is Babylon the Great

Scripture Reading: Revelation 18:1–8

Heart of Victory: Babylon looks invincible until she falls—and the Lamb's call to come out is a call to safety.

There are institutions that feel permanent. Banks that have stood for centuries, empires that span continents. And then, in what feels like an instant, they collapse. The financial system crashes and the empire crumbles. What looked invincible proved to be fragile. What seemed eternal was only temporary. And everyone who put their trust in it is left staring at the rubble, wondering how it all fell apart so fast.

That's the picture John gives us in Revelation 18. After seeing the vision of the prostitute and the beast, after hearing the mystery explained, John now sees another angel coming down from heaven "who had great authority, and the earth was illuminated by his splendor" (18:1). This angel has news to announce, and he announces it with a voice like thunder: "Fallen, fallen is Babylon the Great!" (18:2).

Notice the repetition: "Fallen, fallen." This is not just emphasis. It's finality. Babylon doesn't stumble or decline gradually. She falls — completely and irreversibly. One moment she's the center of wealth, power, and influence. The next moment she's rubble. And the angel tells us why: "She has become a home for demons, a haunt for every unclean spirit, a haunt for every unclean bird, and a haunt for every unclean and despicable beast" (18:2). What once glittered with luxury now crawls with unclean things. What once drew the kings of the earth now houses only demons.

The charge against Babylon is clear: "All the nations have drunk the wine of her sexual immorality, which brings wrath. The kings of the earth have committed sexual immorality with her, and the merchants of the earth have grown wealthy from her sensuality and excess" (18:3). Babylon seduced the nations. She made them drunk on her lies. She partnered with political power and enriched the merchants who served her system. She promised fulfillment, but she delivered bondage. She promised life, but her cup was full of death.

And now, she's fallen.

The Fall Announced, Now Detailed: This is not the first time we've heard about Babylon's fall. Back in Revelation 14, after the 144,000 stood with the Lamb on Mount Zion, an angel flew through the sky announcing, "Fallen, fallen is Babylon the Great, who made all the nations drink the wine of her sexual immorality, which brings wrath" (14:8). That was the announcement. This is the detailed account. John is showing us the same reality from different angles—first the verdict, now the execution. Babylon's fall is so certain that it can be announced in the past tense even before it happens in detail. God has already determined her end. The only question is when the rubble will stop falling.

Then John hears another voice from heaven, and this one speaks directly to God's people: "Come out of her, my people, so that you will not share in her sins or receive any of her plagues" (18:4). This is the call to separation. If you belong to God, you cannot also belong to Babylon. If you follow the Lamb, you cannot also drink from the prostitute's cup. There's no middle ground. Either you come out, or you fall with her.

This command echoes the voice of God through the prophets. When ancient Babylon carried Israel into exile, God called His people to come out: "Flee from the midst of Babylon; let every one save his life! Be not cut off in her punishment" (Jeremiah 51:6, ESV). The same call goes out now. Babylon's sins have "piled up to heaven, and God has remembered her crimes" (18:5). The patience that once held back judgment is exhausted. The cup is full. And anyone who stays in Babylon when the judgment falls will drink from that cup.

The judgment itself is precise: "Pay her back the way she also paid, and double it according to her works. In the cup she mixed, mix a double portion for her" (18:6). This is not arbitrary vengeance. It's exact justice. Babylon made others drink from her cup of immorality and wrath. Now she will drink double from the cup of God's judgment. She lived in luxury, boasting, "I sit as a queen; I am not a widow, and I will never see grief" (18:7). She thought she was invincible. She thought she could defy God and get away with it. She was wrong.

In one day — "in a single day" — her plagues will come: "death, grief, and famine" (18:8). She will be "burned with fire, because the Lord God who judges her is mighty." One day. That's all it takes for the seemingly invincible to fall. Babylon seduced the kings and sat as queen over many nations. She looked so strong that no one could imagine her downfall — yet she's gone in a day.

For those of us living in the shadow of Babylon's influence, this passage is both warning and hope. The warning is stark: come out. Don't be entangled in her sins. Don't drink from her cup. Don't put your trust in her wealth or your hope in her promises. She's falling, and when she falls, everyone still inside will fall with her. Don't find your identity in her approval.

But the hope is just as clear: she will fall. No matter how strong Babylon looks, no matter how permanent her reign seems, she is doomed. God has not forgotten her crimes. Her sins have piled up to heaven. And the Lord God who judges her is mighty. She cannot escape or bribe her way out. She cannot seduce her way to safety. The angel has already announced it: "Fallen, fallen is Babylon the Great." It's done.

So where are you standing? Are you still inside, trying to enjoy her pleasures while avoiding her plagues? That's impossible. Or have you come out completely, leaving behind her seductions, her wealth, her approval, and her lies? Because that's the only safe place when the fire falls.

Babylon is falling and the Lamb is calling. Come out.

Prayer:

Mighty God, You judge Babylon with perfect justice. Thank You for calling us out, for warning us to flee before the plagues fall. Forgive us for the ways we've been entangled in her sins and drunk from her cup, trusting in her promises instead of Yours. Give us courage to come out completely — to leave behind her seductions and to find our security in You alone. Babylon is falling, but Your kingdom stands forever. Keep us safe in You. Amen.

Day 62 – The Lament over Babylon's Wealth

Scripture Reading: Revelation 18:9–24

Heart of Victory: Babylon's wealth vanishes in an hour, but the kingdom of God stands forever — invest wisely.

There's a particular kind of grief that comes when wealth vanishes. Not the grief of losing someone you love — that's deeper, more human. This is the grief of losing what you thought made you secure and gave you status, the things you thought would last forever. It's the shock of watching your portfolio collapse and your business fail, everything you built turning to ash. And when it happens suddenly — when the bottom drops out in a day, in an hour — the grief is mixed with panic. Because if the things you built your life on can disappear that fast, what's left?

That's the grief on display in Revelation 18. Three groups of people watch Babylon burn, and all of them weep — not for her, but for themselves. Not because they loved her, but because they profited from her. And now their profit is gone.

First come the kings of the earth, those who "committed sexual immorality and shared her sensual and excessive ways" (18:9). They stand "far off in fear of her torment" and cry out, "Woe, woe, the great city, Babylon, the mighty city! For in a single hour your judgment has come" (18:10). These are the political leaders who partnered with Babylon, who used her influence to secure power—thinking her strength was theirs. But now she's burning, and they're standing at a distance, afraid to get too close, horrified that the system they depended on has collapsed so quickly.

Then come the merchants, those who "grew wealthy from her" (18:15). They too stand far off, weeping and mourning, because "no one buys their cargo any longer" (18:11). John lists their goods in painful detail: gold, silver, precious stones, pearls, fine linen, purple cloth, silk, scarlet cloth, every kind of fragrant wood, ivory, expensive wood, bronze, iron, marble, cinnamon, spice, incense, myrrh, frankincense, wine, olive oil, fine flour, wheat, cattle, sheep, horses, carriages—and at the end of the list, chillingly, "slaves and human lives" (18:12-13).

This is Babylon's economy. Luxury piled upon luxury, with human beings treated as just another commodity to be bought and sold. The merchants didn't care about justice or dignity. They cared about profit. And Babylon gave them plenty of it. But now the market has crashed. The goods sit unsold. The wealth they accumulated is worthless. And they weep because "in a single hour such great wealth was destroyed" (18:17).

Finally come the seafarers — those who made their living transporting Babylon's goods across the waters. They throw dust on their heads and cry out, "Woe, woe, the great city, where all those who have ships on the sea became rich from her wealth! For in a single hour she was destroyed" (18:19). These are the workers, the sailors, the captains whose livelihoods depended on Babylon's appetite for luxury. They didn't set the system up, but they benefited from it. And now it's gone.

"In a single hour." That phrase echoes through the chapter like a death knell. One hour. That's how long it took for the system that looked so permanent to collapse. The kings thought her power would last, and the merchants thought the market would never crash. They were all wrong.

But while the earth mourns, heaven rejoices. A voice from heaven calls out: "Rejoice over her, heaven, and you saints, apostles, and prophets, because God has pronounced on her the judgment she passed on you!" (18:20). This isn't cruelty. It's justice. Babylon shed the blood of the saints. She persecuted the apostles. She silenced the prophets. She grew wealthy on the backs of slaves. She seduced the nations into idolatry. And now she's receiving what she gave. Heaven celebrates not because God delights in destruction, but because He delights in justice.

Then a mighty angel picks up a stone like a great millstone and throws it into the sea, saying, "In this way, Babylon the great city will be thrown down violently and never be found again" (18:21). This is finality. Not a temporary setback. Not a recession she can recover from. Babylon is gone — completely and forever. The music will stop. The lights will go out. The voice of the bride and bridegroom will be heard in her no more. The merchants who were once her princes will vanish. And why? "Because your merchants were the nobility of the earth, because all the nations were deceived by your sorcery, and in her was found the blood of prophets and saints, and of all those slaughtered on the earth" (18:23-24).

For those of us living in cultures that look a lot like Babylon — cultures built on consumption, wealth, and the pursuit of luxury — this passage is both sobering and clarifying. We're tempted to build our security on the same things the kings, merchants, and seafarers did. We want wealth that makes us comfortable and systems that make us prosperous. And when those things are threatened, we panic and weep, mourning our losses.

But Revelation 18 asks us: what are you really mourning? Are you mourning justice being done, or are you mourning your own loss of comfort? Are you grieving for the oppressed who suffered under Babylon's greed, or are you grieving because you can't buy her cargo anymore?

The call is the same as it was in verse 4: "come out of her." Don't build your life on Babylon's economy or find your security in her wealth. Don't stake your future on systems that can collapse in an hour. Because they will collapse. The only question is whether you're still inside when the collapse comes, or whether you've already come out.

Heaven is rejoicing because justice has been done. The blood of the martyrs has been avenged. The system that oppressed and murdered has fallen. And those who refused to profit from her exploitation and refused to be seduced by her wealth — they're celebrating. Not because they're vindictive, but because they love justice. Because they know that God is right to judge Babylon. Because they've been waiting for this moment.

So where is your treasure? Is it in Babylon's cargo — gold, silver, fine linen, luxury? Or is it in the kingdom of God, where thieves don't break in and moths don't destroy? Because in a single hour, everything Babylon offered can be gone. But the kingdom of God lasts forever.

Prayer:

Father, forgive us for the times we've been seduced by Babylon's wealth, for the times we've built our security on things that can vanish in an hour. Open our eyes to see the injustice embedded in systems of greed and consumption. Keep us from profiting from the oppression of others. Teach us to invest in Your kingdom, where nothing is lost and everything lasts. We don't want to weep over Babylon's fall. We want to rejoice with heaven that Your justice has been done. Amen.

Day 63 – Hallelujah! Salvation and Glory

Scripture Reading: Revelation 19:1–5

Heart of Victory: Heaven celebrates not the destruction itself, but the justice that makes all things right.

Silence can be appropriate after tragedy. After a funeral or after devastating news — silence makes sense. We don't know what to say. Words feel inadequate. So we sit quietly, and the silence itself becomes a kind of tribute to the weight of what has happened.

But after Babylon falls, heaven doesn't fall silent. Heaven erupts in praise.

John hears "something like the loud voice of a vast multitude in heaven, saying, Hallelujah! Salvation, glory, and power belong to our God" (19:1). The word "Hallelujah" means "Praise the Lord," and this is the first time it appears in the New Testament. It bursts onto the scene here, in Revelation 19, as the appropriate response to God's justice. Babylon has fallen, and heaven shouts its praise.

Why? Because "his judgments are true and righteous" (19:2). This is not celebration over random destruction or petty revenge. This is celebration over justice being done. God has "judged the notorious prostitute who corrupted the earth with her sexual immorality" and "has avenged the blood of his servants that was on her hands" (19:2). The martyrs' blood, which cried out from under the altar in Revelation 6, has been vindicated. The saints who suffered under Babylon's persecution have been avenged. And heaven erupts in praise because God is righteous.

Then they say it again: "Hallelujah! Her smoke ascends forever and ever" (19:3). The smoke rising forever is a sign of complete, irreversible judgment. Babylon will never be rebuilt. Her influence will never return. Her seduction will never resume. She is finished, and the smoke of her burning rises as a permanent testament to God's justice. Heaven sees this and praises God again.

Then the twenty-four elders and the four living creatures — those beings who surround the throne in ceaseless worship — fall down and worship God, saying, "Amen! Hallelujah!" (19:4). They affirm what the multitude has declared. They add their voices to the chorus. This is right. This is good. God has done what needed to be done, and all heaven agrees.

And then a voice comes from the throne itself, calling out, "Praise our God, all his servants, and the ones who fear him, both small and great!" (19:5). This is an invitation to join the worship. Not just the angels, not just the elders, not just the living creatures — everyone. Small and great. Powerful and weak. Known and unknown. All are invited to praise the God whose judgments are true and righteous.

For many of us, this scene might feel uncomfortable. We've been taught, rightly, that God is love. We've heard countless sermons on grace, mercy, and forgiveness. And here in Revelation 19, heaven celebrates judgment — praising God as Babylon burns, shouting 'Hallelujah!' over the smoke of her burning. How do we reconcile this?

The answer is that we've sometimes made the mistake of thinking that love and justice are opposites. They're not. God's love is not sentimental. It's not a love that shrugs at evil, overlooks oppression, or ignores the blood of martyrs. God's love is a holy love, and holy love demands justice. To love the oppressed means judging the oppressor and avenging the martyrs' blood. To love righteousness means destroying wickedness.

Heaven praises God for judging Babylon because heaven knows what Babylon did. She corrupted the earth with her lies. She seduced the nations into idolatry. She grew wealthy on the backs of slaves, killed the prophets, slaughtered the saints, and mocked the very name of God with her arrogance. And God, in His justice, has said, "Enough." Heaven celebrates not because destruction is inherently good, but because this destruction is just.

This passage also offers comfort to those who have endured hardship under Babylon's rule. If you've faced oppression, exploitation, or marginalization — if you've witnessed injustice prevail while righteousness is mocked — this moment in Revelation 19 speaks directly to you. God sees, remembers, and will act. The smoke ascending from Babylon isn't an act of cruelty; it's a sign of vindication. It proves that God does not forget or overlook evil — He will not leave it unpunished forever.

And the invitation at the end, "Praise our God, all his servants," is an invitation for you to join the celebration. Not in a spirit of revenge, but in a spirit of justice. Not with bitterness, but with relief. The nightmare is over and the oppressor has fallen. The system that crushed you is gone. And God, who is true and righteous in all His judgments, has made it so.

But even more, this scene prepares us for what comes next. The fall of Babylon is not the end of the story. It's the clearing of the stage for the wedding. With Babylon gone, with the smoke still rising, heaven is getting ready for something far greater than judgment. The Bride is about to be presented. The Lamb is about to receive His reward. And the feast is about to begin.

So join the chorus. Say "Hallelujah" with heaven. Not because you delight in destruction, but because you delight in justice. Not because you're vindictive, but because you trust that God is right to do what He has done. Babylon has fallen. The martyrs are avenged. And the God whose judgments are true and righteous is worthy of all praise.

Prayer:

Holy God, Your judgments are true and righteous. We praise You for avenging the blood of Your servants, for judging Babylon, and for making all things right. Forgive us for the times we've doubted Your justice, for the times we've wanted You to overlook evil rather than deal with it. Teach us to love what You love and to hate what You hate. And when we see injustice now, give us faith to trust that You will act. Hallelujah! Salvation, glory, and power belong to You. Amen.

Day 64 – The Marriage Supper of the Lamb

Scripture Reading: Revelation 19:6–10

Heart of Victory: The Lamb's wedding supper is not a distant hope— it's a certain reality, and we are invited.

There are invitations you wait for your whole life. The acceptance letter from your dream school, or the job offer you've been hoping for. These invitations can redefine your future. They're not just about an event, they're about identity. Belonging and becoming part of something bigger than yourself.

And then there's the invitation in Revelation 19.

After the celebration of Babylon's fall, John hears "something like the voice of a vast multitude, like the sound of cascading waters, and like the rumbling of loud thunder, saying, Hallelujah, because our Lord God, the Almighty, reigns! Let us be glad, rejoice, and give him glory, because the marriage of the Lamb has come, and his bride has prepared herself" (19:6-7). This is not a funeral. This is not a memorial service for Babylon. This is a wedding. And the whole multitude of heaven is shouting with joy because the moment has finally arrived.

The marriage of the Lamb. Think about that image. All through the Old Testament, God described His relationship with His people as a marriage. He was the faithful husband; they were often the unfaithful wife. The prophets pleaded with Israel to return to her first love, to stop committing adultery with idols, to remember the covenant. And Israel kept breaking God's heart, turning away, chasing after other lovers.

But here in Revelation 19, the Bride has been made ready. "She was given fine linen to wear, bright and pure" (19:8). This isn't her own righteousness. The text makes that clear: "the fine linen represents the righteous acts of the saints." The Bride is dressed in righteousness—not her own, but the righteousness that has been given to her, the righteous acts done through her by the power of God. She's clothed in purity because Christ made her pure. And now, finally, the wedding day has come.

The angel tells John, "Write: Blessed are those invited to the marriage supper of the Lamb!" (19:9). And then he adds, "These are the true words of God." This is not poetic exaggeration. This is not metaphor for something less real. This is truth. There is a wedding supper. The Lamb is the Groom. The church is the Bride. And those who are invited — those who belong to Christ, who have been washed in His blood, who have endured — are blessed beyond measure.

This is the moment all of Revelation has been building toward. The seals, the trumpets, the bowls — all of them were clearing the way for this. Babylon had to fall because she was the rival, the seductress, the one trying to steal the affections of God's people. The beast had to be judged because he demanded the worship that belongs only to the Lamb, and the dragon had to be defeated because he was the one who sought to devour the Bride before she could be presented. Now, with all the enemies vanquished, with all the obstacles removed, the wedding can finally happen.

John is so overwhelmed by the vision that he falls at the angel's feet to worship him. But the angel stops him: "Don't do that! I am a fellow servant with you and your brothers and sisters who hold firmly to the testimony of Jesus. Worship God, because the testimony of Jesus is the spirit of prophecy" (19:10). Even in this glorious moment, even as the wedding supper is being announced, the angel redirects worship to where it belongs — to God alone. The testimony of Jesus is what this is all about. Every prophecy, every vision, every word — it all points to Him. And only He is worthy of worship.

For those of us living before the wedding supper, this passage is both invitation and assurance. The invitation is clear: be the Bride. Don't be seduced by Babylon or take the mark of the beast. Be faithful to the Lamb. Let Him clothe you in His righteousness. Let Him prepare you for the wedding day. The invitation has gone out, and it's an invitation to the most glorious event in all of history.

The assurance is just as clear: the wedding is coming. It's not a maybe. It's not dependent on how strong your faith feels or how well you think you're doing. The Lamb has already done what needed to be done to make His Bride ready. He's already purchased her with His blood. He's already given her the fine linen of righteousness. And when the time comes, He will present her to Himself, radiant and pure, and the marriage supper will begin.

But here's the part we need to let sink in: you are invited. If you belong to Christ, you are part of the Bride. This wedding supper is for you. The joy of heaven — the celebration that fills the cosmos with shouts of "Hallelujah!" — includes you. You're not just a spectator. You're not watching from a distance. You are invited to the feast.

And this literally changes everything, redefining your future! It changes how we endure suffering now, because we know the wedding day is coming. It changes how we respond to Babylon's seductions, because we're already engaged to the Lamb, and it transforms our worship because we're preparing for a wedding feast where the only appropriate response is to fall down in awe and give God all the glory.

So hold fast and stay faithful. Keep yourself pure for the Bridegroom. The invitation has been given. The Bride is being prepared. And soon —

sooner than we think — the voice will sound: "The marriage of the Lamb has come!" And we will enter the feast, clothed in righteousness, surrounded by the vast multitude of heaven, shouting with joy because our Lord God, the Almighty, reigns.

Prayer:

Lord Jesus, Lamb of God and Bridegroom of the church, thank You for inviting us to Your wedding feast. Thank You for clothing us in righteousness we could never earn, for preparing us to be Your Bride. Keep us faithful and pure as we watch for the day when the marriage supper begins. We want to be ready. We want to be part of the celebration. Come quickly, Lord. Let the wedding day arrive. Amen.

Day 65 – The Rider on the White Horse

Scripture Reading: Revelation 19:11–16

Heart of Victory: The Rider on the white horse has a name—Faithful and True—and when He rides forth, no beast, no false prophet, and no army can stand before Him.

There are moments when you realize the cavalry is not coming — you are the cavalry. When the rescue isn't arriving from outside, and you have to be the one to stand and fight, risking everything. Those moments test your courage.

But Revelation 19 is not that moment. This is the moment when the cavalry arrives. And it's not just any rescue — it's the King Himself, mounted on a white horse, coming to finish what He started.

John sees heaven opened, and there before him is a white horse. Its rider is called "Faithful and True," and "he judges and makes war with justice"

(19:11). This is Jesus, but not the suffering servant of the Gospels. This is Jesus in His glory, Jesus the warrior King, Jesus whose eyes are "like a fiery flame" and on whose head are "many crowns" (19:12). This is the fulfillment of every messianic promise, every prophecy about the King who would come to reign.

He has a name written on Him that no one knows except Him. There's mystery here — something about Jesus that transcends our ability to fully comprehend. But there are other names we do know. He is called "The Word of God" (19:13), the same title John gave Him in the opening of his Gospel. He is the one through whom all things were made, who became flesh among us, and who reveals the Father. And now He's coming as the Word that judges, the Word that speaks and creation obeys.

He's dressed in a robe dipped in blood — not enemies' blood yet to be shed, but His own blood from Calvary, the proof that this victory was secured before this battle ever begins. This Rider is a conqueror, but His victory was won first on a cross. The blood on His robe is the proof that He has already defeated sin, death, and the devil. And now He's coming to consummate that victory, to bring to completion what He accomplished in His death and resurrection.

The armies of heaven follow Him, "wearing pure white linen" (19:14). These are the saints, the redeemed, the ones who washed their robes in the blood of the Lamb. They're not coming to fight — the battle is already won. They're coming to witness, to participate in the triumph and to be present when the King claims His kingdom.

And then John sees the Rider's weapon: "A sharp sword came from his mouth, so that he might strike the nations with it" (19:15). This is not a physical sword. This is the Word of God, the word of judgment that no one can resist. When Jesus speaks, armies fall. When He commands, kings tremble. His word is enough. He doesn't need a literal weapon, because His word is more powerful than any sword ever forged.

He will "rule them with an iron scepter" (19:15), and "he will trample the winepress of the fierce anger of God, the Almighty." This is the fulfillment of Psalm 2, where the nations rage and God laughs. The Rider on the white horse is the Son to whom the Father has given the nations as His inheritance. And He will rule them with justice — uncompromising, absolute, eternal justice.

On His robe and on His thigh, a name is written: "King of Kings and Lord of Lords" (19:16). This is the ultimate declaration of His authority. Every other king is subject to Him, and every other lord bows before Him. No power in heaven or on earth can stand against Him. He is supreme.

> **Two White Horses, One Victory:** Back in the first seal (6:1–2), a rider on a white horse went out "as a conqueror in order to conquer" — the gospel advancing into the world, claiming hearts and establishing the kingdom. Now, in Revelation 19, another Rider appears on a white horse — but this time it is Christ Himself, coming in person to finish what His gospel began. The first white horse launched the campaign; this one ends it. The word that went forth conquering now returns as the Word of God who strikes the nations. What began at the first seal reaches its consummation here. The gospel was never losing ground. It was always heading toward this Rider. This is not the first time Revelation has shown us Christ's return. In the very first chapter, John wrote, "Look, he is coming with the clouds, and every eye will see him, including those who pierced him" (1:7). During the sixth seal, the kings of the earth hid in caves, crying out to the mountains, "Fall on us and hide us from the face of the one seated on the throne and from the wrath of the Lamb" (6:16). These visions all point to the same moment — the day when Jesus returns, not as the suffering servant but as the conquering King. The Rider on the white horse is the fulfillment of every promise that Christ will come again. And when He does, there will be no doubt, no ambiguity. Every knee will bow.

For those of us waiting for His return, this vision is our hope. We live in a world where evil seems to prosper, the wicked seem to get away with it, and justice feels delayed. And we wonder: when will He come? How long must we wait? How much longer do we have to endure?

Revelation 19 answers clearly: He's coming. The Rider is on His way. And when He arrives, every wrong will be made right. Every enemy will be defeated. Every lie will be exposed. Every injustice will be judged. The Lamb who was slain is the Lion who will roar. The servant who washed feet is the King who wears many crowns. And He is Faithful and True. He will keep His promise. He will return.

This is why we endure and hold fast. This is why we don't lose heart. Because the cavalry is coming, and it's not just any cavalry — it's the King of Kings and Lord of Lords. He rides a white horse, He wears many crowns, and His name is the Word of God. And when He arrives, the battle will be over before it begins.

So keep watching and waiting. Keep your lamps trimmed and your hearts ready. The Rider is coming, and He will not be late. And when you see Him — eyes blazing, sword sharp, robe dipped in blood — you will know that every tear, every trial, and every single moment of suffering was worth it. Because He is Faithful and True, and He is coming to make all things new.

Prayer:

Lord Jesus, King of Kings and Lord of Lords, we wait for Your return. We long to see You riding on the white horse, eyes blazing, wearing many crowns. Come quickly in power to judge the nations and vindicate Your people. We trust that You are Faithful and True and that You will keep Your promise to return. Until that day, keep us faithful and watching, ready for Your arrival. You are the Word of God, and Your word will have the final say. Amen.

Day 66 – The Beast, the False Prophet, and the Birds

Scripture Reading: Revelation 19:17–21

Heart of Victory: The Rider defeats every enemy with a word—our victory is in belonging to Him.

There's something final about a battle where one side doesn't even get to fight. Where the outcome is so certain, so overwhelming, that resistance is futile before it begins. The war is over in a moment. The victor stands unchallenged. And the defeated realize, too late, that they never had a chance.

That's the scene in Revelation 19. After seeing the Rider on the white horse, John sees an angel standing in the sun, calling to all the birds flying high overhead: "Come, gather together for the great supper of God, so that you may eat the flesh of kings, the flesh of commanders, the flesh of the mighty, and the flesh of horses and their riders, and the flesh of everyone, both free and slave, small and great" (19:17-18). This is not a wedding supper. This is the aftermath of a slaughter — a gruesome image of total, irreversible defeat.

Then John sees the beast and the kings of the earth with their armies "gathered together to wage war against the rider on the horse and against his army" (19:19). This is the moment Babylon's system has been building toward. The dragon gave the beast his authority. The false prophet performed signs to deceive the nations. The kings gathered at Armageddon, convinced they could resist God's anointed King. They've assembled their armies, marshaled their forces, and now they face the Rider whose name is Faithful and True.

But there's no battle. There's no drawn-out conflict, no back-and-forth, no suspense about who will win. "The beast was taken prisoner," John writes, "and along with it the false prophet, who had performed the signs in its presence. He deceived those who accepted the mark of the beast and those who worshiped its image with these signs. Both of them were thrown alive into the lake of fire that burns with sulfur" (19:20).

Just like that, it's over. The beast — the one who seemed invincible, who demanded worship and killed the saints — is captured. The false prophet — the one who performed signs, who deceived the nations, and marked people with the beast's name — is captured. And both are thrown into the lake of fire. Not temporarily. Not as a warning. Forever.

"The rest were killed with the sword that came from the mouth of the rider on the horse," and the birds "ate their fill of their flesh" (19:21). The armies that gathered to fight God are defeated by a word. The Rider doesn't swing a sword. He speaks, and they fall. The word that created the universe and holds all things together, the word that spoke light into darkness — that same word speaks judgment, and no one can stand.

This is the end of every counterfeit authority. The beast claimed power but had none, and the false prophet performed signs but couldn't save himself. The kings gathered their armies but couldn't resist the Rider. Every system and every power, every authority that set itself against God — all of them collapse the moment Jesus speaks. And the lake of fire waits for those who refused to repent.

For those of us living in a world that still feels like the beast is winning, this passage is a needed reality check. The beast looks strong and the false prophet looks convincing. But it's all an illusion. The moment the Rider appears, when He speaks, it's over. There's no fight, no contest. The outcome was never in doubt.

This is why Revelation calls us to endurance, not to panic. This is why the call throughout the book has been faithfulness, not victory in our own strength. Because we're not the ones who have to defeat the beast or expose the false prophet. Jesus does that. And when He does it, He does it with a word.

Our job is to refuse the mark and the worship, to reject the seduction. Our job is to hold fast to the testimony of Jesus, even when it costs us everything. Because the day is coming — probably sooner than we may think — when the Rider will appear, and every power that opposed Him will fall. And we want to be standing with Him, not against Him.

The contrast between the two suppers in Revelation 19 is stark. There's the marriage supper of the Lamb, where the Bride is clothed in fine linen and the joy of heaven fills the cosmos. And there's this supper, where the birds gather to eat the flesh of those who opposed God. One is a feast of celebration, the other a feast of judgment. One is for the redeemed. The other is for the rebellious.

And the choice between them has already been made. If you belong to Christ, if you've refused the mark and held fast to His name — you're invited to the wedding. The Lamb has prepared a place for you. The fine linen is ready. The feast is set. And when the Rider appears, you'll be riding with Him, clothed in white, witnessing the final defeat of every enemy.

But if you've taken the mark, worshiped the beast, and aligned yourself with the kings of the earth — there's still time. The lake of fire is real. The judgment is coming. And the Rider's word will be final. Repent now. Turn to the Lamb. Wash your robe in His blood. Because when He appears on the white horse, there will be no second chances.

The beast is doomed and the false prophet is finished. The kings will fall. And the only question that matters is this, "Which supper will you attend?"

Prayer:

Lord Jesus, Rider on the white horse, we worship You. You are the King who needs no army, the Conqueror who defeats with a word. Thank

You for defeating the beast, for exposing the false prophet, and bringing down every power that set itself against You. Keep us from the mark and the deception, holding us faithful until the day You appear. We don't want to stand with the beast. We want to stand with You. Finish what You've begun, speak the word, and bring us to the marriage supper of the Lamb. Amen.

Part Seven: The Thousand Years, Judgment, and New Creation

Revelation 20–22

Heart of Victory: The dragon is finished, the curse is lifted, and God is making all things new—even now drawing us toward the Day when we'll see His face and dwell with Him forever in the city He's prepared.

The dragon is bound. For a thousand years — the church age, the time between Christ's ascension and His return — Satan's power to deceive the nations is restrained. The gospel goes to the ends of the earth. The martyrs who refused the mark are vindicated, seated on thrones, reigning with Christ. This is the first resurrection, the spiritual rebirth of all who come to life in Him. And for those who have been raised, the second death has no power. They are priests of God, reigning with Christ now, even as the battle continues.

But when the thousand years end, Satan is released for one final rebellion. He gathers the nations — Gog and Magog, numberless as the sand — and they march against the camp of the saints. But fire falls from heaven and consumes them before a single blow is struck. And the dragon is thrown into the lake of fire, joining the beast and the false prophet. The ancient serpent, the accuser of the saints, the deceiver of nations — he is finished. Forever.

Then comes the great white throne. Every person who has ever lived stands before the Judge. The books are opened. The record of every life, every deed, and every word. And another book is opened: the book of life. Those whose names are written there stand secure. Those whose names are not found are thrown into the lake of fire, which is the second death. Death and Hades themselves are cast into the fire. And the old creation, the one groaning under the curse, passes away completely.

And then, "Behold, I am making all things new."

A new heaven and a new earth appear. The sea is no more. The holy city, new Jerusalem, descends from heaven, prepared as a bride adorned for her husband. And a voice from the throne declares what we were made for: "God's dwelling is with humanity, and he will live with them. They will be his peoples, and God himself will be with them and will be their God." No more separation. No more distance. God with us, forever.

He wipes away every tear. Death is no more. Grief, crying, and pain are finished. The curse is lifted. The throne of God and the Lamb stands in the city, and His servants worship Him. They see His face. His name is written on their foreheads. And they reign with Him forever and ever, in a city where there is no temple, because God is the temple. And no night, because the glory of God is the light.

The river of the water of life flows from the throne, and on each side of the river stands the tree of life, bearing twelve kinds of fruit, its leaves for the healing of the nations. What was lost in Eden is restored and surpassed, and that which was forbidden is freely given. All that was broken is made whole.

"These words are trustworthy and true," the angel says. Jesus speaks: "Look, I am coming soon." And the Spirit and the Bride respond together: "Come." This invitation echoes through eternity — Come to the water of life. Come freely. Come now.

And the last prayer of Scripture is the prayer the church has prayed for two thousand years: "Come, Lord Jesus." He is coming. The new creation is ready. And we will be home.

Welcome to Part Seven.

Day 67 – Satan Bound and the Reign of the Saints

Scripture Reading: Revelation 20:1–6

Heart of Victory: We reign with Christ now, not because we're powerful, but because He has already won.

There are victories that don't look like victories at the time. A crucified Messiah, or a church scattered by persecution. But what looks like defeat in the moment is actually the decisive turning point. The war is won even when the battles still rage. The kingdom has come even when the king's enemies haven't yet been removed.

That's the vision John gives us in Revelation 20. After seeing the beast and the false prophet thrown into the lake of fire, John sees "an angel coming down from heaven holding the key to the abyss and a great chain in his hand" (20:1). This angel seizes "the dragon, that ancient serpent who is the devil and Satan," and binds him for a thousand years (20:2). The dragon is thrown into the abyss, locked and sealed, "so that he would no longer deceive the nations until the thousand years were completed" (20:3).

A thousand years. The number is symbolic — not a literal countdown but a picture of completeness, of a full and sufficient time. This is the age we're living in now, the time between Christ's victory at the cross and His return in glory. Satan was bound when Jesus rose from the dead. His power to deceive the nations was broken so that the gospel could go out to the ends of the earth. He still prowls like a roaring lion, still accuses and tempts — but he's on a leash. His reach is limited. His time is short. And he knows it.

This binding doesn't mean Satan is inactive. It means his power has been curtailed. Before the cross, the nations were under his dominion. But now the gospel has reached every tribe and tongue. The church has been planted in every corner of the earth. The deceiver who once held the nations captive has been restrained so the light of Christ can shine in the darkness. He's still dangerous. But he's no longer in control.

Then John sees thrones, and "those seated on them were given authority to judge" (20:4). These are the martyrs, the ones "who were beheaded for the testimony of Jesus and for the word of God," the ones who "had not worshiped the beast or its image and had not accepted the mark on their foreheads or their hands" (20:4). They come to life and reign with Christ for a thousand years. This is called "the first resurrection," and those who have part in it are blessed, "the second death has no power over them" (20:6).

What is this first resurrection? It's not a future event after Jesus returns. It's the spiritual resurrection that happens when someone comes to life in Christ. "You were dead in your trespasses and sins," Paul wrote, but God "made us alive with Christ" (Ephesians 2:1, 5). When you're born again, when you're raised from spiritual death to spiritual life, you experience the first resurrection. And if you've been raised with Christ in this way, the second death — eternal judgment — has no claim on you. You're secure and sealed. You reign with Christ now.

This is why the martyrs are highlighted. They're the clearest picture of what it means to reign with Christ. They refused the mark, endured persecution, and gave their lives rather than compromise their witness. And now they're vindicated and seated on thrones. They're given authority to judge. Their suffering was not meaningless. Their faithfulness was not wasted. They reign with Christ because they chose to suffer with Christ.

But this isn't just about martyrs. Every believer who has been raised to life in Christ shares in this reign. You may not have been beheaded, but if you've refused the world's mark and held fast to the testimony of Jesus, if you've endured when it would have been easier to give up —

you're reigning with Christ right now. Not in some distant future. Now. In the midst of the struggle and the daily choice to follow Him — you reign because He reigns.

The phrase "they will be priests of God and of Christ, and they will reign with him for a thousand years" (20:6) is not a promise about the future. It's a description of the present reality for everyone who belongs to Christ. We are priests. Offering sacrifices of praise, interceding for the world, mediating God's presence. We are reigning. Not by wielding earthly power but by exercising spiritual authority, by binding and loosing, and proclaiming the gospel that sets captives free.

And the second death? It has no power over us. We've already passed from death to life. We've been raised and seated with Christ in the heavenly places. The martyrs under the altar asked, "How long until you judge and avenge our blood?" (6:10). Revelation 20 is the answer: not much longer. The thousand years are rolling toward their end. Satan is bound but will soon be released for a final rebellion. And when that happens, the vindication will be complete.

For now, we live in the tension of the "already but not yet." Satan is bound, but we still feel his influence, and we reign with Christ even though the world doesn't acknowledge it. We've experienced the first resurrection, but we're still waiting for the second — when our bodies are raised and death itself is swallowed up in victory. But the victory is sure. The dragon is chained. The martyrs are vindicated. And we who belong to Christ are reigning with Him, even now, as priests of God.

So don't be discouraged when it doesn't feel like you're reigning. Don't lose heart when the battle feels overwhelming. The outcome is already decided. Satan is bound, and you've been raised to life. And the thousand years of Christ's reign — this age we're living in — will end with His return, when every enemy is finally removed and the reign we experience now becomes the reign we experience forever.

Prayer:

Lord Jesus, You have bound the ancient serpent and raised us to life in You. Thank You for making us priests and kings, and for giving us authority to proclaim Your gospel and intercede for the world. When the battle feels overwhelming, remind us that we're reigning with You even now. The dragon is chained. The martyrs are vindicated. And we who belong to You are secure. Finish what You've begun. Complete the thousand years. Return and remove every enemy. Until then, help us live as those who reign with You. Amen.

Day 68 – The Final Rebellion and the Lake of Fire

Scripture Reading: Revelation 20:7–10

Heart of Victory: Satan's end is absolute—he will never accuse, deceive, or threaten God's people again.

Some endings take you by surprise. Others you see coming from miles away. The final rebellion of Satan is not a surprise. John has been clear from the beginning: the dragon is defeated, the beast is judged, and every enemy of God will ultimately fall. And yet, even after a thousand years of being bound, even after Christ has reigned and the martyrs have been vindicated, Satan gets one last chance to show his true nature. And he does exactly what we expect — he deceives and gathers for attack. But this time, there's no drawn-out battle. This time, the end is swift.

"When the thousand years are completed," John writes, "Satan will be released from his prison and will go out to deceive the nations at the four corners of the earth, Gog and Magog, to gather them for battle. Their number is like the sand of the sea" (20:7-8). After centuries of restraint, after the gospel has spread to every nation and the church has proclaimed Christ's victory across the earth — Satan is released. And what does he do? The same thing he's always done. He deceives.

The names "Gog and Magog" come from Ezekiel 38-39, where they represent hostile nations that rise up against God's people. Here in Revelation, they symbolize the final gathering of all who oppose God. The number is staggering — "like the sand of the sea" — a vast, innumerable multitude. After all this time, after all the judgments and Babylon has fallen and the beast has been defeated, there are still people who choose rebellion. They march across the breadth of the earth and surround "the camp of the saints, the beloved city" (20:9).

But before they can strike, "fire came down from heaven and consumed them" (20:9). No battle or prolonged conflict. Just fire from heaven, and it's over. The rebellion ends as quickly as it began. God speaks, and the enemies of His people are consumed.

And then comes the final judgment on Satan himself: "The devil who deceived them was thrown into the lake of fire and sulfur where the beast and the false prophet are, and they will be tormented day and night forever and ever" (20:10). This is not a temporary setback. This isn't a binding or a restriction. This is the absolute, irreversible end of the deceiver. The dragon who has been the enemy since Eden, tempting Adam and Eve, accusing Job, testing Jesus in the wilderness, empowering the beast, and persecuting the church — he's finished. Forever.

The lake of fire is where the beast and the false prophet have been since Revelation 19. Now the dragon joins them. The unholy trinity is complete in its judgment. And they will be tormented forever and ever. Not annihilated or given a second chance — tormented forever.

That is a hard sentence to sit with. We want redemption for everyone. We hope for universal reconciliation. But Revelation doesn't leave room for that hope when it comes to Satan. He is beyond repentance and will not be redeemed. His end is eternal torment in the lake of fire. This is justice. Not for a momentary sin but for millennia of deception, accusation, and destruction. The one who has caused so much pain and has led so many astray, who has opposed God at every turn — he receives what he deserves.

But why does God release Satan at all? If he's been bound for a thousand years, why let him out for one final rebellion? The answer lies in what this reveals. It shows that Christ has reigned for centuries, the gospel has gone to the nations, and every opportunity for repentance has been given — yet there are still those who choose rebellion. The problem isn't just Satan's deception. The problem is the human heart that chooses to be deceived — 'each person is tempted when he is lured and enticed by his own desire' (James 1:14 ESV). The final rebellion proves that sin isn't just about external temptation.

It's about internal rebellion against God.

And this makes the grace of God even more stunning. If, after all this time, people still choose to rebel, then the fact that any of us are saved is pure mercy. We're not saved because we're better than those who rebel. We're saved because God's grace broke through our rebellion, opened our blind eyes, and gave us hearts that want Him. The final rebellion shows us what we would have been without that grace — gathered with Gog and Magog, marching against the beloved city, and consumed by fire from heaven.

But we're not there. We're inside the camp of the saints. We're in the beloved city. Not because we earned it, but because the Lamb purchased us with His blood and the Spirit raised us to life. And now, with Satan thrown into the lake of fire, with the final rebellion ended, the stage is set for the final judgment of all humanity. The books will be opened. The dead will be raised. And every person who ever lived will stand before the great white throne.

For those who belong to Christ, the lake of fire is not a threat, it's a promise. A promise that every enemy will be defeated and every deceiver will be silenced forever. The dragon is finished. The accusation is over. And nothing will ever separate us from the love of God that is in Christ Jesus our Lord.

Prayer:

Almighty God, thank You for defeating the dragon once and for all. Thank You that his accusations are silenced and his power is broken forever. We even praise You for the lake of fire — that final removal of every enemy that secures our eternal peace. Keep us faithful in this age, when the deceiver still prowls. And when he's finally thrown into the fire, let us stand with You, safe inside the beloved city, rejoicing that his end has come. You are just, and Your judgments are true. Amen.

Day 69 – The Great White Throne

Scripture Reading: Revelation 20:11–15

Heart of Victory: The great white throne is not a threat to those whose names are in the Lamb's book—it's the final proof that grace wins.

There are truths we'd rather not think about. We prefer the comforting parts of the gospel — grace, mercy, forgiveness, heaven. We'd rather skip over the uncomfortable realities — judgment and the final reckoning. But Revelation doesn't let us skip. After the dragon is thrown into the lake of fire, and the final rebellion is crushed, John sees something that should make every one of us pause: "Then I saw a great white throne and one seated on it. Earth and heaven fled from his presence, and no place was found for them" (20:11).

This is the great white throne. White, because the One who sits on it is perfectly holy. Great, because His authority is absolute. And the fact that earth and heaven flee from His presence tells us something profound: this is the moment when the old creation gives way completely. There's no hiding place or refuge. No corner of the universe can escape this judgment. Everything stands exposed before the One who sits on the throne.

"I saw the dead, the great and the small, standing before the throne," John writes, "and books were opened. Another book was opened, which is the book of life, and the dead were judged according to their works by what was written in the books" (20:12). Every person who has ever lived — great and small, powerful and weak, famous and forgotten — stands before the throne. The sea gives up its dead. Death and Hades give up their dead. No one is exempt. No one slips through. Everyone is raised, and everyone is judged.

The books are opened. These are the records of every life — every action and word, every thought. The works of each person are laid bare before the Judge. And here's the sobering truth: if you're judged by your works, the verdict is already decided. "All have sinned and fall short of the glory of God" (Romans 3:23). There is no one righteous, not even one. If the books are the only standard, then the lake of fire is the only destination.

But there's another book. The book of life. And this is the book that matters most. "If anyone was not found written in the book of life, he was thrown into the lake of fire" (20:15). The question at the great white throne is not "Did you do enough good works?" The question is "Is your name in the book?" Your name in that book means you belong to the Lamb, washed in His blood and raised to life. And that means the judgment of your works doesn't condemn you. Christ has already borne that judgment on the cross.

This is why Jesus said, "Truly I tell you, anyone who hears my word and believes him who sent me has eternal life and will not come under judgment but has passed from death to life" (John 5:24). If you're in Christ, you don't face the great white throne in terror. You face it with confidence, because your name is written in the Lamb's book of life. The verdict was decided at Calvary. The judgment you deserved fell on Jesus. And now you stand secure.

But for those whose names are not in the book, the great white throne is the place of final reckoning. Death and Hades — the temporary holding places for the unrighteous dead — are themselves thrown into the lake of fire (20:14). This is called "the second death," the final, eternal separation from God. And anyone not found in the book of life shares that fate.

This is a passage we cannot afford to read quickly. It's a warning we desperately need to hear. The great white throne is real. The books will be opened. The judgment is coming. And there are only two destinations — the lake of fire or the new creation. The choice is made now, in this life. Will you trust the Lamb? Will you rest in His blood that covers your sins? Will you live as one whose name is written in His book? Will you enter into final glory?

For believers, this passage should fill us with urgency. People we love — friends, family members, neighbors, coworkers — are heading toward the great white throne. And if their names aren't in the book, they will face the second death. This isn't a truth we should keep to ourselves. This is a truth that should drive us to our knees in prayer and send us out with the gospel on our lips. Because the day is coming when the dead will stand before the throne, and it will be too late to repent.

But it should also fill us with gratitude. We were heading there too. We deserved the lake of fire as much as anyone. But God, in His mercy, wrote our names in the book before the foundation of the world. He sent His Son to take the judgment we deserved. He raised us to life when we were dead in our sins. And now, when the great white throne appears, we don't have to fear. Our names are in the book. Our sins have been dealt with. And the second death has no power over us.

So live with both urgency and assurance. Urgency, because the judgment is real and people need to hear. Assurance, because your name is in the book and your salvation is secure. The great white throne is not a question mark for those who belong to Christ. It's an exclamation point — the final proof that God's justice is perfect, that His mercy is real, and that everyone who calls on the name of the Lord will be saved.

Prayer:

Holy God, You are the righteous Judge, and the great white throne reveals Your perfect justice. Thank You for writing our names in the Lamb's book of life before the foundation of the world. Thank You for taking the judgment we deserved and giving us the righteousness we could never earn. Give us urgency to share the gospel with those who don't yet know You. Give us boldness to warn people about the second death, and give us confidence that our names are secure in Your book. When the throne appears, let us stand without fear, clothed in the righteousness of Christ. Amen.

Day 70 – A New Heaven and a New Earth

Scripture Reading: Revelation 21:1–4

Heart of Victory: The new creation is not a consolation prize—it's the fulfillment of everything God promised, and it's better than we can imagine.

There are moments when you realize the world is broken beyond repair. When another loved one dies. When another relationship shatters. When the news brings another story of violence or injustice. And you think, "It's not supposed to be this way." You're right. It's not. This world — with its death, its sorrow, its pain — was never God's final plan. It's a temporary reality we're passing through, and it's passing away. What's coming is something entirely new.

"Then I saw a new heaven and a new earth," John writes, "for the first heaven and the first earth had passed away, and the sea was no more" (21:1). The old creation — the one marred by sin, groaning under the weight of the curse — is gone. Not merely repaired or improved, but transformed and renewed into something gloriously, wholly new. This isn't the pale, disembodied afterlife of popular imagination — clouds, harps, disembodied souls floating around. This is a new heaven and a new earth, a physical creation remade without the stain of sin, without the shadow of death.

The absence of the sea is significant. In ancient thought, the sea represented chaos, danger, and the realm of death. It's where the beast came from in Revelation 13. It's where the dead were held in Revelation 20. But in the new creation, there is no sea. No chaos or danger. No death lurking beneath the surface. Everything is order, peace, and life.

Then John sees "the holy city, new Jerusalem, coming down out of heaven from God, prepared like a bride adorned for her husband" (21:2). This is the Bride — the church, the people of God — now fully revealed and glorified. John himself later identifies the New Jerusalem as 'the bride, the wife of the Lamb' (21:9), so this isn't a city descending so much as a people arriving. The wedding is complete. The Lamb and His Bride are united. And the city where they dwell is not something we build up to God. It's something God gives to us — a gift from heaven, pure grace.

And then comes the voice from the throne, the announcement that reconstitutes reality itself: "Look, God's dwelling is with humanity, and he will live with them. They will be his peoples, and God himself will be with them and will be their God" (21:3). This is what we were made for. This is the fulfillment of every covenant promise. God dwelling with His people. Not separated by sin or hidden behind a veil. Not distant in heaven while we struggle on earth. God with us. Immanuel. Forever.

This was always the goal. In Eden, God walked with Adam and Eve in the cool of the day. But sin drove them out, and the cherubim guarded the way back. God came down on Mount Sinai, but the people couldn't approach. The glory filled the tabernacle, but only the high priest could enter the Holy of Holies, and only once a year. Jesus came and tabernacled among us, but He ascended back to the Father. Now, finally, the separation is over. God's dwelling is with humanity. Forever.

And with God's presence comes the undoing of every curse: "He will wipe away every tear from their eyes. Death will be no more; grief, crying, and pain will be no more, because the previous things have passed away" (21:4). Read that slowly. Every tear. No more death. No more grief. No more pain. The things that have defined human existence since the fall — the things we've become so used to that we can't imagine life without them — are gone. Not diminished or managed, gone completely.

Imagine it. No more funerals or hospitals. No more broken relationships that can't be healed. No more goodbyes that tear your heart in two. No injustice, no oppression, no evil that goes unanswered. All of it — every tear, every grief, every source of pain — wiped away. Because the One who sits on the throne has made all things new.

This is not escapism, nor is it wishful thinking. This is the promise of God, spoken from the throne, guaranteed by the One who cannot lie. The new creation is coming. Death will be no more. And every tear will be wiped away.

For those of us living in the grip of grief right now, this promise means everything to us. If you've lost someone you love, or maybe you're watching someone suffer, perhaps your own body is failing. Hold on. This isn't the end. The new creation is coming, and in it, there will be no more death. The person you grieve will be raised. The suffering will end. And God Himself will wipe away your tears.

For those of us who have grown weary of the brokenness of this world, this promise is a lifeline. The chaos will be replaced by order, and the violence will give way to peace. The injustice will be swallowed up in righteousness. And we will dwell with God forever, in a place where nothing that hurts us can ever reach us again.

But this promise is also an invitation to live differently now. If the new creation is coming, if God is going to wipe away every tear, and death and grief and pain are going to be no more — then we don't have to live as though this broken world is all there is. We can endure suffering with hope and grieve without despair. We can face death without fear. Because we know what's coming. We know the end of the story. And we know that the One who sits on the throne will make all things new.

Prayer:

Father, thank You for the promise of the new heaven and the new earth. Thank You that death will be no more, that grief and pain will be swallowed up, and that You will wipe away every tear. We're tired of this broken world, Lord. We're ready for You to make all things new. Until that day, give us hope and endurance. Give us eyes to see that the sufferings of this present time are not worth comparing to the glory that will be revealed. Come quickly, Lord. Make all things new. Amen.

Day 71 – Behold, I Am Making All Things New

Scripture Reading: Revelation 21:5–8

Heart of Victory: God's promise to make all things new is not wishful thinking—it's the certain word of the Alpha and Omega.

There are promises people make that they can't keep. "I'll never leave you." "Everything will be okay." We mean well when we say these things, but we're human. We're limited. We can't control the future, and sometimes the promises we make crumble under the weight of circumstances we didn't see coming. But when God makes a promise, it's different. He sees the end from the beginning (Isaiah 46:10). He controls the circumstances. And when He speaks, reality itself bends to His word.

From the throne comes a voice: "Look, I am making all things new" (21:5). Not repairing or patching up — making new. This is the God who spoke light into darkness, who formed the world from nothing. God breathed life into dust. And now He's doing it again — not creating from scratch but renewing what sin has broken, restoring what death has stolen, and making everything new. The whole creation groans under the curse, waiting for this moment (Romans 8:22). And now it's here. God is making all things new.

And then He says to John, "Write, because these words are faithful and true" (21:5). This isn't speculation. This is the word of God, spoken from the throne, and it carries absolute authority. When God says He's making all things new, it's as good as done. When He promises a new heaven and a new earth, it's not a maybe. It's certain.

Then He says, "It is done! I am the Alpha and the Omega, the beginning and the end" (21:6). The same declaration that came from the throne in Revelation 16 when the seventh bowl was poured, "It is done!", comes again here. The judgment is complete. The old creation has passed away. The new creation has arrived. And the One who began all things and will bring all things to their conclusion declares: "It is done."

He is the Alpha and the Omega — the first and last letters of the Greek alphabet. He is the beginning and the end. Everything that exists came from Him, and everything will be consummated in Him. There is no reality outside of Him, no power above Him, no authority beyond Him. He is the source of all things and the goal toward which all things move. And He has declared: "It is done."

And then comes the invitation: "To the thirsty I will give water as a gift from the spring of the water of life" (21:6). This echoes Jesus' words to the woman at the well: "Whoever drinks from the water that I will give him will never get thirsty again. In fact, the water I will give him will become a well of water springing up in him for eternal life" (John 4:14). The thirsty are invited to drink. Freely. As a gift. No payment required. No worthiness demanded. Just come and drink.

And those who drink — those who overcome, who hold fast and endure to the end—will inherit these things: "I will be his God, and he will be my son" (21:7). This is the covenant promise echoing through all of Scripture. "I will be your God, and you will be my people." Now it's fulfilled. Not partially or provisionally—completely. God will be their God, and they will be His children. Forever.

But then comes the sobering list of those who will not inherit the new creation: "But the cowards, faithless, detestable, murderers, sexually immoral, sorcerers, idolaters, and all liars — their share will be in the lake that burns with fire and sulfur, which is the second death" (21:8). This is not a list of people who struggled with sin. This is a list of people who chose sin as their identity, "such were some of you," Paul wrote, "but you were washed" (1 Corinthians 6:11). These are those who refused the washing, who rejected the water of life and chose death instead.

Notice who's first on the list: cowards. Not murderers or idolaters — cowards. Those who knew the truth but were too afraid to stand for it. Those who heard the gospel but refused to confess Christ because of what it might cost them. Those who compromised their witness, took the mark, bowed to the beast — because they feared man more than God. The lake of fire is not just for the overtly wicked. It's for those who were too afraid to be faithful.

This is a warning we need. Revelation is not just about enduring persecution. It's about refusing cowardice. It's about choosing faithfulness even when it's costly and unpopular, even when it puts you at risk. Because in the end, there are only two destinations — the new creation or the lake of fire. And the difference isn't between those who sinned and those who didn't. It's between those who drank from the water of life and those who refused.

So come to the spring and drink freely. Let God satisfy the thirst that nothing else can touch. And when the voice from the throne declares, "I am making all things new," believe it. Because these words are faithful and true. The One who sits on the throne has spoken, and it is done.

Prayer:

Alpha and Omega, beginning and end, thank You for making all things new. Thank You for the spring of the water of life, freely given to all who are thirsty. We're thirsty, Lord. We're tired of this broken world and of death. Give us the water that satisfies forever. Keep us from cowardice. Keep us faithful to the end. And when You declare, "It is done," let us stand as Your children, inheriting the new creation You've promised. Your words are faithful and true. Amen.

Day 72 – The Bride, the Wife of the Lamb

Scripture Reading: Revelation 21:9–14

Heart of Victory: The Bride's beauty is not her own achievement—it's the radiance of the One who prepared her.

There's something breathtaking about a bride on her wedding day. The preparation, the care, the beauty — it comes together in a single breathtaking moment. But the beauty isn't just external. It's the radiance of someone who's been made ready, who's been prepared for this moment, stepping into a covenant that will define the rest of her life. And when one of the angels who held the seven bowls invites John to see the Bride, that's exactly what he shows him—not just beauty, but readiness, permanence, and the glory of being prepared by God Himself.

"Come, I will show you the bride, the wife of the Lamb," the angel says (21:9). Notice the tense — not "the bride who will become the wife" but "the bride, the wife." The wedding has happened. The covenant is sealed. What John is about to see is not the church preparing for marriage but the church already united to Christ, now revealed in all her glory.

Two Women, One Choice: The angel showing John the Bride is the same angel who showed him the great prostitute in chapter 17. There, the angel said, "Come, I will show you the judgment of the great prostitute" (17:1). Here, the same angel says, "Come, I will show you the bride, the wife of the Lamb" (21:9). This is deliberate. Revelation places these two women side by side as the ultimate contrast: Babylon the prostitute, drunk on the blood of the saints, adorned in counterfeit splendor — and New Jerusalem the Bride, radiant with God's own glory, descending from heaven. One seduces and destroys. The other reflects and gives life. Every believer in every age faces the same choice between them.

The angel carries John away in the Spirit to a great, high mountain and shows him "the holy city, Jerusalem, coming down out of heaven from God, arrayed with God's glory" (21:10-11). This is stunning. The Bride is a city. Not a single person but a community—the people of God, redeemed from every tribe and nation, now dwelling together in perfect unity. And she doesn't shine with her own light. She's "arrayed with God's glory." Her radiance comes from Him. Her beauty is His reflection.

John describes her brilliance as "like a precious jewel, like a jasper stone, clear as crystal" (21:11). This echoes the description of God Himself in Revelation 4, where the One on the throne had "the appearance of jasper" (4:3). The Bride reflects the glory of the One she's married to. She bears His likeness. She shines with His light. This is what we were created for — not to generate our own glory but to reflect His.

The city has "a great high wall with twelve gates" and "twelve angels at the gates" (21:12). On the gates are written "the names of the twelve tribes of the sons of Israel." This is the fulfillment of God's covenant with Abraham—a people from every nation, grafted into the olive tree of Israel (Romans 11:17), becoming the true children of promise. The gates bear the names of the twelve tribes because this is the true Israel, the people God has been building since the beginning.

And the wall has "twelve foundations, and on the foundations were the twelve names of the Lamb's twelve apostles" (21:14). The church is built on the foundation of the apostles' teaching (Ephesians 2:20). The gospel they proclaimed, the Christ they testified to, and the truth they handed down—that's the foundation on which the Bride stands. We're not building something new. We're part of something that has been under construction for two thousand years and built on the foundation of those who saw Jesus, touched Him, and proclaimed His resurrection.

The number twelve appears over and over — twelve gates, twelve tribes, twelve foundations, twelve apostles. It's the number of completion, of God's people fully gathered, fully formed. Nothing is missing. No one is left out. The Bride is complete, and she's standing on firm ground.

But notice what's not here. There's no mention of the Bride's achievements. No list of her good works. No catalog of her righteousness. She shines with God's glory, standing on the apostles' foundation. She bears the names of the tribes of Israel. Everything about her points away from herself and toward the One who prepared her. This is a Bride who has been made ready, not a Bride who made herself ready.

And this should fill us with both humility and hope. Humility, because we're not the source of the beauty. We don't generate the light. We don't lay the foundation. Everything we are as the Bride comes from Christ. He cleanses and adorns us. He prepares us. We bring nothing to the wedding except the sin He washes away.

But this should also fill us with hope. Because if the Bride's beauty comes from Christ, then it's not dependent on us getting everything right. It's not conditional on our perfection. He makes us radiant and clothes us in fine linen—He's the one who presents us to Himself without spot or wrinkle (Ephesians 5:27). And He will finish what He's started.

Right now, the church doesn't always look like a radiant Bride. We're divided and struggling. We fail and stumble. But that's not the end of the story. The Bride John sees is the church as she will be — perfected, glorified, and arrayed with God's glory. And every believer who belongs to Christ will be part of that city, standing on that foundation, shining with that light.

Do not despair when the church appears weak. Don't lose heart when you feel like a failure. The Bride is being prepared. The foundations are secure. One day, you will stand as part of the holy city, descending from heaven, radiant with the glory of God. Not because you earned it, but because the Lamb loved you and gave Himself for you.

Prayer:

Lord Jesus, Lamb of God and Bridegroom of the church, thank You for making us Your Bride, for cleansing us, preparing us, and clothing us in glory that is Yours alone. We don't deserve this. We didn't earn it. But You loved us and gave Yourself for us. Finish what You've begun. Perfect us. Sanctify us. And on the day when the Bride is fully revealed, let us stand as part of the holy city, radiant with Your glory, founded on Your apostles, bearing the names of Your people. We are Yours. Amen.

Day 73 – The City of Glory and Its Gates

Scripture Reading: Revelation 21:15–21

Heart of Victory: The city God prepares for us is measured with infinite care and adorned with infinite beauty—we are worth more than we know.

Some things can't be measured. Love and glory, beauty beyond words. We try — we say "I love you this much" or "that's beautiful beyond description" — but the measurements always fall short. Yet when John sees the New Jerusalem, the angel measuring it shows us that what seems immeasurable is, in fact, perfectly measured by God. Every dimension matters. Every detail counts. This is not a city thrown together. It is a city designed, crafted, and prepared with infinite care.

The angel has "a golden measuring reed to measure the city, its gates, and its wall" (21:15). And what he finds is staggering: "The city is laid out in a square; its length and width are the same. He measured the city with the reed at 12,000 stadia. Its length, width, and height are equal" (21:16). Twelve thousand stadia is about 1,400 miles. This is a perfect cube — as long as it is wide, as wide as it is high. A massive, symmetrical structure that echoes the Holy of Holies in the temple, which was also a perfect cube (1 Kings 6:20). The entire city is the Holy of Holies. The entire city is the dwelling place of God.

The wall measures "144 cubits according to human measurement, which the angel used" (21:17). The number 144 is twelve times twelve — the tribes of Israel multiplied by the apostles of the Lamb. It's the fullness of God's people, the complete gathering of everyone He has redeemed. And the fact that it's measured "according to human measurement" reminds us that this city is for us. It's not an abstract heavenly ideal. It's a real place for real people, prepared by God for His redeemed humanity.

Then John describes the materials, and they're almost too lavish to comprehend. "The foundation of the city wall was adorned with every kind of jewel" (21:19). Jasper, sapphire, emerald, topaz, onyx, carnelian — the list goes on. Twelve foundations, each adorned with a different precious stone. These aren't decorations. These are declarations of worth. The city is built on foundations more valuable than anything earth has ever produced. And we, the redeemed, stand on those foundations.

"The twelve gates were twelve pearls; each individual gate was made of a single pearl" (21:21). A pearl is formed through suffering — a tiny grain of irritation covered over and over with layers of beauty. Whether or not John intends this picture, the image fits perfectly: we enter through suffering transformed into glory. The martyrs who were killed for their testimony enter through gates that tell their story, where pain is redeemed and even death is swallowed up in beauty.

And then, the street. Not streets, plural. One street. "The main street of the city was pure gold, transparent as glass" (21:21). Gold so refined, so pure, that it's transparent. The street we walk on in the New Jerusalem is made of what we considered most valuable on earth, but here it's pavement. What we hoarded, fought over, and killed for — it's what we walk on. Because in the presence of God, the values are reversed. What seemed precious becomes ordinary. And what we overlooked — faithfulness, love, and endurance becomes the true treasure.

This city is almost too much to take in. It's a perfect cube, vast beyond imagination. Its foundations are jewels, its gates are pearls, and a street is transparent gold. And every detail speaks of the infinite worth God places on His people. He didn't just throw open heaven's doors and say, "Come in." He built a city. He designed it with care and adorned it with beauty. And He did it all for us.

This should silence every lie that whispers, "You're not worth it." If God has prepared a city like this — a city with foundations of jewels, gates of pearls, streets of gold — then you are worth more than you can imagine. Not because of what you've done, but because of what He's done. He has loved you with an everlasting love (Jeremiah 31:3) and redeemed you with His Son's blood, and has a place prepared that defies description.

But this city also reminds us that we're not home yet. We're pilgrims, strangers and exiles (Hebrews 11:13; 1 Peter 2:11). We live in tents, not in the city. We see by faith, not by sight. And every disappointment and loss we experience here, every grief — it's a reminder that this world is not the city God has prepared. We're longing for something better. And one day, we'll walk through gates of pearl onto streets of gold, and we'll be home.

So hold loosely to what this world offers. It's all temporary. It's all passing away. The gold we accumulate here will be left behind. The status we chase will be forgotten. But the city God is preparing — the one with foundations of jewels and gates of pearls — that city will last forever. And if your name is written in the Lamb's book of life, you'll walk its streets, stand on its foundations, and dwell in the presence of God forever.

Prayer:

Father, thank You for preparing a city for us, for the care You've taken, the beauty You've crafted, and the glory You've designed. We confess we've chased after things that won't last — gold that tarnishes and treasures that fade. Teach us to long for the city You've prepared, the one with foundations of jewels and gates of pearls. Keep us faithful on the journey. Keep us pilgrims who know we're not home yet. And when we finally arrive, let us walk through those gates in wonder, knowing we're finally home. Amen.

Day 74 – No Temple, No Night

Scripture Reading: Revelation 21:22–27

Heart of Victory: We don't need a temple—we have God Himself, and His presence is our eternal light.

We build structures to contain what feels too big to grasp. Temples to house the divine, sanctuaries where we can encounter what seems distant. But what happens when God is no longer distant, when His presence no longer needs to be contained, mediated, or accessed through ritual? What happens when the separation is finally gone?

"I did not see a temple in it," John writes, "because the Lord God the Almighty and the Lamb are its temple" (21:22). This is startling. The temple has been central to worship throughout the Old Testament. The tabernacle in the wilderness. Solomon's temple. The rebuilt temple after the exile. The temple was where God's presence dwelled and worshipers came to meet with Him through sacrifice. But in the New Jerusalem, there is no temple. Why? Because God Himself is the temple. His presence fills everything. There's no need for a building to house Him, no need for a special place to encounter Him. He is there. Everywhere. Always.

This is what we've been longing for. Not a better temple, but no temple. Not better access to God, but unmediated presence. The veil has been torn, the barrier removed, and now we dwell with Him face to face. The separation that began in Eden is finally over.

"The city does not need the sun or the moon to shine on it," John continues, "because the glory of God illuminates it, and its lamp is the Lamb" (21:23). No created light. The glory of God is the light, and the Lamb radiates it. This echoes Isaiah's prophecy: "The sun will no longer be your light by day, and the brightness of the moon will not shine on you. The LORD will be your everlasting light, and your God will be your splendor" (Isaiah 60:19).

In the beginning, God created light before He created the sun. Light existed independently of any source we know. And now, in the new creation, we return to that original reality. "God is light, and in him there is no darkness at all" (1 John 1:5). We don't need the sun because we have the source of all light. We don't need the moon because the glory of God never sets.

"The nations will walk by its light," John says, "and the kings of the earth will bring their glory into it" (21:24). This is the fulfillment of God's promise to Abraham—that through his offspring, all the nations of the earth would be blessed (Genesis 22:18). The nations that once raged against God now walk by His light. The kings who once resisted Him now bring their glory to honor Him. What began with one man, one family, and one nation, has expanded to include everyone. And they all come to the light.

"Its gates will never close by day, and there will be no night there" (21:25). The gates are always open. No threat requires them to shut. No enemy approaches to be kept out. The city is perfectly secure, not because of walls or guards, but because nothing unclean can enter. "Nothing unclean will ever enter it, nor anyone who does what is detestable or false, but only those written in the Lamb's book of life" (21:27).

This is both comfort and warning. Comfort, because if your name is in the book, you will enter. The gates are open to you. The light shines for you. God's presence is yours forever. But it's also a warning, because the book is the only way in. There's no sneaking past the gates. No claiming your own goodness. No appeal to your own merit. Either your name is written there, or it's not. And if it's not, you will stand outside in the darkness, where there is no light, no presence, and no hope.

But for those whose names are written — for those who belong to the Lamb — this is the promise: no more barriers or distance. No more darkness. God is the temple. The Lamb is the light — and we'll walk in His presence forever, never separated or alone.

This should change how we worship now. If the whole point is unmediated access to God, then our worship shouldn't be about rituals or buildings or special places. It should be about encountering Him. Right now. Right here. The veil is torn. The way is open. And while we don't yet see the fullness of His glory, we can draw near with confidence because Jesus has opened the way. The temple we need is not made with hands — it never was (Acts 7:48; 17:24). It's Christ Himself.

And this should change how we think about eternity. Heaven is not a place where we float on clouds or sing one endless worship song. It's a place where we walk with God. Where we dwell in His presence without any barrier. Where His light illuminates everything and the darkness is gone forever. This is what we were made for. This is what we're longing for. And this is what's coming.

Prayer:

Lord God Almighty, You are the temple and the Lamb is the light. Thank You for tearing the veil, for opening the way, for removing every barrier between You and us. We don't want better access, we want You. We don't want a shinier temple, we want Your presence. Hasten the day when there's no more separation, no more darkness and no more night. Until then, help us draw near with confidence, knowing that the way is open because Jesus has made it so. You are our everlasting light. Shine on us now, and shine forever. Amen.

Day 75 – The River and the Tree of Life

Scripture Reading: Revelation 22:1–5

Heart of Victory: The curse is lifted, the healing is complete, and we will see His face—this is what we're longing for.

Some stories end where they began. Not because nothing changed, but because everything has been restored. The journey comes full circle, and what was lost is found again — but better, fuller, richer than before. That's what happens in Revelation 22. We're back in a garden, but it's not Eden. It's Eden surpassed. It's what the garden was always meant to become.

John sees "a river of the water of life, clear as crystal, flowing from the throne of God and of the Lamb down the middle of the city's main street" (22:1-2). This is the river Ezekiel saw in his vision, flowing from the temple and bringing life wherever it went (Ezekiel 47:1-12). But now the source is not a temple, it's the throne. The river flows directly from

God and the Lamb, and it flows through the city, accessible to everyone. You don't have to journey to a distant temple to find this water. You live beside it and you drink from it every day.

"On each side of the river was the tree of life bearing twelve kinds of fruit, producing its fruit every month" (22:2). The tree of life — the one Adam and Eve were barred from after the fall, guarded by cherubim with flaming swords (Genesis 3:24) — is here. Whether one tree spanning both banks or many trees lining the river, the tree of life is abundant and accessible — bearing fruit continuously. What was forbidden in Eden is freely given in the New Jerusalem. What was lost is restored, and more than restored.

And then this stunning detail: "The leaves of the tree are for healing the nations" (22:2). Healing. Not because anyone is sick — the text has already told us there's no more pain, no more crying, no more death. But because the effects of the curse need to be undone completely. The wounds inflicted by sin, the brokenness passed down through generations, the fractures between nations and peoples — all of it is healed. The leaves of the tree restore what the fall broke.

"No longer will there be a curse," John writes (22:3). The curse that fell on Adam and Eve and spread to all creation with its thorns and sweat and death, it's gone. Lifted. Completely reversed. And in its place, "the throne of God and of the Lamb will be in the city, and his servants will worship him" (22:3). This is what we were created for. Not independence from God. Not autonomy. But worship and service. Dwelling in His presence and finding our greatest joy in honoring Him.

"They will see his face," John says, "and his name will be on their foreheads" (22:4). This is the culmination of every promise. In the Old Testament, no one could see God's face and live. Moses asked to see God's glory, and God said, "You cannot see my face, for humans cannot see me and live" (Exodus 33:20). But now, in the New Jerusalem, we see His face. Not through a veil. Not from a distance. Face to face.

And His name is on our foreheads. This is the ultimate mark — not the mark of the beast, but the mark of belonging to God. It's the seal that was promised in Revelation 7, now fully revealed. We bear His name. We belong to Him. And nothing will ever change that.

"Night will be no more," John writes. "People will not need the light of a lamp or the light of the sun, because the Lord God will give them light, and they will reign forever and ever" (22:5). No night. No darkness. No shadow. Just light. The light of God's presence, the light of His glory, shining on His people forever. And we reign. Not in the sense of wielding power over others, but in the sense of sharing in Christ's authority, participating in His rule, exercising the dominion we were created to have (Genesis 1:28) — not over people, but over creation, under God, for His glory.

This is the fulfillment of everything. The river that brings life. The tree that heals. The throne from which God reigns. The servants who worship. The faces that see Him. The names marked on foreheads. The light that never fades. The reign that never ends. This is what we're heading toward. *This is* what's coming. And nothing on earth compares to it.

For those of us who are tired — tired of fighting sin and enduring suffering, tired of living in a broken world — this vision is medicine. The river is flowing and the tree is bearing fruit. The healing is coming. And one day, you will see His face. *We* will see His face. Not through any mediation or any worship song, however beautiful. And you will know that you're home.

So hold on. The night is almost over and the dawn is coming. The river is flowing from the throne, and it's heading straight for you.

Prayer:

Father, we long for the river of life and the tree that heals. We're tired of the curse and brokenness, weary of living in shadow. Hasten the day we see Your face. Your name on our foreheads and dwelling in Your light forever. Until then, give us strength to endure. Give us hope to hold on. And remind us that the river is flowing, the tree is bearing fruit, and the healing is coming. We want to see Your face. Amen.

Day 76 – These Words Are Trustworthy and True

Scripture Reading: Revelation 22:6–11

Heart of Victory: Every word of this prophecy is trustworthy because the God who spoke it is faithful—and His promises of victory, judgment, and restoration will stand when everything else has passed away.

There are books you read and forget. And then there are books that won't let you go — books that grab you by the shoulders and shake you. Revelation is that kind of book. It doesn't offer polite suggestions or interesting theories. It makes claims that require you to decide: do you believe this, or don't you? Will you stake your life on these promises, or will you hedge your bets? Because if these words are true, everything changes.

"These words are trustworthy and true," the angel tells John (22:6). This is the third time in three chapters that this phrase appears (19:9, 21:5, 22:6). It's as if God knows we need the reminder. Because some of what Revelation describes sounds too good to be true. A new heaven and a new earth, with no more death or pain? It sounds like wishful thinking. But the angel repeats it: "These words are trustworthy and true." This isn't fantasy or wishful thinking. The symbols are real and the promises are certain. This is the future God has promised, and He will bring it to pass.

Then Jesus Himself speaks: "Look, I am coming soon! Blessed is the one who keeps the words of the prophecy of this book" (22:7). Notice that Jesus doesn't say "Blessed is the one who understands everything" or "Blessed is the one who decodes every symbol." He says "Blessed is the one who keeps the words." Keeping means obeying and living in the light of what you've read. Revelation isn't meant to be solved like a puzzle. It's meant to be kept like a treasure, guarded like a command, and lived like a promise.

John is so overwhelmed that he falls down to worship the angel. And the angel stops him: "Don't do that! I am a fellow servant with you, your brothers the prophets, and those who keep the words of this book. Worship God" (22:9). Even the angel who showed John these glorious visions refuses worship. All glory belongs to God. This is the test of every claim to divine revelation, *every* experience that says it's from God. Does it direct worship toward God, or does it draw attention to itself? True revelation always points away from the messenger and toward the One who sent it.

Then the angel gives a puzzling command: "Don't seal up the words of the prophecy of this book, because the time is near" (22:10). This is the opposite of what the angel told Daniel. This stands in deliberate contrast to Daniel. When Daniel received his visions, the angel said, 'Seal up the words of the scroll until the time of the end' (Daniel 12:4). But John is told not to seal it. Why? Because the time is near. The decisive moment has already happened. Jesus has died, risen, and ascended. The kingdom has been inaugurated. The end has begun. And now the message needs to go out — open and available to everyone.

And then comes a verse that sounds harsh: "Let the unrighteous go on in unrighteousness; let the filthy still be filthy; let the righteous go on in righteousness; let the holy still be holy" (22:11). This isn't permission to keep sinning. It's a declaration that the time for decision is running out. People are hardening into their choices. The unrighteous are becoming fixed in their unrighteousness. The holy are being confirmed in their holiness. And the window for change is closing.

This serves as both a warning and motivation. The warning is straightforward: don't delay. Don't think you have endless time to repent, believe, or deepen your commitment to following Jesus. Soon, the angel will declare, "Let the filthy still be filthy," sealing the final decision. The motivation is just as evident: continue growing in holiness and moving forward. Protect what you've received. Since the time is near, and you'd want to be discovered faithful when Jesus returns.

For those who have read Revelation — who have experienced the seals, trumpets, bowls, and visions of judgment and glory — this is the moment to ask, "What now? How should I respond to what I've seen?" The answer is straightforward: hold on to these words and live guided by them. Let these words influence your worldview, decisions, endurance, and worship. Do not seal them away or dismiss them as merely interesting or irrelevant. Keep them close. Protect them. Treasure them. Meditate on them day and night.

Because these words are trustworthy and true. The Lamb who was slain is returning as the Lion, the dragon is defeated, and Babylon is fallen. The new creation is coming. And blessed is the one who keeps these words, lives as though they're true, and watches for the return of the One who said, 'Look, I am coming soon."

Prayer:

Lord Jesus, You are coming soon. Thank You for giving us these words, trustworthy and true. Help us keep them, not just know them. Help us live in light of Your return, not as people who are anxious or afraid, but as people who are ready. Don't let us seal this book. Don't let us set it aside. Keep it open in our hearts. Keep us holy. Keep us watching. And when You come, find us faithful. Amen.

Day 77 – "Surely I Am Coming Soon"

Scripture Reading: Revelation 22:12–17

Heart of Victory: Jesus is coming soon, and He invites us to come freely to the water of life—now, before it's too late.

The best news in the world can also be the most urgent. "The plane is boarding." "He's on his way home." These aren't statements you can casually acknowledge and then forget. They demand a response. They create urgency. And when Jesus says, "Look, I am coming soon," it's not an interesting theological point to file away. It's the declaration that changes everything — if you believe it.

"Look, I am coming soon, and my reward is with me to repay each person according to his work" (22:12). Jesus is coming, and He's bringing rewards. This isn't about earning salvation — that's already been settled by grace through faith. This is about how we lived once we were saved. Did we build on the foundation with gold, silver, and precious stones? Or with wood, hay, or straw? (1 Corinthians 3:12). Jesus is coming to reward faithfulness — and the greatest reward is the One who brings it (Genesis 15:1)

Then He declares His identity: "I am the Alpha and the Omega, the first and the last, the beginning and the end" (22:13). This is the same title God gave Himself in Revelation 1:8. Jesus is not a messenger bringing news about God. He is God. He is the source of all things and the goal toward which all things move. And He's coming.

"Blessed are those who wash their robes," He says, "so that they may have the right to the tree of life and may enter the city by the gates" (22:14). Notice the present tense, "those who wash." This is ongoing. We don't wash our robes once and then coast. We keep coming back to the blood of the Lamb. We continuously confess sin and receive cleansing. And those who do — those who continually wash their robes in His blood — have the right to the tree of life. They will enter the city.

But "outside are the dogs, the sorcerers, the sexually immoral, the murderers, the idolaters, and everyone who loves and practices falsehood" (22:15). This is the contrast. Inside the city are those who have washed their robes, while outside the city stand those who refused. And the difference is stark. One group eats from the tree of life. The other stands in the darkness outside the gates.

Jesus emphasizes His role: "I, Jesus, have sent my angel to attest these things to you for the churches" (22:16). This whole book — all the visions, all the warnings, with each and every promise — comes from Jesus. He's the one who sent the revelation. He's the one attesting to its truth. He's "the root and descendant of David, the bright morning star." He is the fulfillment of every promise God made to David. He is the light that signals the end of night and the beginning of the new day.

And then comes the invitation: "Both the Spirit and the bride say, 'Come!' Let the one who hears say, 'Come!' Let the one who is thirsty come. Let the one who desires take the water of life freely" (22:17). This is the heartbeat of the gospel. Come. Not "try harder." Not "clean yourself up first." And certainly not "prove you're worthy." Come. The Spirit invites. The Bride invites. And anyone who hears should join the chorus, "Come."

This invitation echoes through all of Scripture. "Come, everyone who is thirsty, come to the water" (Isaiah 55:1). "Come to me, all of you who are weary and burdened" (Matthew 11:28). And now, at the end of Revelation, the invitation goes out one more time: Come. The water is free. The gate is open. And Jesus is returning soon to bring His reward.

For those of us who have already come, this passage is a call to perseverance. Keep washing your robes and living in light of His return, inviting others to come. Jesus is coming soon, and He's bringing rewards. Live in a way that will earn His "Well done, good and faithful servant (Matthew 25:21)."

But for those who haven't yet come—who are still standing outside, holding back, still unsure—hear the invitation: Come. Come now. Come freely. Come before the door closes, before the opportunity passes, before Jesus returns and the time for deciding is over. The Spirit is calling. The Bride is calling. And Jesus Himself is saying, "I am coming soon." Come while you can.

Because the alternative is unthinkable. To stand outside the city in the darkness, excluded from the tree of life, with no hope of being with Jesus — that is a fate too terrible to risk. So come. Drink from the water of life. Wash your robes in the blood of the Lamb. And wait with confidence for the One who said, "I am coming soon."

Prayer:

Lord Jesus, You are coming soon. Thank You for the invitation to come freely, to drink from the water of life, to wash our robes in Your blood. We come. We're thirsty. We're weary. And we need You. Help us to keep coming, day after day. To keep washing and continue living in light of Your return. And help us to join the invitation, to call others to come while there's still time. You are the bright morning star, the beginning and the end. Come quickly, Lord. Amen.

Day 78 – The Last Words and the Last Prayer

Scripture Reading: Revelation 22:18–21

Heart of Victory: The last prayer of Scripture is the prayer we should pray every day—"Come, Lord Jesus."

Last words carry weight. A deathbed confession. A final letter. We pay attention to last words because they reveal what matters most. And as Revelation draws to a close, the final words aren't about decoding symbols or mapping out timelines. They're about guarding this book and longing for Jesus to return. That's what matters and that is what we're left with.

John issues a serious warning: "I testify to everyone who hears the words of the prophecy of this book: If anyone adds to them, God will add to him the plagues written in this book. And if anyone takes away from the words of the book of this prophecy, God will take away his share of the tree of life and the holy city, which are written in this book" (22:18-19). This warning applies first to Revelation itself — don't tamper with this prophecy — but it reflects a principle that runs through all of Scripture: show proper reverence for God's Word, not adding to it to make it more acceptable, nor subtracting from it to avoid uncomfortable truths.

Revelation has been hard to hear. It's confronted us with judgment, suffering, and the cost of faithfulness. It's called us to endure persecution, refuse the mark, and hold fast when everything in us wants to compromise. And the temptation is always there to soften it, to edit it, or to make it say something less demanding. But John's warning is clear: don't.

This is God's word. Guard it and protect it. Let it say what it says, even when it's hard.

Then Jesus speaks one more time: "Yes, I am coming soon" (22:20). This is the third time in this chapter He's said it (22:7, 12, 20). And each time, it's a promise and a warning. A promise for those who belong to Him — He's coming to rescue and reward us, and to make all things new. A warning for those who don't — He's coming to judge, to settle accounts and to separate the righteous from the wicked. "I am coming soon." Believe it. Live like it's true. Because it is.

And John's response is perfect: "Amen! Come, Lord Jesus!" (22:20). Just "Come." This is the prayer that should be on our lips every day. Come, Lord Jesus. Come and make all things new. Come and wipe away every tear. Come and finish what You started. Come and take us home. This is the longing of the church, the cry of the Bride. This is the heartbeat of everyone who has walked through Revelation and seen the vision of the new creation. Come, Lord Jesus.

Then John closes with a blessing: "The grace of the Lord Jesus be with all the saints" (22:21). After all the visions of judgment and warnings about the lake of fire, and all the calls to endure, John ends with grace. Because that's where it all begins. Grace that saves us and sustains us. Grace that will bring us home. We don't earn the tree of life or entrance to the city. We don't earn the right to see His face. It's all grace, from beginning to end.

And this is how we're meant to live in the meantime — between "I am coming soon" and "Come, Lord Jesus." We guard the word. We refuse to add to it or subtract from it. We let it say what it says, even when it's uncomfortable. We live in light of His return. We watch. We wait. And we pray, every single day, "Come, Lord Jesus."

Because that prayer draws a line. When you pray "Come, Lord Jesus," you're saying you're ready. You're saying this world isn't enough. You're saying you want Him more than you want comfort, more than you want security, and more than you want the approval of people who will never understand. You're saying, "I'm done with Babylon and the beast. I'm done with compromise. Come, Lord Jesus. Take me home."

And one day — maybe sooner than we think — He will. The sky will open. The trumpet will sound. And the One who said, "I am coming soon" will appear. And we'll see His face and hear His voice. We'll stand in His presence. And everything Revelation promised will be ours — the new heaven and the new earth, the tree of life standing in the midst with the river flowing from the throne through the city where God dwells with His people forever.

So guard the word. Don't add to or subtract from it. Let Revelation say what it says. And pray the prayer the church has prayed for two thousand years: "Come, Lord Jesus." He's coming. And when He does, every tear will be wiped away, every enemy will be defeated, and we will be home.

Prayer:

Lord Jesus, You said You are coming soon. We believe You and trust You. And we're praying with the church across every generation: Come, Lord Jesus, and finish what You started. Come and make all things new. Take us home. Until that day, help us guard Your word. Help us live in light of Your return and help us watch and wait with hope. The grace of the Lord Jesus be with us. Amen. Come, Lord Jesus.

Part Eight: Echoes of the Old Testament

From Promise to Fulfillment

Heart of Victory: Revelation is not a stand-alone vision—it's the climax of God's redemptive story, the fulfillment of every prophetic hope.

Revelation is not a random book. It is the last chapter of a story that starts in Genesis, moves through the prophets, and reaches its fulfillment in Christ. Every vision John describes, and every symbol he uses echo the words of prophets who saw only hints of what we now see clearly. Revelation fulfills the hope found in the Old Testament.

In Daniel's night visions, a Son of Man comes to the Ancient of Days and receives an everlasting kingdom. In Revelation, that same Son of Man walks among the lampstands, with eyes like fire and a voice like "rushing waters" (NIV). The person Daniel saw is the same one John sees: Jesus, exalted and reigning (Daniel 7:13–14; Revelation 1:13–16).

When Israel was trapped at the Red Sea between Pharaoh's army and certain death, God saved them. The waters parted, the enemy drowned, and Moses and the people sang a victory song. In Revelation, the redeemed stand on a sea of glass, holding harps and singing the Song of Moses and the Lamb. The pattern repeats, but this time the deliverance is even greater — not just from Egypt, but from sin, death, and the dragon.

Ezekiel saw a vision of a restored temple and a river flowing from it, bringing life everywhere. In Revelation, there is no temple because God Himself is the temple. The river flows from the throne of God and the Lamb, and the tree's leaves bring healing to the nations. What Ezekiel saw in part, Revelation shows completely.

The prophets spoke of the Day of the Lord, a day of darkness, cosmic upheaval, and divine judgment. Joel described the sun turning dark and the moon turning to blood (Joel 2:31), and Isaiah pictured the earth reeling like a drunkard (Isaiah 24:20). And in Revelation, when the sixth seal is opened, the sun turns black, the moon becomes like blood, and the stars fall from the sky. The Day of the Lord arrives, not as a myth, but as reality. The harvest is final.

Daniel saw four great beasts rise from the sea, representing terrifying empires that destroyed and crushed. He also saw the Ancient of Days judge and destroy the beasts. In Revelation, the beast rises from the sea, demands worship, and fights against the saints. But the Lamb defeats him, and the beast is thrown into the lake of fire. Every beastly kingdom falls, but only the Lamb's kingdom endures.

Isaiah spoke of a new heaven and a new earth, where the wolf lies with the lamb, all weeping ends, and God's people live in peace forever (Isaiah 65:17–25). In Revelation, John sees this new heaven and new earth. The old things are gone, death is finished, and God dwells with people forever.

Part Eight does not introduce new ideas. It helps us see the story we have been reading all along. Revelation does not create new images; it brings them together. It does not replace Old Testament promises; it fulfills them. All the echoes and fulfilled prophecies point to one truth: Jesus is the faithful witness, the firstborn from the dead, and the ruler of the kings of the earth. He is the Alpha and the Omega, the Lion of Judah, and the Lamb who was slain. He is the fulfillment of every hope and the answer to every longing—the completion of every promise God made.

The Old Testament looked forward to Him. Revelation shows Him. Now, at the end of the story, we see what the prophets longed for: the victory of the Lamb, the vindication of the saints, and the renewal of everything.

Welcome to the Final Part.

Day 79 – The Son of Man and the Ancient of Days

Scripture Reading: Daniel 7:9–14; Revelation 1:12–18; 14:14

Heart of Victory: Jesus is the Son of Man Daniel saw —fully human, fully divine, reigning with everlasting dominion.

There are moments in Scripture when heaven's curtain is drawn back, revealing what truly happens behind the scenes. Daniel experienced such a moment. In a night vision, he saw thrones being arranged, and the Ancient of Days took His seat. His garments were white as snow, and His hair was like pure wool. The throne was ablaze, and its wheels shone like flames. Thousands of angels attended Him, and ten thousand times ten thousand stood before Him (Daniel 7:9-10). This represents God — timeless, everlasting, and majestic beyond measure.

But then Daniel saw someone else. "One like a son of man," he writes, "was coming with the clouds of heaven. He approached the Ancient of Days and was escorted before him. He was given dominion, glory, and a kingdom, so that those of every people, nation, and language should serve him. His dominion is an everlasting dominion that will not pass away, and his kingdom is one that will not be destroyed" (Daniel 7:13-14).

A son of man — a human figure — approaching God and receiving the kingdom. This wasn't just any king. This was someone who shared God's authority, reigning forever while the nations served. Daniel saw it and wondered: who is this?

Revelation gives the answer. When John turns to see the voice speaking to him, he sees "someone like the son of man" standing among the seven golden lampstands (Revelation 1:12-13). The description is unmistakable. His head and hair are white like wool, white as snow. His eyes are like a fiery flame. His feet are like fine bronze refined in a furnace. His voice is like the sound of cascading waters. And from His mouth comes a sharp double-edged sword (Revelation 1:14-16).

This is Daniel's vision fulfilled. The Son of Man is Jesus. And He doesn't just approach the Ancient of Days — He bears the very appearance of the Ancient of Days. White hair. Blazing eyes. A voice that shakes the earth. Jesus is not simply a messenger sent by God. He is God, the Son, exalted and reigning. He shares the throne with the Father, reigning as equal in glory and power. And His kingdom will never end.

John's response is the same as Daniel's: "When I saw him, I fell at his feet like a dead man" (Revelation 1:17). You can't stand in the presence of the exalted Christ and remain casual. You can't see the Son of Man in His glory and stay upright. The only appropriate response is to fall.

But Jesus doesn't leave John there. He places His right hand on him and says, "Don't be afraid. I am the First and the Last, and the Living One. I was dead, but look—I am alive forever and ever, and I hold the keys of death and Hades" (Revelation 1:17-18). This is the stunning mystery: the Son of Man who receives the eternal kingdom is the one who died on a cross. The Ancient of Days in human form is the Lamb who was slain. And now He's alive, forever, holding the keys to death itself.

Later in Revelation, John sees another vision of the Son of Man. "I looked, and there was a white cloud, and one like the son of man was seated on the cloud, with a golden crown on his head and a sharp sickle in his hand" (Revelation 14:14). He's seated, reigning. He wears a crown, ruling. And He holds a sickle, ready to harvest. The kingdom Daniel saw being given to the Son of Man is here. And the harvest is coming.

This connection between Daniel and Revelation is crucial. For centuries, God's people waited for the fulfillment of Daniel's vision. They looked for the Son of Man who would receive the kingdom. And they longed for the day when God's reign would break into history and overthrow every beastly empire. And then Jesus came. He lived among us. He died on a cross. He rose from the dead. And He ascended to the right hand of the Father, where He received — just as Daniel saw — dominion, glory, and an everlasting kingdom.

What does this mean for us? It means the one we worship is not a distant God disconnected from human suffering. He is the Son of Man — fully human, like us. He walked where we walk, wept where we weep, and died the death we deserve. But it also means He is the Ancient of Days — fully God, eternal, all-powerful, reigning. He is not just a good teacher or a moral example. He is the exalted Lord, the King of kings, and the one to whom every knee will bow.

And because He is both — fully human and fully divine — He can sympathize with our weaknesses while also holding the keys to death and Hades. He understands what it's like to be tempted, rejected, and broken (Hebrews 4:15). But He also has the authority to deliver us, to raise us, and to seat us with Him in the heavenly places (Ephesians 2:6).

So when you feel weak, remember: the Son of Man who walked this earth is the one who now reigns on the throne. When you face suffering, remember: the one who sympathizes with you is the Ancient of Days who will bring justice. And when you're afraid of death, remember: He walked out of the tomb. The keys are His. And He's coming back to complete what He started.

Prayer:

Lord Jesus, Son of Man and Ancient of Days, You are the fulfillment of every prophetic hope. Thank You for becoming like us and sharing in our humanity, and dying our death. Thank You for rising in glory and reigning on the throne, holding the keys to death and Hades. We fall before You in worship, trusting You with our lives. And we wait for the day when every knee will bow, and every tongue confess that You are Lord. Come, Lord Jesus. Amen.

Day 80 – The New Exodus and the Song of Moses

Scripture Reading: Exodus 14:26–15:2; Revelation 15:1–4; 11:18

Heart of Victory: The Exodus was a shadow—the Lamb's deliverance is the substance, greater in every way.

Some stories get told over and over because they define who we are. For Israel, the Exodus was that story. Trapped between Pharaoh's army and the Red Sea, with no way forward and no way back, they stood on the edge of destruction. And then God acted. The waters parted. They walked through on dry ground. And when Pharaoh's chariots followed, the sea closed over them. Israel was saved and Egypt was judged. And the people sang.

"I will sing to the LORD," Moses proclaimed, "for he is highly exalted; he has thrown the horse and its rider into the sea. The LORD is my strength and my song; he has become my salvation" (Exodus 15:1-2). This wasn't just relief. This was worship. God had done what no one else could do. He delivered His people from slavery, brought them through the sea, and drowned their enemies. The song wasn't about Israel's courage. It was about God's power.

For generations, that song echoed through Israel's worship. Passover after Passover, they remembered the night God struck Egypt with plagues and passed over His people. Year after year, they told the story of the sea that parted and the God who saved. The Exodus became the lens through which Israel understood God. Deliverance comes from Him. He judges oppressors and leads His people out of bondage.

And then Revelation picks up the same pattern. John sees "something like a sea of glass mixed with fire, and those who had conquered the beast, its image, and the number of its name, standing on the sea of glass with harps from God" (Revelation 15:2). This is the same imagery. A sea. Victorious people standing on the other side. Enemies defeated. And what are they doing? They're singing. "They sang the song of God's servant Moses and the song of the Lamb" (Revelation 15:3).

The Song of Moses and the Lamb. Not two songs, but one — the same song, echoing across centuries, celebrating the same kind of deliverance. Moses sang because God brought Israel through the Red Sea. The redeemed in Revelation sing because the Lamb has brought them through something greater.

What's the greater deliverance? Not just freedom from an earthly empire, but freedom from sin, death, and the dragon. The plagues God sent on Egypt find their echo in the bowls of wrath poured out on those who worship the beast. The sea that swallowed Pharaoh's army finds its echo in the lake of fire that consumes God's enemies. And the people standing safely on the other side? They're not just free from slavery — they're free from the second death.

Listen to their song: "Great and awe-inspiring are your works, Lord God, the Almighty; just and true are your ways, King of the nations. Lord, who will not fear and glorify your name? For you alone are holy. All the nations will come and worship before you because your righteous acts have been revealed" (Revelation 15:3-4).

This is Moses' song, but it's bigger. Moses sang about one nation delivered from one empire. The Lamb's people sing about every nation delivered from every power that opposes God. Moses sang about Pharaoh drowning in the sea. The Lamb's people sing about the dragon, the beast, and the false prophet cast into the lake of fire. Moses sang about crossing into the Promised Land. The Lamb's people sing about entering the New Jerusalem.

The pattern is the same. Oppression. Judgment. Deliverance. Song. But the scale is cosmic. What God did for Israel at the Red Sea was a preview, a shadow, a sign pointing forward to the ultimate deliverance

He would accomplish through the Lamb. And now, in Revelation, we see the full picture. The Exodus wasn't just a one-time event in ancient history. The Exodus was, as the writer of Hebrews understood, a shadow of the good things to come (Hebrews 10:1). It was the pattern of how God saves His people — through judgment on His enemies and grace for those He calls His own. Even earlier in Revelation, when the seventh trumpet sounds, the heavenly voices declare that the time has come to judge, to reward the saints, and to destroy those who destroy the earth (11:18). The Exodus pattern is woven throughout the whole book.

And here's what this means for us: if you're in Christ, you're part of the New Exodus. You've been delivered. Not from Egypt, but from something worse—slavery to sin and the tyranny of death. The bowls of wrath have fallen on the one who held you captive. The sea has parted. You've walked through on dry ground. And the enemy who pursued you? He's been swallowed up. The dragon is defeated. The beast is thrown down. And you're standing on the sea of glass, holding a harp, ready to sing.

So sing. Sing the Song of Moses and the Lamb. Sing because God is great. Sing because His ways are just. Sing because He alone is holy. Sing because the nations will come and worship Him. Sing because you've been delivered from a slavery far worse than Egypt, and you're heading toward a home far better than Canaan.

The Exodus isn't over. It's been fulfilled. And one day, when the New Jerusalem descends and God makes His dwelling with His people, we'll sing that song again — not as those who are hoping for deliverance, but as those who have received it fully. The Lamb has led us through. The enemy is drowned. And we're home.

Prayer:

Lord God Almighty, You delivered Israel from Egypt, and You have delivered us from sin and death through the Lamb. Great and awe-inspiring are Your works. Just and true are Your ways. We stand on the sea of glass because You brought us through. You defeated our enemy. You drowned the dragon. And now we sing — not because of our strength, but because of Yours. Teach us to sing the Song of Moses and the Lamb every day, worshiping You for the deliverance only You could accomplish. Amen.

Day 81 – The Temple, the City, and God's Presence

Scripture Reading: Ezekiel 47:1–12; Revelation 21:22–27; 22:1–5

Heart of Victory: Ezekiel saw a temple; John sees God Himself dwelling with His people—no separation, no distance, forever.

Some visions demand patience. Ezekiel, exiled in Babylon, was shown a vision of a restored temple — chapter after chapter of measurements, gates, and rooms. It's easy to get lost in the details. But then, in chapter 47, something stunning happens. Ezekiel sees water trickling from under the threshold of the temple. As he follows it, the water deepens — ankle-deep, knee-deep, waist-deep, until it becomes a river he cannot cross. And wherever the river flows, life follows. Trees grow on both banks, bearing fruit every month, and their leaves are for healing (Ezekiel 47:1-12).

There's a promise here. God's presence brings life. Where He dwells, death is reversed. The temple is the source of the river, and the river transforms everything it touches. Ezekiel's vision gave hope to a people who had lost everything—their land, their city, their temple. One day, God said, I will return. And when I do, life will flow from My presence.

But here's what's stunning. When John sees the fulfillment of Ezekiel's vision in Revelation, there's no temple. "I did not see a temple in it," John writes, "because the Lord God the Almighty and the Lamb are its temple" (Revelation 21:22). This isn't a loss, it's actually the ultimate gain. The temple was never the goal. The temple was always a pointer — a way for God to dwell among His people despite the separation caused by sin. But now, in the New Jerusalem, that separation is gone. The veil has been torn and the distance has been erased. God doesn't need a building to house His presence, because He dwells with His people directly, fully — forever.

And the river? It's still there. John sees "the river of the water of life, clear as crystal, flowing from the throne of God and of the Lamb down the middle of the city's main street" (Revelation 22:1). This is Ezekiel's river, but now the source isn't a temple. It's the throne — God and the Lamb reigning together, and from their throne, life flows. The river Ezekiel saw trickling from the temple has become a torrent flowing through the entire city.

And just like in Ezekiel's vision, there are trees. "On each side of the river was the tree of life bearing twelve kinds of fruit, producing its fruit every month. The leaves of the tree are for healing the nations" (Revelation 22:2). The tree of life — the one Adam and Eve were barred from after the fall (Genesis 3:24) — is here, lining the river and completely accessible to everyone. What was lost in Eden is restored in the New Jerusalem. And the leaves? They're for healing. Not because anyone is sick, but because the effects of the curse are being undone completely.

Ezekiel's vision pointed forward to this. The temple he saw was never meant to be just a building in Jerusalem. It was a picture of what was coming — a reality where God's presence wouldn't be confined to one place but would fill everything. Where the river of life wouldn't be a trickle but a flood, and healing wouldn't be partial but complete.

In the old covenant, you went to the temple to meet with God. But in the new creation, God comes to you. His dwelling is with humanity. His throne is in the city where His people live. The river flows down the main street. The tree grows where everyone can reach it. This isn't about making a pilgrimage to a holy place. This is about living in the presence of God every moment, forever.

John emphasizes this: "The city does not need the sun or the moon to shine on it, because the glory of God illuminates it, and its lamp is the Lamb" (Revelation 21:23). No created light is necessary. God Himself is the light. And "the nations will walk by its light, and the kings of the earth will bring their glory into it" (Revelation 21:24). The vision Ezekiel saw of nations coming to worship at the temple? It's fulfilled. But they're not coming to a building. They're coming to God Himself.

For those of us who long for God's presence, this is the ultimate hope. Right now, we see through a glass darkly (1 Corinthians 13:12 KJV). We pray, and sometimes it feels like God is distant. We worship, and we wonder if He's listening. We read His word, and we strain to hear His voice. But this won't last. One day, the river will flow past our feet. The tree will be within our reach. And we will see His face. Not mediated through prayer or worship or Scripture — as precious as those are. His face, directly. And we will know that we're home.

Ezekiel's vision was never just about bricks and mortar. It was about the presence of God returning to His people. And in Revelation, that vision is fulfilled beyond anything Ezekiel could have imagined. No temple is needed, because God Himself is the temple. No distant source is needed, because the river flows directly from His throne. And we, who once stood outside the garden, barred from the tree of life, will eat from it freely, healed and whole, in the presence of the One we were made to worship.

Prayer:

Lord God Almighty, You are our temple. You are the source of the river of life. Thank You for tearing down every barrier, removing every veil, and making it possible for us to dwell in Your presence forever. We long for the day when the river flows through the city, and the tree bears fruit for all, and we see Your face and know we're home. Until that day, help us live as those who are heading toward Your presence, not away from it. You are our dwelling place, now and forever. Amen.

Day 82 – The Day of the Lord and the Final Harvest

Scripture Reading: Joel 2:28–32; Isaiah 13:9–13; Revelation 6:12–17; 14:14–20

Heart of Victory: The Day of the Lord is both terror and triumph—judgment for God's enemies, rescue for His people.

The prophets spoke of a day that made people tremble. Not just any day, but the Day of the Lord. It would be a time when God settles accounts, judges the wicked, and the earth itself shakes. Joel described it: "The sun will be turned to darkness and the moon to blood before the great and terrible day of the LORD comes" (Joel 2:31). Isaiah saw it too: "The stars of heaven and its constellations will not give their light. The sun will be dark when it rises, and the moon will not shine" (Isaiah 13:10). This is not just a symbol for political change. It is a real, cosmic disruption. Creation itself groans under the weight of God's judgment.

The Day of the Lord was both a promise and a warning — longed for by the oppressed, dreaded by the unfaithful. It all depended on which side of God's covenant you were standing on.

Then John sees it. When the Lamb opens the sixth seal, "there was a violent earthquake. The sun turned black like sackcloth made of hair; the moon became like blood; and the stars of heaven fell to the earth as a fig tree drops its unripe figs when shaken by a high wind" (Revelation 6:12-13). This is the language Joel used. This is Isaiah's vision. The Day of the Lord has come. The signs the prophets described are happening, and everyone is terrified.

"The kings of the earth, the nobles, the generals, the rich, the powerful, and every slave and free person hid in the caves and among the rocks of the mountains. And they said to the mountains and to the rocks, 'Fall on us and hide us from the face of the one seated on the throne and from the wrath of the Lamb, because the great day of their wrath has come! And who is able to stand?'" (Revelation 6:15-17).

This is the great day of wrath — not only God's, but the Lamb's. The one who was slain, who bore the sins of the world and offered Himself as the sacrifice, is also the Judge. On the Day of the Lord, no one can stand before Him unless they are covered by His blood.

Later in Revelation, John sees another image of the Day of the Lord: the final harvest. "I looked, and there was a white cloud, and one like the son of man was seated on the cloud, with a golden crown on his head and a sharp sickle in his hand. Another angel came out of the temple, crying out in a loud voice to the one who was seated on the cloud, 'Use your sickle and reap, for the time to reap has come, since the harvest of the earth is ripe'" (Revelation 14:14-15).

The harvest is the fulfillment of every prophetic warning. The grain is separated from the chaff. The wheat is gathered into the barn, and the wicked are thrown into the winepress of God's wrath. "So the angel swung his sickle at the earth and gathered the grapes from the vineyard of the earth, and he threw them into the great winepress of God's wrath. Then the press was trampled outside the city, and blood flowed out of the press up to the horses' bridles for about 180 miles" (Revelation 14:19-20).

This is graphic and final. This is the Day of the Lord in all its terror. The prophets warned about it, and Jesus spoke of it (Matthew 24:29–31). Revelation shows it not as mere symbol, but as certain reality — the symbols point to something that will actually happen. The harvest is coming. Judgment is certain, and no one escapes.

But if you belong to Christ, the Day of the Lord is not a day of terror. It's a day of vindication. The same day that brings wrath on God's enemies brings rescue for His people. The same cosmic upheaval that drives the wicked into caves also causes the saints to lift their heads, because their redemption is drawing near (Luke 21:28).

Joel saw this too. After describing the darkness, the blood, and the terror, he said, "Then everyone who calls on the name of the LORD will be saved" (Joel 2:32) — the same promise Peter proclaimed at Pentecost (Acts 2:21) and Paul echoed in Romans 10:13. That is the escape. That is the hope. It is not about hiding in caves or begging the rocks to fall, but about calling on the name of the Lord. And everyone who does, everyone who trusts in the Lamb and washes their robes in His blood, everyone who holds fast to His name, will be saved.

The Day of the Lord is coming. The cosmic signs will unfold. The harvest will be reaped. The question is not whether it will happen; it will. The real question is: will you be standing, or will you be hiding? Will you be calling on His name, or calling for the rocks to fall?

The prophets warned us, and Jesus confirmed it. Revelation reveals it, and now we wait, not in terror but in hope. The Day of the Lord is when everything wrong is made right. Every enemy is defeated, and the people of God are finally and fully vindicated.

Prayer:

Lord God, the Day is coming. The sun will turn dark, the moon will become blood, and the stars will fall. We do not fear that day, because we call on Your name. We trust in the Lamb. We have washed our robes in His blood. When the harvest comes, we will stand, not because we are righteous, but because He is. Hasten that day, Lord. Bring the harvest. Vindicate Your people. Let us stand before You without fear, clothed in the righteousness of Christ. Amen.

Day 83 – The Beastly Kingdoms and the Lamb's Kingdom

Scripture Reading: Daniel 7:1–8, 15–27; Revelation 13:1–10; 17:9–14

Heart of Victory: Beastly kingdoms roar for an hour, but the Lamb's kingdom stands forever—choose wisely.

Empires rise and fall. Babylon conquered the known world, then crumbled. Persia rose in its place, then fell to Greece. Rome seemed eternal, but it collapsed. History is littered with the ruins of kingdoms that thought they would last forever. But they all had one thing in common: they were beasts.

Daniel saw them in a vision. Four great beasts rose from the sea — terrifying and violent and devouring. The first was like a lion with eagle's wings. The second like a bear, raised up on one side. The third like a leopard with four wings and four heads. And the fourth? Daniel couldn't even describe it. It was different from all the others, "extremely terrifying, with iron teeth and bronze claws, devouring, crushing, and trampling with its feet whatever was left" (Daniel 7:19). This fourth beast had ten horns, and out of them came another horn — small at first, but growing larger, speaking arrogantly, waging war against the saints (Daniel 7:8, 21).

These beasts represented kingdoms — oppressive empires that rose to power, crushed God's people, and demanded worship. But then Daniel saw something else. "The Ancient of Days took his seat. His clothing was white like snow, and the hair of his head like whitest wool. His throne was flaming fire; its wheels were blazing fire" (Daniel 7:9). The Judge arrived. And the beasts? They were destroyed. "I watched, then, because of the sound of the arrogant words the horn was speaking. As I continued watching, the beast was killed and its body destroyed and given over to the burning fire" (Daniel 7:11).

The beasts fell. The kingdom of God endured.

And then Revelation shows us the same pattern. John sees "a beast coming up out of the sea. It had ten horns and seven heads. On its horns were ten crowns, and on its heads were blasphemous names" (Revelation 13:1). This is Daniel's beast. The same arrogant imagery. The same violence. It rises from the sea, demands worship, wars against the saints, and conquers them — for a time (Revelation 13:7).

Revelation doesn't present this as a one-time event. The beast is a pattern. Every empire that opposes God and persecutes the church, demanding their allegiance — it's the beast rising again. Rome was a beast. So were the empires that followed. And so will be the empires that come. The beast keeps appearing because the dragon keeps empowering it. But every time, it falls.

Later, an angel explains the mystery to John. The beast "was, and is not, and is about to come up from the abyss and go to destruction" (Revelation 17:8) — a mocking echo of God's own title, 'who is, and who was, and who is to come' (Revelation 1:4). The beast imitates God but ends in destruction. God endures forever. The beast rises and falls, rises and falls. It looks invincible. It seems eternal. But it's always heading toward destruction. "The ten horns you saw are ten kings who have not yet received a kingdom, but they will receive authority as kings with the beast for one hour. These have one purpose: to give their power and authority to the beast. They will make war against the Lamb, but the Lamb will conquer them because he is Lord of lords and King of kings" (Revelation 17:12-14).

One hour. That's how long the beast's kingdom lasts in the grand scheme of eternity. One hour. It feels like forever when you're living under its oppression and unstoppable when it's killing the saints. But it's temporary. And the Lamb? He conquers.

This is the stark contrast Daniel saw and Revelation confirms. Beastly kingdoms are fleeting, but the Lamb's kingdom is everlasting. Empires rise with violence and crush anyone who resists. But they all fall. The Lamb, on the other hand, conquers not by violence but by sacrifice. He doesn't demand worship — He inspires it. He doesn't crush the weak— He lifts them up. And His kingdom? It never ends.

"The kingdom, dominion, and greatness of the kingdoms under all of heaven will be given to the people, the holy ones of the Most High. His kingdom will be an everlasting kingdom, and all rulers will serve and obey him" (Daniel 7:27). This is the promise. The beasts will devour each other, and though they are permitted to war against the saints for a time (Revelation 13:7), they cannot devour the people of God ultimately. The kingdoms of this world will crumble, but the kingdom of the Lamb will stand forever.

So when you see empires that look invincible, remember: they're temporary. They rise for an hour and then fall. When you see powers that demand allegiance and threaten those who refuse, remember: they're temporary. When you see violence, arrogance, and blasphemy parading as strength, remember: the Lamb conquers. Not with iron teeth and bronze claws, but with the power of His own blood.

And when you're tempted to give in and to compromise your witness because the beast seems too strong — remember Daniel's vision. The Ancient of Days takes His seat. The books are opened. And the beast is thrown into the fire. Every. Single. Time.

The kingdoms of this world will become the kingdom of our Lord and of His Christ (Revelation 11:15 KJV). And those who belong to the Lamb will reign with Him forever.

Prayer:

Lord Jesus, Lamb of God and King of kings, You are the one who conquers. Thank You for defeating every beast, for overcoming every empire, and for establishing a kingdom that will never end. When we're tempted to fear the beast, remind us that its hour is short. When we're pressured to compromise, give us the strength to hold fast. And when the beast finally falls — as it always does — let us stand with You, the saints of the Most High, reigning in Your everlasting kingdom. Amen.

Day 84 – A New Heaven and a New Earth

Scripture Reading: Isaiah 65:17–25; Isaiah 11:1–10; Revelation 21:1–5

Heart of Victory: Isaiah promised a new creation; Revelation reveals it fulfilled—the same God, faithful from beginning to end.

Isaiah saw it coming. Centuries before John received his vision on Patmos, Isaiah stood among a broken people and spoke words that sounded impossible. "For I am about to create new heavens and a new earth; the past events will not be remembered or come to mind. Then be glad and rejoice forever in what I am creating" (Isaiah 65:17-18). The old order of sin, death, and suffering would pass away. Something entirely new was coming, and when it arrived, the former things — the pain, the grief, the brokenness — would be forgotten.

Isaiah described a world transformed. "No infant will die prematurely, and no old person will not live a full life" (Isaiah 65:20). Death loses its grip. "They will build houses and live in them; they will plant vineyards and eat their fruit" (Isaiah 65:21). Work becomes meaningful, not futile. "The wolf and the lamb will feed together, and the lion will eat straw like cattle, but the serpent's food will be dust!" (Isaiah 65:25). Even the animal kingdom is at peace, and the serpent — the ancient enemy — is defeated.

This wasn't just poetry. This was prophecy. God was making a promise: the curse will be lifted. Creation will be renewed. And peace will reign.

Isaiah saw it again in another vision. "A shoot will grow from the stump of Jesse, and a branch from his roots will bear fruit" (Isaiah 11:1). From the line of David, a King would come and under His reign, "the wolf will dwell with the lamb, and the leopard will lie down with the goat. The calf, the young lion, and the fattened calf will be together, and a child will lead them" (Isaiah 11:6). This is Eden restored. This is creation as it was meant to be. "They will not harm or destroy each other on my entire holy mountain, for the land will be as full of the knowledge of the LORD as the sea is filled with water" (Isaiah 11:9).

For generations, God's people held onto these promises. When empires crushed them and exile scattered them, when suffering overwhelmed them — they remembered Isaiah's words. One day, God would make all things new. One day, the wolf would lie down with the lamb. One day, death would be no more.

And then John sees it. "Then I saw a new heaven and a new earth; for the first heaven and the first earth had passed away, and the sea was no more" (Revelation 21:1). This is Isaiah's vision fulfilled. Not spiritualized. Not metaphorical. Real. The old order is gone. The curse is lifted. And God is making all things new.

"Look, God's dwelling is with humanity, and he will live with them. They will be his peoples, and God himself will be with them and will be their God. He will wipe away every tear from their eyes. Death will be no more; grief, crying, and pain will be no more, because the previous things have passed away" (Revelation 21:3-4).

Every tear wiped away. No more death. No more grief. Isaiah promised it. John sees it. And the One on the throne declares it: "Look, I am making everything new" (Revelation 21:5). Not patching. Not merely renovating. Making new — transformed and renewed from the throne down. Everything.

This is what the whole Bible has been building toward. From Genesis 3, when sin entered the world and the curse fell, God has been working toward this moment. The sacrifices pointed to it (Hebrews 10:1). The prophets spoke of it. Jesus accomplished it on the cross. And now, in Revelation, we see it completed. The new heaven and the new earth. The dwelling of God with humanity. The end of death. The beginning of eternal life.

And here's the stunning continuity: it's the same God. The God who spoke through Isaiah is the God who speaks through John. The God who promised a shoot from Jesse's stump is the God who sent the Lamb. The God who said "I am about to create new heavens and a new earth" is the God who says "I am making everything new." He hasn't changed His mind. He hasn't altered the plan. He's been faithful, from beginning to end.

For those of us who live between Isaiah's promise and its fulfillment, this is everything. We're not waiting for a new plan. We're waiting for the completion of the plan God announced from the beginning. The new creation is coming. Death is being undone. And one day — closer than it's ever been — we'll stand in that city, with no more tears, no more pain, no more death. And we'll look back on all the suffering, all the grief, all the brokenness, and we'll know: it was worth it. Because God kept His promise. He made all things new.

Isaiah saw it dimly. John saw it clearly. And we? We're living in the in-between, holding onto the promise, waiting for the day when the dwelling of God is with humanity, and He wipes away every tear.

Prayer:

Father, You are making all things new. Thank You for the promise You gave through Isaiah, for the vision You gave to John, and for the certainty that You will complete what You've begun. We long for the new heaven and the new earth. We're tired of death, of grief, and of pain. We want the wolf to lie down with the lamb. We want to see Your face and to dwell with You forever. Hasten that day, Lord. Wipe away every tear. Make all things new. Amen.

Conclusion: Living the Heart of Victory

We've reached the end.

For twelve weeks — 84 Days — we've walked through the book of Revelation together. We've seen the glorious Christ among His churches. We've stood in the throne room and heard the endless praise. We've watched the seals break open, the trumpets sound, and the bowls pour out. We've witnessed the dragon's fury, the beast's blasphemy, and Babylon's fall. And we've seen it all end the way it always had to end: with the marriage supper of the Lamb, the new heaven and the new earth, and the promise that He is coming soon.

If you're still standing — if you made it all the way through — that is no small thing. You've done something a lot of people are intimidated to do. You've read the book of Revelation. Not just skimmed it. Not just cherry-picked the comforting parts. You've read it, wrestled with it, and (I hope) let it read you. You finished something hard. You stayed faithful. You endured. Sound familiar? That's exactly what Revelation calls us to do.

And now the question is: what do we do with what we've seen?

The Heart of Victory

From the very first Day, we've been talking about "the heart of victory." That phrase has shown up at the beginning of every single Day — a one-sentence distillation of what each passage reveals about Christ's victory and what that means for us. But now, at the end of this journey, I want to ask you to think about "the heart of victory" not as a concept to understand, but as a posture to live.

What does it look like to live with the heart of victory? It looks like worship. It looks like witness. It looks like endurance. And it looks like hope.

Let me say a word about each of these.

Worship. The book of Revelation is, before anything else, a call to worship. The throne room scenes aren't just poetic interludes. They're the interpretive key to everything else. When John wants to help the churches understand suffering, he takes them to the throne room. When he wants to help them understand judgment, he takes them to the throne room. Why? Because worship reorients everything. When you see God on His throne — sovereign, holy, glorious — and when you see the Lamb who was slain now standing at the center of all power and praise, you can't help but fall on your face. And when you stand back up, the world looks different. The threats look smaller and the suffering looks bearable. The promises look certain.

Living with the heart of victory means making worship central to your life. It means letting the reality of God's throne reshape how you see everything else. It means joining your voice to the song that's already being sung in heaven, "Worthy is the Lamb who was slain, to receive power and wealth and wisdom and might and honor and glory and blessing" (Revelation 5:12, ESV). You don't wait until everything is fixed to worship. You worship now, in the mess, in the middle of the fight, because worship is what declares where your hope truly lies.

Witness. Revelation was written to encourage the church's faithful witness in a hostile world. The martyrs under the altar, the two witnesses in sackcloth, the saints who overcame by the blood of the Lamb and the word of their testimony — these are the heroes of Revelation. Not the powerful. Not the comfortable. The faithful witnesses.

Living with the heart of victory means refusing to be silent about Jesus. It means bearing witness to who He is, what He's done, and what He's promised, even when that witness is costly. Even when people mock you. Even when it costs you opportunities, relationships, or safety. The beast demands allegiance. Babylon seduces with comfort. And the call of Revelation is clear: don't give in. Hold fast. Keep testifying. The outcome is never in doubt. Jesus wins. And everyone who belongs to Him shares in His victory.

This doesn't mean being obnoxious or unnecessarily provocative. But it does mean living openly as a follower of the Lamb in a world that worships the beast. It means letting your life — and your words — point people to Jesus.

Endurance. If there's one theme that shows up more than any other in Revelation, it's endurance. "Here is a call for the endurance of the saints," John says (Revelation 14:12 ESV). Not success. Not comfort. Endurance. The ability to keep going when everything in you wants to quit.

The heart of victory isn't triumphalism. It's not pretending that following Jesus is easy or that faithfulness guarantees earthly prosperity. The heart of victory is knowing that the final chapter has already been written and that you're going to make it to the end — not because you're strong, but because the One who holds you is stronger than anything that comes against you.

Living with the heart of victory means staying faithful when it's hard. When your prayers feel unanswered. When the wicked seem to prosper. When you're tired of being the odd one out. When suffering drags on longer than you thought you could bear. You endure. Not because you're a hero, but because you know the end of the story. Christ is coming. Every tear will be wiped away. Every wrong will be made right. And you will stand before His throne, clothed in white, with His name on your forehead, reigning with Him forever.

Hope. And that brings us to hope. Not wishful thinking. Not optimism. Hope — the confident expectation that what God has promised, He will do.

Revelation ends with an invitation and a prayer. "The Spirit and the Bride say, 'Come.' And let the one who hears say, 'Come'" (Revelation 22:17 ESV). And then, a few verses later, Jesus says, "Surely I am coming soon," and John responds, "Amen. Come, Lord Jesus!" (22:20 ESV).

That's the heartbeat of the Christian life. Come, Lord Jesus. Not someday. Not eventually. Soon. We're not trying to make ourselves comfortable in this world as though it's our permanent home. We're strangers and exiles, longing for the city that is to come. We're watching for the Bridegroom. We're keeping our lamps burning. We're ready.

Living with the heart of victory means orienting your entire life around the certainty of Christ's return. It means making decisions — about work, money, relationships, time — in light of the fact that He's coming back. It means praying every day, "Come, Lord Jesus." And meaning it.

Go Back and Read It Again

Here's my challenge to you: don't let this be the last time you read Revelation.

Now that you've been through it once, go back and read it again. But this time, read it on your own. Read it slowly, prayerfully, with confidence instead of confusion. Watch for the patterns we've talked about. Notice the echoes of the Old Testament. Pay attention to where the text takes you back to the throne room, over and over again. Let the repetition sink in. Let the vision of Jesus saturate your imagination. And let Revelation's vision of Christ's present victory continue to reorient how you face Monday mornings, difficult relationships, and an uncertain world. We're not decoding prophecy; we're living in victory.

You'll see things you missed the first time. That's how Scripture works. The more you read it, the more it opens up. Revelation is a book you can spend your whole life with and never exhaust.

And as you read, ask the Spirit to help you see Jesus. That's the whole point. This book exists to unveil Him — His glory, His authority, His love, His victory. Every beast, every bowl, every battle — it all exists to magnify the Lamb. So keep looking at Him. Keep marveling at Him. Keep falling in love with Him.

Hold Fast

There's a phrase that shows up repeatedly in the letters to the seven churches: "Hold fast." Hold fast to what you have. Hold fast until I come. Don't let go.

That's the word for us as we close this book. Hold fast.

Hold fast to Jesus. Don't be seduced by Babylon's wealth or comfort. Don't be intimidated by the beast's threats. Don't compromise or grow weary. Don't let your love grow cold. Hold fast to the One who loved you and gave Himself for you.

Hold fast to the gospel. The message that saves you is the same message that sustains you. Christ died for sinners. He rose from the dead. He reigns at the Father's right hand. He's coming back. That's the good news and the foundation. That's what you build your life on, and that's what you cling to when everything else is shaking.

Hold fast to hope. Not naive hope that pretends suffering isn't real. Not false hope that puts its confidence in politics or progress. But true hope — the kind of hope that looks at the chaos of the world and the pain of your own life and says, "Even so, come, Lord Jesus." The kind of hope that believes God's promises even when they seem impossible. The kind of hope that sees the end from the beginning and knows that every tear will be wiped away, every wrong will be made right, and every child of God will stand before His throne in joy.

The Certainty of His Coming

Jesus is coming back.

That's a promise. And it's the promise that holds everything else together.

He's coming back to judge the living and the dead. He's coming back to destroy the beast, burn up Babylon, and throw the devil into the lake of fire. He's coming back to wipe away every tear, to make all things new, and to dwell with His people forever in a world where there's no more death, no more mourning, no more crying, no more pain.

And when He comes, we will see His face.

That's the promise that makes everything else worth it. Not just that we'll be safe or that we'll be happy — but that we'll see Him. We'll see the One we've loved, the One we've worshiped, the One we've longed for. We'll see Him face to face, and we'll be with Him forever.

So live like someone who knows the end of the story. Live like someone whose hope is fixed on what's coming, not on what's passing away. Live like someone who's watching for the Bridegroom, who's listening for the trumpet, who's ready.

Come, Lord Jesus

I want to leave you with one more challenge. Make the prayer of Revelation 22:20 your daily prayer. Every morning when you wake up, every night before you sleep, and as many times in between as you can remember — pray it.

"Come, Lord Jesus."

Three words. But they carry the weight of everything we've seen in Revelation. They're a prayer of longing and hope. A prayer of surrender.

A prayer that says, "Your kingdom come. Your will be done. On earth as it is in heaven."

"Come, Lord Jesus."

Say it when the world feels overwhelming. Say it when suffering feels unbearable. Say it when you're tempted to give up, to compromise, to settle for something less than what He's promised. Say it when you're confused, when you're scared, when you don't know what else to pray. Say it when you're full of joy, when you're overwhelmed with gratitude, when you catch a glimpse of His glory and it takes your breath away.

"Come, Lord Jesus."

That's the prayer of the church — the prayer of the Bride. That's the prayer of everyone who's been through Revelation and seen what's coming and can't wait for it to arrive.

And one day — sooner than we think — He will answer that prayer.

He will come. The sky will split open. The trumpet will sound. And every eye will see Him (Revelation 1:7). The King who was slain. The Lamb who conquered. The One who is and who was and who is to come.

And we will be with Him forever.

That's the end of the story. That's the victory. And that's the hope that changes everything.

Until that day, hold fast. Keep worshiping. Keep witnessing. Keep enduring. Keep hoping. And keep praying, "Come, Lord Jesus."

The grace of the Lord Jesus be with you. Amen.

Carl Copsey
DeRidder, LA

DIGGING DEEPER

If you're the kind of reader who finishes a book and immediately wants to know more, these pages are for you. I've included the historical background behind this book's interpretive approach, a chapter to how Revelation uses symbols, a glossary for quick reference, and a reading list for wherever your interest takes you next. None of this is required reading — but all of it is here because I wish someone had handed it to me when I first started studying Revelation.

I'd strongly encourage you to read at least the first two.

Standing on Old Ground traces how Christians have read Revelation across two thousand years — and shows that the approach you've just experienced isn't new at all. If anything in this book felt unfamiliar compared to what you grew up hearing, this chapter explains why and puts it in its proper historical context.

Signified starts with a single Greek word in Revelation 1:1 that most English translations obscure — and shows why that one word changes how you read the entire book. If you walk away with nothing else from these pages, understanding what John means by "signified" may transform how you approach Revelation for the rest of your life.

DIGGING DEEPER: Standing on Old Ground

How Christians have read Revelation across two millennia — and why this approach, though it may feel unfamiliar, is actually very old

If you've spent much time in evangelical churches over the last century, there's a good chance the interpretive approach in *The Heart of Victory* feels unfamiliar. Maybe even surprising. You might have grown up hearing about the rapture, the seven-year tribulation, the Antichrist rising in the end times, and a literal thousand-year reign of Christ on earth after His return.

Those ideas didn't appear in this book. Not because I'm unaware of them or trying to hide something, but because I don't believe that's what Revelation teaches. Instead, this book has read Revelation symbolically, emphasizing Christ's present reign, the Church's calling to faithful witness, and the certain hope of His return to make all things new.

And if that approach felt different to you, I want you to know something important: **the way we've read Revelation in this book isn't new.** In fact, it's very, very old.

For most of Christian history — across roughly eighteen of the last twenty centuries, by most estimates — the dominant streams of the Church have read Revelation much the way we've read it here. Not as a detailed prediction of future events in a specific chronological sequence, but as a symbolic unveiling of Christ's victory, the cosmic conflict between the Lamb and the dragon, and the ultimate triumph of God's kingdom.

This chapter isn't an attack on other views. Good, faithful Christians disagree about how to interpret Revelation, and I respect that. But I want you to understand that if this book's approach felt unfamiliar, it's not because it's a novel interpretation. It's because much of contemporary evangelicalism has, in the last 150 years, shifted toward a different way of reading Revelation — one that, historically speaking, is actually the newcomer.

So let's talk about history. Not to win an argument, but to help you see that when you read Revelation the way *The Heart of Victory* has guided you, you're reading with the majority voice of the historic Christian church.

The First Three Centuries: Revelation as Pastoral Encouragement

When the Apostle John wrote Revelation in the late first century (probably around AD 95), the Church was under pressure. Some faced outright persecution. Others confronted the seductive pull of emperor worship, economic pressure to compromise, and the constant temptation to blend Christianity with the surrounding pagan culture.

Revelation wasn't written to satisfy curiosity about the distant future. It was written to strengthen Christians facing immediate trials. The question wasn't "What will happen in 2,000 years?" but "How do we stay faithful right now when Rome demands our worship and threatens our livelihoods?"

The Church Fathers Read It Symbolically

When the early Church fathers — the Christian leaders and theologians in the centuries immediately following the apostles — wrote about Revelation, they read it as symbolic encouragement for the Church in every age. They debated some details (particularly whether the thousand years was present or future), but they shared a common approach: symbolic interpretation, Christ-centered focus, and pastoral application.

Irenaeus of Lyons, writing in the late second century, believed in a future resurrection and a literal thousand-year reign of Christ on earth (what we now call historic premillennialism). But he read Revelation's beasts, symbols, and imagery as representing spiritual realities and patterns of opposition to God. He didn't treat Revelation as a chronological timeline of future political events. His focus was on Christ's victory and the Church's triumph through suffering.

Origen of Alexandria, a generation later, read Revelation spiritually, understanding its symbols as revealing timeless truths about the cosmic battle between good and evil, Christ's victory, and the Church's calling to faithful witness. He explicitly rejected overly literal interpretations of Revelation's imagery.

Victorinus of Pettau, who wrote the earliest surviving commentary on Revelation and was martyred around 304, recognized that the book recapitulates — it goes over the same ground from different angles rather than presenting a strict chronological sequence. He saw the seven seals, seven trumpets, and seven bowls not as consecutive events but as overlapping visions of the same realities.

The pattern in these early centuries was clear: **Revelation was read as symbolic, pastoral, and applicable to the Church's present experience.** Whether they believed the thousand years was happening now or would happen in the future, they agreed that the beasts represented recurring patterns of opposition to God, that the woman clothed with the sun represented the Church or God's people, and that the message was victory through faithful witness — not escape through a secret rapture or a detailed calendar of future political developments.

Augustine and the Patristic Consensus

The most influential voice in shaping how the Western Church would read Revelation for the next 1,500 years was Augustine of Hippo, writing in the early fifth century.

In his massive work *The City of God*, Augustine laid out a way of reading Revelation that would become the dominant interpretation throughout the medieval period and into the Reformation. He taught that the thousand years in Revelation 20 represents the present church age, from Christ's first coming to His second coming. Satan is bound in the sense that his power is limited — he cannot prevent the gospel from spreading to the nations. The first resurrection is spiritual — coming to life in Christ through faith. Christ reigns now from heaven, and believers reign with Him through their union with Him. And the "last days" began with Christ's first coming and continue until His return.

This wasn't Augustine inventing something new. He was systematizing and defending what had become the broad consensus of the Church. And his influence was enormous. For over a millennium, when Christians read Revelation, they read it through an Augustinian lens.

What This Meant Practically

When medieval Christians read about the dragon pursuing the woman, they understood it as the ongoing reality of spiritual warfare — Satan's attempts to destroy the Church through persecution and deception in every generation.

When they read about Babylon the great, they saw it as a symbol of worldly systems opposed to God — whether Rome in the first century, or the seductions of wealth and power in their own time.

When they read about the New Jerusalem descending, they understood it as the future hope of the Church — God's people renewed and dwelling with Him forever in the new creation.

Revelation wasn't a puzzle about distant future events. It was a pastoral letter about present realities and certain hope.

The Reformation: Continuity with the Past

When the Protestant Reformation exploded across Europe in the 16th century, the Reformers challenged many aspects of medieval theology and practice. But on the question of how to read Revelation, there was remarkable continuity with Augustine and the patristic consensus.

Martin Luther, while initially skeptical of Revelation's apostolic authorship (a question eventually resolved in its favor), read the book symbolically when he did engage it. He saw the beast as representing the papacy and false religious systems, but he didn't develop a futurist timeline of end-times events.

John Calvin wrote commentaries on nearly every book of the New Testament — except Revelation. Not because he rejected it — scholars have debated the exact reason — but likely because he found it difficult and was wary of adding to the speculative interpretations already in circulation. It's also worth noting that Calvin died at fifty-four after years of serious illness; it's entirely possible he simply never got to it. His broader theological framework, however, supported the Augustinian reading: Christ reigns now, the Church endures through suffering, and believers await His return to consummate all things.

The major Reformed and Presbyterian confessions from this period — documents like the Westminster Confession of Faith (1646) — affirmed that Christ ascended to heaven and now reigns, that the kingdom of God is present through the Church, and that believers await His glorious return. This is fundamentally the same framework Augustine articulated.

The Reformers read Revelation as the early Church had — symbolically, focusing on Christ's victory and the Church's calling, not as a detailed prophetic calendar of future events.

The Puritan Era and Beyond: Holding the Line

The Puritans — those rigorous, Bible-saturated English Reformed Christians of the 17th century — continued reading Revelation symbolically and Christocentrically, though many developed a more optimistic view of history than Augustine had.

John Owen, one of the greatest Puritan theologians, wrote extensively about Christ's heavenly priesthood and present reign — truths that Revelation's throne-room visions illuminate and that Owen's theology assumed and reinforced. He understood Revelation as revealing Christ's current authority and the Church's security in Him.

Matthew Henry, whose commentary on the whole Bible became a standard reference for generations of pastors, read Revelation as a symbolic unveiling of the conflict between Christ and Satan, the Church and the world, with assured victory for God's people.

Many Puritans embraced postmillennialism — the belief that the gospel would increasingly triumph in history, that the Church would experience significant victory before Christ's return, and that the "thousand years" represented a future golden age of gospel success on earth. This was different from Augustine's amillennialism, which saw the thousand years as the entire church age from Christ's first to second coming. But what the Puritans shared with Augustine — and what matters for our purposes — was the symbolic reading of Revelation, the emphasis on Christ's present reign, and the rejection of speculative futurism.

The pattern held for centuries. From the Church fathers through Augustine, from the medieval period through the Reformation, from the Puritans into the 18th century, Christians debated whether they were amillennial, premillennial (not to be confused with dispensational premillennialism), or postmillennial — but they shared a common approach: reading Revelation symbolically, emphasizing Christ's victory, and applying its message to the Church's present calling, not treating it as a detailed prediction of future events in chronological sequence.

This wasn't perfect unanimity on every detail. But the broad interpretive framework remained remarkably stable.

The 19th Century: A New Approach Emerges

Something shifted in the 19th century, particularly in Britain and America. A new way of reading biblical prophecy began to gain traction, and it would eventually reshape how millions of evangelical Christians understood not just Revelation but the entire Bible's teaching on the end times.

This approach is called dispensationalism, and it's probably the view you've been most exposed to if you grew up in evangelical churches in the 20th or early 21st century.

But before we talk about dispensationalism, we need to make an important distinction. Some Christians throughout history — including some early Church fathers like Irenaeus — have believed in a future, literal thousand-year reign of Christ on earth. This view is called historic premillennialism, and it's not the same thing as dispensational premillennialism.

What's the Difference? Historic premillennialism teaches that Christ will return before the millennium, and there will be a future, literal thousand-year reign. But — and this is crucial — it reads Revelation's imagery symbolically, emphasizes Christ's present reign from heaven, sees one people of God across both testaments, doesn't separate Israel and the Church into different destinies, and doesn't teach a pre-tribulation rapture. In other words, historic premillennialists read Revelation much the way Augustine and the Reformers did, even though they disagree about the timing of the millennium.

Dispensational premillennialism, which emerged in the 1800s, introduces a significantly different set of assumptions. It adds a secret rapture before a seven-year tribulation, a strict separation between Israel and the Church as two peoples with different plans, a reading of Revelation 4–22 as entirely future events, a division of history into distinct "dispensations" with different ways God relates to humanity, and a much more literalistic reading of prophetic symbols.

The key difference isn't about *when* the millennium happens. It's about *how you read Revelation*. Historic premillennialists read symbolically and Christocentrically, like Augustine and the Reformers did. Dispensationalists read futuristically and literalistically in a way that's genuinely new.

The Heart of Victory doesn't take a position on whether you should be amillennial (like Augustine), postmillennial (like many Puritans), or historic premillennial (like Irenaeus). What it rejects is the dispensational approach that emerged in the 19th century. And it's that approach we need to understand.

The Origins of Dispensationalism

John Nelson Darby, a former Anglican priest who joined the Plymouth Brethren movement in the early 1800s, developed the system that would become dispensationalism. His key innovations included dividing history into distinct "dispensations" (ages in which God relates to humanity differently), separating Israel and the Church as two distinct peoples with two different destinies, the "secret rapture" — believers being caught up to heaven before a seven-year tribulation — a literal, future thousand-year reign of Christ on earth after His return, and reading Revelation 4–22 as future events that haven't happened yet.

Darby traveled extensively, teaching his system throughout Britain and America. But it was the Scofield Reference Bible in 1909 that really spread dispensational teaching to the masses. C.I. Scofield's study notes, printed right alongside the biblical text, taught millions of Christians that dispensationalism was simply "what the Bible teaches."

Why It Spread

Dispensationalism offered something appealing to many Christians, especially in America. It provided confidence about the future in uncertain times, a detailed "plan" that made prophecy seem clear and understandable, hope of escape from suffering through the pre-tribulation rapture, and a "literal" reading that felt more straightforward than symbolic interpretation. It also fit well with certain American cultural values: individualism, a sense of being in the "last generation," and a fascination with trying to match current events to biblical prophecy.

The 20th century saw explosive growth in dispensational teaching through Bible prophecy conferences, the Scofield Bible's enormous influence, popular books like Hal Lindsey's *The Late Great Planet Earth* (1970), and eventually the *Left Behind* series by Tim LaHaye and Jerry Jenkins (1995–2007), which sold over 60 million copies.

For many contemporary evangelicals, dispensationalism is the only interpretive framework they've ever encountered. If you've heard terms like "the rapture," "the tribulation," "the Antichrist," and "the millennial kingdom" your whole Christian life, you were probably being taught dispensational theology — even if no one ever used that label.

Understanding the Shift

Here's what's crucial to understand: **dispensationalism is roughly 175 years old.** That doesn't automatically make it wrong (the Reformation itself recovered biblical truths that had been obscured). But it does mean that when you encounter a different approach — like the one in *The Heart of Victory* — you're not encountering innovation. You're encountering how Christians read Revelation for the vast majority of church history.

The approach this book takes isn't a 21st-century invention. It's the continuation of an 1,800-year tradition.

Why It Matters

You might be wondering: "Why does this history lesson matter? Can't good Christians disagree about Revelation's interpretation?"

Absolutely, yes. And they do. I have friends and brothers in Christ who hold dispensational views, and I respect them deeply. This isn't about declaring one view "Christian" and another view "heretical." Both perspectives exist within evangelical Christianity.

And to be clear: **this book does take the position on the millennium being present (amillennialism), not future (historic premillennialism or postmillennialism).** Good, faithful Christians who read Revelation symbolically and Christocentrically have held different views on that question throughout church history.

What *The Heart of Victory* rejects is the dispensational framework that emerged in the 19th century — the sharp separation between Israel and the Church, the pre-tribulation rapture, the reading of Revelation 4–22 as entirely future events, and the attempt to map prophetic symbols onto contemporary political developments.

But the history matters, and here's why.

It provides perspective. If the interpretive approach in this book felt strange to you, now you know why — and you know it's not because it's novel. For most of church history, Christians have read Revelation much the way we've read it here. Understanding that can give you confidence that this approach isn't fringe or unorthodox. It's actually the historic mainstream.

It frees you from timeline anxiety. Dispensationalism tends to generate a lot of anxiety about "are we in the last days?" and attempts to match current events to prophetic timelines. Every generation of dispensationalists has been convinced they were living in the final generation before Christ's return — and every generation has been wrong. The historic Christian reading frees you from that. It says: **we've**

been in the "last days" since Christ's first coming. He could return today, or He might tarry another thousand years. Either way, our calling is the same: faithful witness, patient endurance, confident hope. We're not decoding prophecy; we're living in victory.

It centers you on Christ. The historic approach keeps Revelation's focus where John put it: **on the Lamb who was slain and now reigns.** It's not primarily about identifying the Antichrist or calculating tribulation timelines. It's about seeing Jesus clearly — His authority, His love, His justice, His certain triumph — and letting that vision transform how you live.

It connects you to the Church. When you read Revelation the way this book has guided you, you're reading with Augustine, with the Reformers, with the Puritans, and with the majority of Christians across two millennia. There's something deeply encouraging about that. You're not alone in this interpretation. You're part of a long tradition of faithful believers who have found comfort, strength, and hope in Revelation's message.

A Word About Humility

I want to be clear about something: **I could be wrong about some of this.** Faithful Christians have disagreed about Revelation's interpretation for centuries, and they'll continue to disagree until Christ returns and we see clearly what we now see only dimly.

I'm not asking you to close your mind to other views or to treat this book's interpretation as the only legitimate option. I *am* asking you to recognize that what you've encountered here isn't a fringe position. It's rooted in the soil of historic Christianity.

If you've been taught dispensational theology your whole life and this book challenged that, I hope you'll wrestle with these questions thoughtfully, prayerfully, and with humility. Read widely. Study

Scripture carefully. Consult church history. And ultimately, land where your conscience, informed by God's word, leads you.

But don't dismiss the historic Christian reading of Revelation simply because it's unfamiliar to you. That unfamiliarity might say more about contemporary evangelical culture than about the legitimacy of the interpretation.

Reading with the Church

There's a phrase from the early Church fathers: 'the rule of faith' (regula fidei). Originally it referred to the apostolic teaching passed down as the interpretive guide to Scripture — what we now summarize in the great creeds (the Apostles' Creed and the Nicene Creed). At its heart, it points to the core beliefs that have united Christians across time and space.

When it comes to Revelation's details, Christians have always had some freedom to disagree. But the core message has remained constant: Jesus Christ is Lord, and He reigns now from heaven's throne. The Church is called to faithful witness through suffering and opposition. Victory is certain — the Lamb has overcome, and His people share in His triumph. And Christ will return to judge the living and the dead, raise His people to resurrection life, and dwell with them in the new creation forever.

These truths have united Christians for 2,000 years. The details of *how* and *when* these things unfold have been debated, but the *what* and *who* have remained clear.

When you read Revelation with that core message in focus — Christ's victory, your calling to faithfulness, the certainty of His return — you're reading with the historic Church. And that's exactly what *The Heart of Victory* has aimed to help you do.

Closing Thoughts

If this appendix has been helpful, I encourage you to dig deeper. Read some of the early Church fathers on Revelation — Victorinus, for instance, or selections from Augustine's *City of God*. Read the Reformers. Study church history. You'll find Christians who were amillennial, postmillennial, and historic premillennial — all reading Revelation symbolically and Christocentrically.

You'll find that what seemed "new" in this book is actually very old. And you'll discover that when you read Revelation as a symbolic unveiling of Christ's present reign and certain triumph, you're not reading against the Church's tradition — you're reading *with* it.

> **A Note on Millennial Views:** The approach in *The Heart of Victory* — symbolic interpretation, recapitulation, Christ-centered focus, emphasis on present reign and future hope — is compatible with different views on the timing of the millennium. Whether you land on amillennialism (like Augustine), postmillennialism (like many Puritans), or historic premillennialism (like Irenaeus), you're standing on old ground as long as you're reading Revelation symbolically and rejecting the dispensational approach that emerged in the 19th century. The debates between these three views are legitimate theological discussions within the historic Christian framework. What matters most is reading with the Church's wisdom rather than with contemporary speculation.

The heart of Revelation is victory. That's what the Church has believed and proclaimed for two millennia. And that's the message we desperately need to hear today.

The Lamb reigns. The kingdom is His. And those who belong to Him will share in His eternal triumph.

That truth doesn't change, no matter how we debate the details.

The goal isn't to "win" an interpretive debate. It's to read Revelation faithfully, worship Christ rightly, and live with confident hope. If this book has helped you do that, its purpose is fulfilled — regardless of what label you put on your eschatology.

Grace and peace to you in Christ, the King who reigns and is coming soon.

DIGGING DEEPER: Signified

How John tells us to read Revelation — right from the very first verse

"The revelation of Jesus Christ, which God gave him to show to his servants the things that must soon take place. He made it known by sending his angel to his servant John." — Revelation 1:1 (ESV)

"The revelation of Jesus Christ that God gave him to show his servants what must soon take place. He made it known by signifying it through his angel to his servant John." — Revelation 1:1 (literal translation, emphasis added)

The Word We Miss

Most English translations of Revelation 1:1 use phrases like "made it known" or "communicated" to translate the Greek word John uses to describe how this revelation came to him. And those translations aren't wrong — they capture part of what the word means.

But they miss something crucial.

The Greek word is esēmanen, from the verb sēmainō. While the word can mean 'to make known' in a general sense — which is why most translations render it that way — its more precise and distinctive meaning is 'to signify': to communicate through signs, to indicate by symbols, to reveal truth through figurative representation.

John is telling us something essential about Revelation in the very first verse: **this book came to him in signs and symbols.**

Not literal descriptions of future events. Not straightforward predictions we can decode like a news report. But **signified** — communicated through symbolic visions that require interpretation, that draw on Old Testament imagery, that reveal spiritual truth through carefully chosen signs.

If you miss that word in verse 1, you'll misread the entire book.

What "Signify" Means in Scripture

The word *sēmainō* appears elsewhere in the New Testament, and every time it carries this sense of communicating through symbolic indication rather than plain, literal statement. Let me show you.

In John 12:33, after Jesus says, "When I am lifted up from the earth, I will draw all people to myself," John adds this explanatory note: *"He said this to show (sēmainō) by what kind of death he was going to die."* Jesus didn't say plainly, "I will be crucified." He said, "I will be lifted up." That's symbolic language — *signified* truth. John has to explain what the sign means: Jesus was indicating His death by crucifixion.

The same thing happens in John 21:19. After Jesus tells Peter, "When you are old, you will stretch out your hands, and another will dress you and carry you where you do not want to go," John explains: *"This he said to show (sēmainō) by what kind of death he was to glorify God."* Again, Jesus didn't say literally, "Peter, you will be crucified." He spoke in symbolic terms — stretching out hands, being carried where you don't want to go. John tells us Jesus was *signifying* the kind of death Peter would die.

In Acts 11:28, the prophet Agabus *"stood up and foretold (sēmainō) by the Spirit that there would be a great famine over all the world. (ESV)"* Prophetic communication through the Spirit, indicating future events — this is the realm where *sēmainō* operates.

Even in a mundane context in Acts 25:27, the word appears when Paul says it seems unreasonable to send a prisoner without *"indicating (sēmainō) the charges against him."*

Here's the pattern: *sēmainō* means to communicate truth through signs, symbols, indications — not always through direct, literal statement. It's the language of symbolic communication, prophetic vision, and figurative representation.

And that's exactly the word John uses in Revelation 1:1 to describe how this entire book came to him.

What This Tells Us About Reading Revelation

When John says God "signified" this revelation to him, he's giving us a massive interpretive key right at the start. And it changes everything about how we approach the book.

First, expect symbolic language. If the book was *signified*, then we should expect symbols. We should expect visions that communicate truth through carefully chosen imagery rather than literal descriptions. When John sees a beast with seven heads and ten horns (Revelation 13:1), he's not describing a literal biological creature. He's seeing a *sign* — a symbolic representation of earthly power that opposes God. The heads and horns signify authority and strength, and the imagery is drawn from Daniel's visions (Daniel 7), connecting Revelation to the Old Testament prophetic tradition of symbolic communication. When John sees a woman clothed with the sun, with the moon under her feet and a crown of twelve stars on her head (Revelation 12:1), he's not seeing a literal astronomical phenomenon. He's seeing a *sign* (the text explicitly calls her "a great sign" in 12:1) — symbolic imagery representing God's people, drawing on Old Testament pictures of Israel as a woman and the twelve tribes. The book was signified. Therefore, read it symbolically.

Second, don't impose literalism where God gave symbolic signs. One of the most common mistakes in reading Revelation is trying to interpret literally what God communicated symbolically. People try to identify the beast with a specific modern political figure. They calculate the number 666 as if it's a literal code pointing to someone's name. They treat the locust-scorpion creatures in Revelation 9 as descriptions of modern military technology. But that's not how *signified* revelation works. When God communicates through signs, we need to interpret the signs — not decode them as if they're literal descriptions in disguise. The number 666 isn't a puzzle to solve by adding up letters in someone's name. It's a symbolic number — six being the number of humanity, falling short of the divine seven — indicating incompleteness, failure, and the beast's ultimate inadequacy before a holy God. It *signifies* humanity's rebellion and the beast's ultimate inadequacy. The locusts in Revelation 9 aren't helicopters or missiles. They're symbolic creatures — signs drawn from Joel's locust plague (Joel 1–2), representing demonic torment and spiritual warfare. God gave this book in symbols. To read it rightly, we must interpret the symbols, not literalize them.

Third, look to the Old Testament for the symbol key. Because Revelation was *signified* — communicated through symbolic signs — we need to understand where those signs come from. And overwhelmingly, they come from the Old Testament. Revelation is saturated with Old Testament imagery. Scholars have identified somewhere between 400 and 700 allusions to the Old Testament in Revelation's 404 verses — G.K. Beale, whose commentary on Revelation is the most comprehensive on this question, places the number at the higher end. That's not coincidental. John is drawing on a rich symbolic vocabulary that God's people already knew. The seven lampstands echo the menorah in the tabernacle, representing God's people as light-bearers. The sealed scroll draws on Ezekiel 2–3 and Daniel 12, representing God's sovereign plan. The four living creatures connect to Ezekiel 1, representing creation worshiping its Creator. The great prostitute draws on Isaiah's and Ezekiel's imagery for unfaithful Jerusalem, representing worldly seduction. The river of life and tree of life reach all the way back to Genesis 2 and forward through Ezekiel 47, representing restored Eden. John isn't inventing new symbols. He's using a symbolic language his first-century Jewish-Christian readers would have recognized immediately because they knew their Scriptures. The symbols in Revelation aren't arbitrary. They're drawn from God's previous revelation, particularly the Old Testament prophets who also received signified visions.

Fourth, recognize that symbols reveal truth, not timelines. When God signifies truth through symbols, the symbols reveal theological and spiritual realities — not necessarily chronological events. The vision of the woman and the dragon in Revelation 12 isn't predicting a specific future event that will happen at a particular moment in time. It's revealing a truth that spans the entire church age: Satan pursues God's people to destroy them, but God protects them, and Satan fails. That's been true since Christ's ascension. It's true now. It will be true until Christ returns. The *signified* vision reveals a **pattern**, not a **timetable**. The seven seals, seven trumpets, and seven bowls aren't three consecutive series of future judgments happening one after another in chronological sequence. They're three different *signs* — three symbolic ways of depicting the same reality from different perspectives: God's judgment on rebellion throughout the church age, culminating in Christ's return. Signified revelation reveals timeless truths, not timelines we can chart on a calendar.

Why This Matters

If John tells us right at the beginning that this book was *signified* — given to him in symbolic form — then any interpretive approach that insists on reading Revelation literally is fighting against the text itself.

Dispensationalism's insistence that we must read Revelation's symbols as literal descriptions of future political and military events isn't just a different interpretation. It's a refusal to read the book the way John tells us to read it.

When dispensationalists identify the beast with a specific modern world leader, they're treating as literal what God gave as symbol. When they interpret the locusts as literal military technology, they're imposing literalism on signified revelation. When they construct detailed timelines of future events based on Revelation's visions, they're using symbolic imagery in a way it was never intended to be used.

John tells us up front: this was signified. Read it accordingly.

The Irony of "Literal" Interpretation

Ironically, those who insist most loudly on a "literal" reading of Revelation often end up reading it in the most bizarre, convoluted ways imaginable.

A "literal" seven-headed beast becomes a metaphor for a political system or alliance. A "literal" 144,000 becomes symbolic of Jewish evangelists in the tribulation (even though the text says nothing about evangelism). A "literal" thousand years becomes a future earthly millennium (even though the text places it after the final battle).

The so-called "literal" method ends up being highly selective — literal when it supports the system, symbolic when literalism becomes impossible.

But if we start where John starts — recognizing that the book was *signified* — we can read the symbols as symbols, interpret them through their Old Testament background, and receive the truth they're meant to communicate. A seven-headed beast is a sign of beastly, blasphemous power that opposes God — a pattern that repeats throughout history. The 144,000 is a symbolic number (12 × 12 × 1,000) representing the complete people of God, sealed and secure. And the thousand years is a symbolic period representing Christ's reign from His ascension to His return.

Reading Revelation as signified revelation isn't less faithful to the text. It's more faithful — because it reads the book the way John tells us to read it.

Trust the Symbols

Here's the practical takeaway: **Don't try to decode Revelation. Learn to read its symbols.**

When you encounter a strange image — a beast, a number, a color, a creature — don't immediately ask, "What modern thing does this literally refer to?" Instead, ask: Where does this image come from in the Old Testament? What did this symbol mean in its original context? What truth is this sign revealing about God, Christ, the Church, or spiritual realities? How does this symbol function within Revelation's larger message?

When you read this way — respecting that the book was *signified* — Revelation stops being a confusing puzzle and starts becoming what it was always meant to be: a powerful revelation of Jesus Christ, His victory, and His certain triumph.

The symbols aren't obstacles to understanding. They're the means by which God chose to communicate deep spiritual truth in vivid, memorable ways.

Conclusion

The first verse of Revelation gives us the first and most important key to reading the entire book: **it was signified.**

God gave this revelation to Jesus Christ. Jesus made it known to John. And He did so by *signifying* it — communicating through signs, symbols, and figurative visions.

That's not a weakness of the book. It's a feature. Symbolic communication allows Revelation to speak to every generation of Christians facing opposition, temptation, and suffering. The symbols reveal truths that transcend any one historical moment while remaining powerfully applicable to all.

If you've been trying to read Revelation literally — matching its symbols to current events, calculating timelines, identifying modern figures — you've been working against John's own instructions. He tells you right at the start: this was signified.

Read it that way. Interpret the symbols through Scripture. Let the signs reveal the truth they were designed to communicate. And discover that when you stop trying to decode Revelation and start simply reading it as signified revelation, its message becomes clear:

Christ reigns. His people are secure. His victory is certain. And those who hold fast will share in His triumph when He returns to make all things new.

That's the heart of what was signified to John on Patmos. And it's the message we desperately need to hear today.

The book was signified. And the One who signified it is coming soon.

DIGGING DEEPER: Key Terms

The Heart of Victory: A Daily Journey Through the Book of Revelation

---

A

Abyss/Bottomless Pit — The place of confinement for evil spirits and Satan, symbolizing complete separation from God's presence and temporary restraint of evil (Revelation 9:1–2, 11; 20:1–3).

Alpha and Omega — The first and last letters of the Greek alphabet, used by Christ to declare His eternal nature as the beginning and end of all things (Revelation 1:8; 21:6; 22:13).

Angel — A heavenly messenger or servant of God. Revelation features many angels delivering messages, executing judgments, and leading worship before God's throne.

Antichrist — The term 'antichrist' never actually appears in Revelation — it appears only in 1 John and 2 John (1 John 2:18, 22; 4:3; 2 John 7). In Revelation, the same reality is represented by the beast from the sea (Revelation 13). The popular association of 'the Antichrist' with Revelation's beast reflects later theological synthesis rather than Revelation's own vocabulary.

Apocalypse — From the Greek word meaning "revelation" or "unveiling." The genre of literature that reveals hidden spiritual truths through symbolic imagery.

Armageddon — The symbolic location of the final battle between good and evil (Revelation 16:16), representing God's ultimate triumph over rebellion.

B

Babylon — The symbolic name for the world system opposed to God, representing human civilization in rebellion against divine authority (Revelation 17–18).

Beast — Primarily refers to two figures in Revelation 13: the beast from the sea (representing political/military power) and the beast from the earth (representing false religious authority).

Book of Life — The heavenly record containing the names of all who belong to Christ through faith, determining entrance into eternal life (Revelation 3:5; 13:8; 20:12, 15; 21:27).

Bowls of Wrath — The seven final judgments poured out by angels, representing God's complete and final response to persistent rebellion (Revelation 16).

Bride — The Church in her perfected state, prepared for eternal union with Christ the Bridegroom (Revelation 19:7; 21:2, 9).

C

Church — The assembly of believers throughout history, represented by both the seven churches of Asia Minor and the universal Bride of Christ.

"Come Out of Her, My People" — The divine call to separate from Babylon's influence and worldly allegiance before her judgment falls (Revelation 18:4), urging believers to maintain distinct loyalty to Christ.

Crown — Symbol of victory and authority. Revelation mentions different types: the crown of life (2:10), golden crowns of the elders (4:4), and the many crowns of Christ (19:12).

D

"Do not be afraid" — Christ's repeated reassurance to John and implicitly to all believers facing the book's overwhelming visions (Revelation 1:17), establishing that Revelation is meant to comfort, not terrify, those who belong to Him.

Dragon — Satan, described as a great red dragon with seven heads and ten horns, representing his power and deceptive authority (Revelation 12).

E

Elders — The twenty-four crowned figures around God's throne, likely representing the complete people of God from both Old and New Testament eras (Revelation 4:4).

Eternal Life — The quality of life that begins now through faith in Christ and continues forever in perfect fellowship with God.

F

False Prophet — The second beast (Revelation 13:11–18), representing deceptive religious authority that serves worldly power rather than God.

First Resurrection — The spiritual resurrection that occurs when believers come to faith, giving them authority to reign with Christ (Revelation 20:4–6).

Four Horsemen — The riders released when the first four seals are opened, representing conquest, war, famine, and death — forces that operate throughout history under God's sovereign control (Revelation 6:1–8).

G

Gog and Magog — Symbolic names for the nations that gather in final rebellion against God before being decisively defeated, demonstrating the ultimate futility of opposing God's kingdom (Revelation 20:8).

Great Tribulation — The period of intense suffering and persecution faced by God's people throughout history (Revelation 7:14). The text identifies those who 'have come out of the great tribulation' as those who have washed their robes in the Lamb's blood — a description applicable to all faithful believers across every age, not limited to a specific future period.

Great White Throne — The final judgment where all are evaluated according to their deeds and relationship with Christ (Revelation 20:11–15).

H

Harlot — Another name for Babylon, representing unfaithful systems that seduce people away from devotion to God (Revelation 17).

Heaven — Not merely a future destination, but the present reality of God's throne room where His will is perfectly accomplished.

Hidden Manna — The promise given to the overcomers in Pergamum (Revelation 2:17), representing spiritual sustenance and the intimate fellowship with God that the world cannot understand or access.

I

Image of the Beast — The false representation of worldly power that demands worship and allegiance (Revelation 13:14–15).

Incense — The prayers of the saints rising before God's throne, symbolizing the power and importance of believers' intercession in God's purposes (Revelation 5:8; 8:3–4).

J

Jerusalem, New — The bride-city representing the perfected people of God, where heaven and earth unite in perfect fellowship (Revelation 21–22).

Judgment — God's righteous response to sin and rebellion, often portrayed through seals, trumpets, and bowls, designed to call people to repentance.

K

Kingdom of God/Heaven — God's sovereign rule that is present now and will be consummated in the future, where His will is perfectly accomplished.

L

Lake of Fire — The final destination of all that opposes God, representing complete separation from His presence and love (Revelation 20:14–15).

Lamb — Christ in His sacrificial role, who was slain but now lives and reigns. The dominant Christological title in Revelation, appearing over 25 times — more than any other title for Christ in the book. The Lamb who was slain is also the Lion who conquers (Revelation 5:5–6), uniting sacrifice and sovereignty in one image.

Lampstands — The seven golden lampstands representing the seven churches, symbolizing that the Church exists to bear Christ's light to the world (Revelation 1:12, 20; 2:1).

Little Scroll — The opened scroll in Revelation 10, distinct from the sealed scroll of chapter 5, which John eats and finds both sweet and bitter — representing the joy and cost of bearing God's word to the nations (Revelation 10:8–11).

Living Creatures — Four beings around God's throne (lion, ox, man, eagle) representing all of creation in worship (Revelation 4:6–9).

M

Mark of the Beast — The identifying sign of allegiance to worldly systems rather than God, contrasted with the seal of God on believers' foreheads (Revelation 13:16–18).

Martyr — One who suffers or dies for faith in Christ. In Revelation, martyrs are portrayed as victorious witnesses rather than mere victims.

Michael — The archangel who leads God's army against Satan in the heavenly battle (Revelation 12:7).

Millennium — The symbolic thousand-year period representing the complete reign of Christ with His people (Revelation 20:1–6).

Morning Star — Christ Himself, given as a promise to the overcomers in Thyatira (Revelation 2:26–28), representing His glorious presence and the dawn of God's eternal day (Revelation 22:16).

Mount Zion — The heavenly Jerusalem where the Lamb stands with the 144,000, representing the complete assembly of God's redeemed people in victory (Revelation 14:1).

N

New Creation — God's renewal of all things, where the old order of sin and death passes away (Revelation 21:1, 5).

New Heaven and New Earth — The ultimate restoration where God dwells perfectly with His people in an environment unmarked by sin.

Nicolaitans — False teachers mentioned in the letters to Ephesus and Pergamum (Revelation 2:6, 15), representing compromise with worldly practices and the accommodation of pagan customs within the church.

No More Sea — The absence of the sea in the new creation (Revelation 21:1), representing the removal of chaos, danger, and separation, replaced by complete peace and unhindered access to God.

O

Overcomer — Believers who remain faithful to Christ despite trials and persecution, receiving promised rewards (Revelation 2–3).

P

Patmos — The small island in the Aegean Sea where John received the visions of Revelation while in exile for his faith (Revelation 1:9).

People of God — All who belong to Christ through faith, represented as a kingdom of priests serving God.

Pillar in the Temple — The promise given to overcomers in Philadelphia (Revelation 3:12), symbolizing permanent security, stability, and honored position in God's eternal presence.

Plagues — Divine judgments that serve as warnings and calls to repentance, often echoing the plagues of Egypt.

Prophecy — Not merely prediction of future events, but revelation of God's truth that calls for present faithfulness and worship.

Prophet — One who speaks God's truth. All believers are called to prophetic witness through faithful testimony.

Prostitute — See Harlot.

R

Recapitulation — The pattern in Revelation where the same spiritual realities are shown repeatedly from different perspectives, with each cycle adding new insight rather than presenting sequential chronological events. This explains why Revelation contains multiple visions of the end rather than a single timeline.

Redemption — God's act of purchasing humanity back from sin through Christ's sacrifice, central theme of Revelation.

Repentance — Turning from sin to God, the appropriate response to divine judgment and grace.

Resurrection — Both the spiritual awakening to new life in Christ and the final bodily resurrection of all people.

Revelation — The unveiling or disclosure of hidden truth, particularly about Christ's victory and God's ultimate purposes.

River of Life — The water flowing from God's throne through the New Jerusalem, symbolizing eternal life and spiritual refreshment provided by God's presence (Revelation 22:1–2).

S

Sackcloth — The prophetic garment of mourning worn by the two witnesses (Revelation 11:3), symbolizing both lament over sin and the call to repentance that characterizes faithful witness in a fallen world.

Saints — All believers, called to holiness and faithfulness, not a special class of super-Christians.

Satan — The dragon, serpent, and devil who opposes God but is ultimately defeated through Christ's victory.

Scroll (Sealed Scroll) — The book containing God's redemptive plan and the unfolding of history, sealed with seven seals and held in God's right hand (Revelation 5). Only the Lamb is worthy to open it, revealing that Christ alone can accomplish God's purposes and bring history to its appointed end.

Sea of Glass — The crystal-clear expanse before God's throne, representing the purity and transcendence of heaven's reality (Revelation 4:6; 15:2).

Seal — Both the protective mark God places on believers and the judgments that open the scroll of history.

Second Death — The final, eternal separation from God experienced by those whose names are not written in the Book of Life, contrasted with believers who are exempt from this judgment (Revelation 20:6, 14; 21:8).

Seven — The number of completion and perfection throughout Revelation (seven churches, seals, trumpets, bowls, etc.).

Seven Spirits — The fullness of the Holy Spirit before God's throne, representing the Spirit's complete and perfect work in the world (Revelation 1:4; 3:1; 4:5; 5:6). The sevenfold Spirit likely draws on Isaiah 11:2, where the Spirit rests on the Messiah in His fullness.

Stars — The seven stars representing the angels or messengers of the seven churches, held in Christ's right hand, symbolizing His authority over and care for His Church (Revelation 1:16, 20).

Sword — God's word, particularly as it proceeds from Christ's mouth to execute judgment and justice (Revelation 1:16; 19:15).

Synagogue of Satan — Those who claim to be God's people but oppose the true church, mentioned in the letters to Smyrna and Philadelphia (Revelation 2:9; 3:9), representing false religion that persecutes genuine faith.

T

Temple — In Revelation's new creation, Christ Himself serves as the temple, eliminating the need for a physical building (Revelation 21:22).

Testimony — The faithful witness believers bear to Christ's truth, particularly in the face of opposition.

Throne — Symbol of God's sovereign authority and rule, appearing over 40 times in Revelation as the center of all reality.

Tree of Life — Located in the new Jerusalem, representing eternal life and healing for all nations (Revelation 22:2).

Trumpets — Seven calls to attention that announce God's judgments and interventions in history.

Two Witnesses — The prophetic testimony of God's people, empowered by the Spirit to bear faithful witness despite opposition (Revelation 11:3–12).

V

Victory — The central theme of Revelation: Christ's triumph over sin, death, and Satan, shared by all who belong to Him.

Visions — Symbolic revelations given to John to communicate spiritual truths about God's character and purposes.

W

War — Both the spiritual battle between good and evil and the final defeat of all opposition to God.

Wedding Supper of the Lamb — The great celebration of Christ's union with His Church, representing the joy and intimacy of eternal fellowship with God (Revelation 19:9).

White — Color symbolizing purity, victory, and righteousness throughout Revelation.

Witness — The calling of all believers to testify faithfully to Christ's truth, regardless of consequences.

"Who has ears to hear" — The repeated refrain in the seven letters (Revelation 2–3), calling every believer in every age to attentive, responsive obedience to Christ's words, not just the original congregations.

Woman Clothed with the Sun — The symbolic figure in Revelation 12 representing God's people (Israel/Church) giving birth to the Messiah while under attack from the dragon, illustrating the cosmic conflict between God's kingdom and Satan's rebellion.

Word of God — Christ Himself as the ultimate revelation of God, and the faithful testimony believers are called to maintain.

Worship — The appropriate response to God's revelation of His character and works, central activity of heaven and earth.

Worthy/Worthiness — The central question of Revelation 4–5: "Who is worthy to open the scroll and break its seals?" (5:2). Only the Lamb who was slain is worthy to accomplish redemption and bring God's purposes to fulfillment, establishing the foundation for all heavenly worship.

Wrath — God's righteous anger against sin and rebellion, always measured and ultimately designed to accomplish justice.

Interpretive Framework

Symbolic Interpretation — Understanding Revelation's imagery as representing spiritual and theological truths rather than literal future events.

Present Application — Reading Revelation as revealing current spiritual realities and calling for immediate faithfulness rather than distant speculation.

Christocentric Focus — Interpreting all of Revelation in light of Christ's central victory and ongoing reign.

Church Age Perspective — Understanding most of Revelation's events as occurring throughout the entire period between Christ's first and second comings.

Optimistic Eschatology — Believing that God's kingdom advances triumphantly through history rather than merely rescuing believers from a defeated world.

Numbers in Revelation

Numbers in Revelation carry symbolic weight drawn from Old Testament usage. Understanding their symbolic meaning prevents both over-literal and under-serious readings of the text.

One — Unity and singularity of God; the one throne, one Lamb, one Lord.

Two — Witness and testimony; the two witnesses, two-edged sword, representing adequate testimony.

Three — Divine perfection and completeness; the Trinity, three woes, three unclean spirits.

Three and a Half — Period of testing and persecution; 42 months, 1,260 days, time, times, and half a time. A broken seven — real but limited suffering that falls short of completeness.

Four — Universal scope and completeness; four living creatures, four corners of earth, four winds.

Six — Imperfection and incompleteness; 666 as the number of man falling short of divine perfection (seven).

Seven — Perfection and completion; appears over 50 times in Revelation. Seven churches, seals, trumpets, bowls, spirits, stars, lampstands.

Ten — Completeness in earthly matters; ten horns, ten crowns, ten days of tribulation.

Twelve — God's people and divine government; twelve tribes, twelve apostles, twelve gates, twelve foundations, 144,000 (12 × 12 × 1,000).

Twenty-Four — Complete representation of God's people; twenty-four elders (12 tribes + 12 apostles).

Forty-Two — See Three and a Half; period of testing (42 months).

144,000 — The complete number of God's sealed people (12 × 12 × 1,000), representing all believers.

666 — The number of man, representing human rebellion and imperfection, falling short of seven (perfection).

1,000 — Completeness and perfection in time; the millennium as Christ's complete reign.

1,260 — See Three and a Half; days of witness and protection during persecution.

Note: This glossary reflects the theological framework of "The Heart of Victory," which emphasizes Revelation's symbolic nature, present application, and optimistic view of God's advancing kingdom rather than literal future-predictive interpretation.

DIGGING DEEPER: Further Reading and Resources

The Heart of Victory: A Daily Journey Through the Book of Revelation

If this 84-day journey left you wanting more, this section is for you. You don't need to read everything listed here — this is a menu, not a checklist. The resources are organized by relevance to what you've just studied, starting with the books most closely aligned with **The Heart of Victory** and moving outward from there. Read selectively, follow your interests, and remember that studying Revelation is ultimately about encountering the risen Christ who stands at the center of history and eternity.

Revelation Commentaries

These commentaries engage the text of Revelation directly and will deepen your understanding of the book you've just studied.

★ HIGHLY RECOMMENDED — **Revelation** by Joel R. Beeke. The finest Reformed commentary available — rigorous exegesis married to warm Puritan devotion, consistently moving from "What does this mean?" to "How should this change us?"

Our God Reigns: A Fresh Look at the Book of Revelation by Sam Storms. Deeply pastoral, thoroughly biblical, and wonderfully accessible — the natural next step if you appreciated the devotional approach of this book.

The Overcomers: God's Vision for You to Thrive in an Age of Anxiety and Outrage by Matt Chandler. A chapter-by-chapter walk through Revelation showing that believers are not victims but overcomers, uniquely placed in this moment of history to push back darkness with courage and confidence.

More Than Conquerors: An Interpretation of the Book of Revelation by William Hendriksen. The classic that explains Revelation's recapitulation structure — how the visions cycle through the same realities from different angles — with remarkable clarity for lay readers.

★ HIGHLY RECOMMENDED **The Book of Revelation: A Shorter Commentary** by G.K. Beale. The sweet spot between accessibility and depth, showing how deeply Revelation is rooted in the Old Testament with pastoral heart throughout.

★ HIGHLY RECOMMENDED **Triumph of the Lamb: A Commentary on Revelation.** by Dennis E. Johnson Chapter-by-chapter exposition that keeps the focus on practical application — clear writing on complex passages, excellent for personal study or teaching others.

Revelation (Reformed Expository Commentary) by Richard D. Phillips Verse-by-verse Reformed exposition with a preacher's clarity, emphasizing Christ's current reign and the Church's calling to faithful witness.

★ HIGHLY RECOMMENDED **The Returning King: A Guide to the Book of Revelation** by Vern Poythress A fair-minded guide that shows multiple interpretive options while helping readers understand Revelation's structure and theology.

Reversed Thunder: The Revelation of John and the Praying Imagination by Eugene H. Peterson Revelation not as a puzzle to decode but as a vision to inhabit — teaching you to pray through John's apocalypse rather than merely study it.

Revelation: Four Views, A Parallel Commentary by Steve Gregg Four major interpretive approaches presented side-by-side for each passage — the best tool for understanding why faithful Christians disagree about Revelation.

Eschatology and Last Things

These works provide the broader theological framework that shapes how we read Revelation's message about God's kingdom and final purposes.

★ HIGHLY RECOMMENDED — **The Promise of the Future** by Cornelis P. Venema The standard reference for Reformed eschatology — comprehensive treatment of every major topic with scholarly precision and pastoral warmth.

★ HIGHLY RECOMMENDED **Kingdom Come: The Amillennial Alternative** by Sam Storms The accessible introduction to amillennial eschatology — defending symbolic interpretation with biblical arguments and historical perspective.

A Case for Amillennialism: Understanding the End Times by Kim Riddlebarger The most thorough accessible defense of amillennial eschatology available, with especially helpful treatment of Revelation 20 and a valuable historical survey of how interpretation has developed.

★ HIGHLY RECOMMENDED **The Doctrine of Last Things** by Samuel E. Waldron Precise Reformed thinking on death, resurrection, judgment, and eternal states — complex theology in language ordinary readers can follow.

The Bible and the Future by Anthony A. Hoekema Comprehensive biblical theology of last things that transforms future hope into present-tense faithfulness — essential for complete eschatological understanding.

★ HIGHLY RECOMMENDED **The End Times Made Simple** by Dean Davis Complex eschatology made understandable for everyday readers, explaining why Christians throughout history have read prophecy differently than modern dispensationalism teaches.

Postmillennialism: An Eschatology of Hope by Keith A. Mathison An accessible introduction to postmillennial thinking within Reformed theology, emphasizing the gospel's transforming power and Christ's current reign.

Biblical Theology and Background

These resources illuminate the Old Testament roots, literary structure, and canonical context that enrich your reading of Revelation.

The Climax of Prophecy: Studies in the Book of Revelation by Richard Bauckham Thematic studies that unlock Revelation's message — particularly insightful on Old Testament imagery, the book's structure, and the theology of worship.

The Theology of the Book of Revelation by Richard Bauckham A concise synthesis of Revelation's theological themes — God's character, Christ's victory, the Spirit's work, and the Church's calling — in accessible form.

All Things New: Revelation as Canonical Capstone by Brian J. Tabb Demonstrates how Revelation brings together creation, exodus, temple, exile, and restoration themes as the fitting conclusion to Scripture's story.

Echoes of Exodus: Tracing a Biblical Motif by Alastair Roberts and Andrew Wilson Traces how exodus themes echo throughout Scripture — helping you recognize the Exodus connections John assumes his audience will catch.

Seeing Things John's Way: The Rhetoric of the Book of Revelation by David A. deSilva How John strategically structures his visions and imagery to call readers toward faithful endurance — bridging ancient rhetoric and modern reading.

Reading Revelation Responsibly by Michael J. Gorman How to read Revelation ethically — calling believers to cruciform witness that mirrors the Lamb's sacrificial victory rather than worldly power.

The Victory Theme

These books develop the central theme of Christ's triumph that runs through every page of Revelation.

Worthy Is the Lamb: The Finished Work of Christ in Revelation by Ray Summers Relentlessly Christ-centered exposition showing how every vision, judgment, and promise points to the Lamb who was slain.

★ HIGHLY RECOMMENDED **The High King of Heaven: A Biblical Theology of the Kingdom of God** by Dean Davis Traces the kingdom theme from Genesis through Revelation, showing how God's redemptive plan holds together across the entire canon.

Study Bibles

These study Bibles provide reliable notes and cross-references for ongoing Revelation study.

ESV Study Bible Comprehensive notes from a Reformed, generally amillennial perspective with excellent cross-references and Old Testament connections.

Reformation Study Bible edited by R.C. Sproul Reformed theology throughout, emphasizing God's sovereignty, Christ's finished work, and the Church's calling to faithful witness.

CSB Study Bible Thoughtful evangelical notes across various perspectives with the clear, readable translation used throughout this devotional.

NIV Cultural Backgrounds Study Bible edited by Craig S. Keener and John H. Walton Illuminates Revelation through first-century culture — imperial worship, apocalyptic symbolism, and Roman-world context.

Primary Sources

For readers who want to hear from the earliest Christian interpreters of Revelation directly.

Commentary on the Apocalypse by Victorinus of Pettau The earliest surviving commentary on Revelation, written by a bishop who was martyred around AD 304 — a firsthand witness to what the early church believed about John's visions.

The City of God (especially Book 20) by Augustine Augustine's landmark treatment of the millennium and last things, which shaped Christian eschatology for over a thousand years and established the amillennial reading as mainstream Christian orthodoxy.

Against Heresies (selections on eschatology) by Irenaeus Writing in the second century, Irenaeus provides one of the earliest theological engagements with Revelation's prophetic themes from a pastor who was two generations removed from the apostles.

Understanding Other Perspectives

Fair study means understanding how other faithful Christians read the same text. These works represent perspectives that differ from this book but deserve thoughtful engagement.

The Meaning of the Millennium: Four Views edited by Robert G. Clouse Representatives of each major millennial position make their case and respond to each other — charitable disagreement at its best.

Three Views on the Millennium and Beyond edited by Darrell Bock A more recent survey focusing on contemporary evangelical perspectives, showing where the conversation has moved.

Revelation by John F. Walvoord Classic dispensational premillennial interpretation from one of its most influential proponents — the dispensational commentary to consult.

Revelation by Grant R. Osborne Thoughtful premillennial scholarship that considers multiple options before presenting conclusions — premillennialism at its most careful.

The Blessed Hope by George Eldon Ladd The classic statement of historic premillennialism — distinct from dispensationalism, rooted in older church tradition, and worth understanding as a serious alternative framework.

Progressive Dispensationalism by Craig Blaising and Darrell Bock Shows how dispensational thinking has evolved from within the movement itself, moving closer to historic positions on several key points.

The Last Days According to Jesus by R.C. Sproul Partial preterism examined with characteristic Sproul clarity — helpful for appreciating first-century fulfillment of prophetic texts.

Living in the Shadow of the Second Coming: American Premillennialism 1875–1982 by Timothy Weber The definitive history of how dispensational premillennialism rose to dominance in American evangelicalism — essential context for understanding why so many readers approach Revelation the way they do.

Choose what serves you best from this list. Read thoughtfully. Disagree charitably where you must. And let everything you read drive you deeper into worship of the Lamb who was slain and now lives forever.

May your study deepen your worship, strengthen your faith, and enhance your witness to the victorious Lamb. The heart of victory that beats through every page of Revelation is yours in Christ Jesus.

DIGGING EVEN DEEPER

There's More Where This Came From

If these 84 days left you hungry for more — good. That's exactly what Revelation is supposed to do.

I've created a growing collection of free resources to complement what you've just read: printable versions of the glossary and reading list, additional study guides, and new tools I'll continue adding as the Kingdom Journey series grows. **The Heart of Victory** is only the beginning.

Visit **carlcopsey.com** to access everything.

While you're there, I'd love to hear your story. How has walking through Revelation changed the way you see Christ's victory in your everyday life? Drop me a note. Every message matters, and knowing how God is using this book in real lives is the greatest reward a writer could ask for.

ABOUT THE AUTHOR

Carl has been studying Scripture and theology for most of his adult life — not in a seminary classroom, but through years of self-study, correspondence courses, and a relentless hunger to understand God's word. That pursuit eventually led him to teach on the book of Revelation, eschatology, and other biblical topics, both online and in person. His goal has always been the same: making deep theology clear and accessible for everyday believers.

He lives in DeRidder, Louisiana, with his wife Rebecca, where they care for his uncle. Their two sons, MoeCharles and Quinten, are both recently married — MoeCharles to Camille, and Quinten to Bella — and both couples serve in Christian ministry and education, carrying forward the biblical convictions their family holds dear.

Carl has loved writing since he was young, though life required him to set it aside for many years. The Heart of Victory marks his return — not just to writing, but to the work he believes he was made for: serving the church with solid biblical teaching, starting with the part of Scripture that most needs to be understood without fear or confusion.

He handles every aspect of his books through Pilgrim's Path Press.

9 798899 539000 8